Virtual Communion

Virtual Communion

Theology of the Internet and the Catholic Sacramental Imagination

Katherine G. Schmidt

LEXINGTON BOOKS/FORTRESS ACADEMIC
Lanham • Boulder • New York • London

Published by Lexington Books/Fortress Academic
Lexington Books is an imprint of The Rowman & Littlefield Publishing Group, Inc.
4501 Forbes Boulevard, Suite 200, Lanham, Maryland 20706
www.rowman.com

6 Tinworth Street, London SE11 5AL, United Kingdom

Copyright © 2020 by The Rowman & Littlefield Publishing Group, Inc.

All rights reserved. No part of this book may be reproduced in any form or by any electronic or mechanical means, including information storage and retrieval systems, without written permission from the publisher, except by a reviewer who may quote passages in a review.

British Library Cataloguing in Publication Information Available

Library of Congress Control Number: 2020932599

ISBN 978-1-9787-0162-5 (cloth : alk. paper)
ISBN 978-1-9787-0164-9 (pbk : alk. paper)
ISBN 978-1-9787-0163-2 (electronic)

∞™ The paper used in this publication meets the minimum requirements of American National Standard for Information Sciences—Permanence of Paper for Printed Library Materials, ANSI/NISO Z39.48-1992.

Contents

List of Table		vii
Acknowledgments		ix
Introduction		xi
1	Theological Concerns	1
2	Ecclesial Perspectives on Media and Communications	25
3	Incarnation, Virtuality, and the Church	59
4	Virtuality and Sacramentality	71
5	The Social Dynamics of Life Online	91
6	The Suburbanization of American Catholic Life	109
7	The Standards of Communion	123
Conclusion		163
Bibliography		167
Index		173
About the Author		175

List of Table

Table 2.1 World Communications Day Speeches and Topics
          1967–2018   41

Acknowledgments

I would like to thank the community of the University of Dayton for all of their love and support as I worked on this project. My mentors—Vince Miller, Sandra Yocum, and Bill Portier—were especially supportive of not only this project but of all of my work as a graduate student and beyond. Without the encouragement and insight of Vince Miller especially, I would not have been able to write *Virtual Communion*.

Special thanks to Adam Sheridan, whose wisdom and creativity has been a source of inspiration to me as a scholar for a decade. Long road trips and sumptuous meals with Tim Gabrielli solidified so many of my thoughts on this subject and kept me sane during the writing process. My work is also bolstered by the constant friendship of Emily McGowin and Derek Hatch, who make up just part of a much bigger community of scholars with whom I have been lucky to study and teach.

Finally, the support of two women—my mother, Marsha Miskec Schmidt, and my cousin, Jennifer Miskec—helped me have the confidence to write on this topic. In this project and in my teaching life, I strive to represent the beauty and grace of all the Miskec women.

Introduction

Many in the Catholic Church will remember March 13, 2013. On that evening, Francis spoke his first words as pontiff, introducing the world to his humble style through a small wave and a slight smile. His first speech is really a prayer—for Pope Benedict XVI, for the Church of Rome and city of Rome, and for Francis himself. He paused before offering his own blessing to allow those gathered in St. Peter's Square to pray for him as he embarked on an office he never sought. Francis then gave his own blessing, his first "Urbi et Orbi," before bidding the crowd goodnight and telling them "sleep well."

Between these two moments of prayer the cardinal who had introduced the new pope (known in this capacity as the Protodeacon) stepped in to provide a prologue to Francis' first blessing as pope. The official transcript includes the following to convey what happened instead of Cardinal Jean-Louis Tauran's actual words:

> The Protodeacon announced that all those who received the blessing, either in person or by radio, television or *by the new means of communication* receive the plenary indulgence in the form established by the Church. He prayed that Almighty God protect and guard the Pope so that he may lead the Church for many years to come, and that he would grant peace to the Church throughout the world.[1]

As much as I will remember Francis' first words for their beautiful simplicity, I will also remember the words of Cardinal Tauran. For in what most people might only recall as a *pro forma* interlude to Francis' first papal prayer, I heard with clarity an ancient church grant an indulgence through the internet.[2]

In Cardinal Tauran's announcement, we can see the church dealing with various media as they came along: radio, television, and "new means of communication," now so various as to need a generalized phrase to capture them. The Protodeacon was speaking to people in St. Peter's Square holding cell phones that transmitted pictures and sounds to their loved ones, and to people watching the announcement while huddled over laptops and iPads in offices and on buses. I have no evidence of who wrote this sentence about indulgences, and I have no evidence if he included "new means of communication" for more than what he assumed were practical reasons. I take this sentence, however, as a call for theologians to be ever attentive to the means of communication as they relate the economy of grace. This project is a response to that call.

I remember exactly where I was when I first learned about the internet. I stood in the room of a teenage girl, the daughter of a family friend who had called my technologically savvy father over for help. "She wants to be on the Web," her father told mine, "but I'm having trouble with the connection." I learned that "the Web" was a way for people to talk to each other through their computers. I stared in awe at the blank screen of the monitor, turned off for my father's inspection, trying to ignore the passing thought, *Why wouldn't they just use the telephone?*

My sensitivity and attraction to the internet as a subject of study has not little to do with the fact that the internet and I grew up together. I think of myself as a second-generation digital immigrant, fluent in the language and culture of the internet but old enough to remember a time before it. My technological biography is just different enough from the students I now teach (mostly born in the late 1990s) that I can still be to be impressed and puzzled by it, such that I would see it as a topic for research at all.

In what follows, I argue that internet technology is in need of theological reflection that centers on the category of mediation. I will not be discussing the place of projectors, big screens, iPads, etc. in the worship space. I have opinions about these things, but they are not altogether scholarly. I will leave such questions up to pastors, lay leaders, theologians, and other experts in liturgical matters. Instead, I am interested in technology as a culture, and its relationship to the church. The Christian tradition has a vested interest in technological culture not only because the church is in the world and cannot be otherwise, but also because questions about technology invite questions about mediation. And religion is about mediation.

I would like to argue two related points as foundational to a theology of the internet. First, I would like to advance the idea that Christian liturgy can be understood as virtual. This is an expansion and concretization of the idea of religion as mediation. Second, I would like to propose that the virtual nature of Christian liturgy—and indeed, the virtual nature of the church itself—turns toward a self-reflective theological analysis of the internet. I propose under this second point that the internet has changed what it means to be social to such a degree that we must now understand its social spaces as ancillary to the liturgical spaces of the tradition.

The thesis I advance is as follows: As virtual space, the internet can be understood theologically through the doctrinal loci of the Incarnation and the church. These two doctrines pervade both scholarly and ecclesial discussions of technology and the internet to date, and remain the central doctrinal categories with which theologians should assess internet culture. In its broader sacramental imagination and its ecclesiology, the church relies on virtual space insofar as it relies on the productive tension between presence and absence. Furthermore, the social possibilities of the internet afford the church great opportunity for building a social context that allows the living out of Eucharistic logic within what I term "ancillary spaces." These spaces are necessary to the life of the church, and rather than lamenting the disappearance of their traditional iterations, I suggest that we pay close attention to their new residence in the digital context.

Chapter 1 presents the state of the theological question. I argue here that theological reflection on internet technology centers on five main concerns: anonymity, vitriol, authority, access, and disembodiment. The two dominant doctrinal loci for addressing these concerns have been the Incarnation and the church. Though I begin to offer some thoughts on each of the five theological concerns, I propose in the conclusion of this chapter that theologians focus more on the ways in which Catholicism is beholden to mediation, given that so much theological work has focused on the mediating structures of the internet as sites for theological concern.

Chapter 2 reviews ecclesial documents on technology and social communication. Here I argue that church teaching on these matters has focused mostly on the doctrines of Incarnation and the church as well to address the technological issues of a given time. Throughout the twentieth century, the church remained cautiously optimistic about the role of technology in society. After the Second Vatican Council, and especially during the pontificates of John Paul II and Francis, official church statements acknowledge the inevitable interconnectedness of social communications and the church, as well as the possibilities for living out the mission of the church in precisely that context.

Chapter 3 is a theological account of mediation, with particular attention to the doctrinal locus of the Incarnation. Drawing on the work of computer scientists, I argue that the sacramental imagination of the church, as Incarnational, is reliant upon an understanding of mediation now conceptually available because of digital culture. In chapter 4, I apply the category of "virtual" to two ecclesial spaces: (1) Paul's letters and (2) replica grottoes of Lourdes. I argue that the sacramental imagination that characterizes Catholicism relies upon a virtual logic insofar as it trades on the productive relationship between immediacy and hypermediacy.

Chapter 5 turns to the social dynamics of the internet. It reviews relevant scholarship from internet studies and other (non-theological) fields that attempt to describe and critique the emerging social life of online environments. Chapter 6 provides a sociological argument about the state of the Catholic Church in the United States, namely that its primary social context is suburbanization. I present this sociological and historical narrative in the context of scholarship about the internet in order to introduce the argument of the final chapter.

Chapter 7 is the theological culmination of the project. I argue that by understanding the sacramental economy of the church in terms of symbolic exchange, the church will be poised to address the sociological challenges facing the living out of the Eucharistic logic that forms the liturgical assembly. The first half engages the work of Henri de Lubac, whose Eucharistic ecclesiology presents an optimistic vision of the church. De Lubac argues for Eucharist-centered ecclesiology, but I argue that he is insufficiently attentive to the sociological challenges to the church's living out of Eucharistic logic. I go on to argue that Louis-Marie Chauvet's sacramental theology is helpful in addressing these challenges. Specifically, Chauvet's focus on "symbolic exchange" gives us a standard for communion by which we can assess both the church and the culture in which it carries out its mission. Therefore, symbolic exchange is a theological hermeneutic for the phenomenon of the internet and its possibilities vis-à-vis the Catholic Church.

I conclude with the observation that there are two forces at work in this project. I began my research with the desire to bring theological categories to bear on the social phenomenon of the internet. In the end, however, I discovered that this analysis alone is insufficient in light of the spirit of the Second Vatican Council, and indeed a much longer history of the church's relationship with the world. I hope to demonstrate that a fuller theological engagement with internet culture means bringing the categories of digital life to bear on the life of the church. It is only in being open to this second dynamic that theologians can contribute to a church that preserves timeless truths at the same time that it acknowledges itself as a community in space and time.

NOTES

1. "Pope Francis: His First Words," *Radio Vaticana*, accessed June 25, 2015. http://en.radiovaticana.va/storico/2013/03/13/pope_francis_his_first_words_/en1-673112. Emphasis mine.

2. I opt not to capitalize the word "internet" throughout this project. One sees "internet" capitalized in both scholarly and popular texts, although other authors have

chosen not to as well. For me, this is not just a matter of style. By leaving "internet" in the lower case, I mean to give grammatical expression to the observation of cultural trends, namely the "becoming ordinary" of the internet. When capitalized, "internet" retains an otherness that cannot speak to the way in which it has become a part of daily existence in so many places in the world.

Chapter 1

Theological Concerns

The present technological moment attracts the thoughts of a great variety of writers and scholars. Academic theologians, pastoral ministers, and theologically inclined scholars of other disciplines are among the voices one finds in the choir of reflection about the internet. These accounts, by and large, reflect the sensibilities of *Gaudium et Spes* in their earnest attempt to understand the modern world in the light of faith. They pay close attention to the "griefs and anxieties" engendered by our technological milieu, and find some space to laud its contribution to the "joys and hopes" of humanity. The former, however, has tended to dominate theological reflection on the topic to date, and there is surely much in present technological culture calling for critical thought. Theological critique inevitably rests upon theological assumptions, two of which I aim to explicate here. However, we would do well to remember that especially in a culture that is increasingly hostile to outward displays of religiosity, theological critique is always tempted to a certain mentality of entrenchment and defensiveness.

The two theological loci that dominate theological discussion on the topic of the internet are the church (specifically in its local form) and the Incarnation. One must be careful not to divide these two, as it is theologically inappropriate to consider one without the other: Christian ecclesiology is necessarily incarnational, and the doctrine of the Incarnation carries ecclesiological consequences. This reciprocity appears in the theological work examined below. In short, much of what has been said by theologians on this topic has focused on those aspects of the internet which relate to these doctrinal positions. Theologians have appealed to the central doctrine of the Incarnation—God made flesh in Jesus Christ—in order to critique the apparently disembodied character of virtual life. They have appealed to the centrality of the church, especially in its local form, in order to critique virtually mediated social relationships, positing the church as the ideal social institution and mediator of relationships. With so much of our daily lives being mediated virtually, theologians have sought to bring the critical power of the Christian tradition to bear on our technological culture, focusing specifically on what the Incarnation and the church mean for us and our relationship to the internet.

What follows is a discussion of five characteristics of the internet around which theological reflection has clustered: anonymity, vitriol, authority, access, and disembodiment. This five-part taxonomy is necessary but problematic. It is necessary because it reflects the major themes found in theologies of the internet to date. These five aspects provide insight into the theological stakes of the internet itself. It is problematic because none of the authors surveyed here take on all five aspects together as I do here. More often than not, two or more are considered together to make a larger point. I have chosen to separate them in order to tease out commonalities among theologies of the internet. These five aspects reflect the two doctrinal loci above. Each one has serious theological implications for both incarnational and ecclesiological reasons. Although individual theologians have given different arguments and inflections to these characteristics, all of them are grounded in the desire to promote the centrality of the embodied revelation in Jesus Christ, as well as the place of the church as the mediating institution of that revelation for communities of faith.

I focus on more general theological accounts of the internet, spending less time with those which ask questions about the role of technology in specific pastoral situations. One of the primary assumptions of this entire project is that in order to address any of these questions on the pastoral level, we must be willing to examine the theological stakes of whatever technology we find relevant to the church. The same goes for moral evaluations of our online interactions. We have become mired in discussions of pornography, personal distraction via technological gadgets, video game violence, and the like without asking deeper questions about what the internet actually *is* from a specifically theological point of view. We have been too eager to point out new sins and old sins-done-new that we find online without undertaking any prolonged reflection on how to interpret this technological and cultural moment within the economy of grace. We have begun the task set out in *Gaudium et Spes*, as we have found and continue to find the anxieties of our age. We have yet to delve deeply into the possibilities of that moment, and to look for moments of hope in the light of the gospel.

The theological work surveyed here is important and worthwhile. It demonstrates the beginning of an effort, as a discipline, to engage in the complex technological culture in which we write, study, and teach. We are only beginning to examine the important theological questions raised by our virtual life together, and the extant theological treatments of the internet demonstrate what doctrines are proving to be most important for these questions.

ANONYMITY

The internet affords users an unprecedented degree of anonymity for their interpersonal communication and their engagements with content which is mediated by the internet. In terms of the former, one is able to access all kinds of content—images, sounds, videos, etc.—without anyone knowing it has been accessed. One can also produce and distribute content relatively anonymously.[1] Interpersonal communication of all kinds online is also done anonymously in many contexts, through the use of handles, screennames, and avatars. This anonymity can be both intentional and unintentional. Sometimes, a user intentionally hides her identity from others or to avoid attaching herself to any piece of content. Other times, the very nature of the medium itself requires that a user's identity is hidden from others.

"Anonymity," however, can be a misleading category here. Etymologically, anonymity refers to the state of being without a *name*. In the case of online interpersonal communication, therefore, most cases of "anonymity" are actually moments of pseudonymity. By appropriating this term from its traditional usage in literature, we get a better sense of what really is at stake in so-called "anonymous" exchanges: disguise. Online anonymity is not entirely about individuals operating without names per se, but about their ability to produce words and images without accountability. For example, users regularly comment on articles or videos online under their real names. Even when an individual uses his real name to post a comment online, he remains anonymous to nearly every person who reads it. The user will never meet the readers in person and though they may attempt to hold him accountable with a counter-comment, the user can simply ignore them or remove himself from the conversation with no real social consequences.

Social consequences are at the very heart of this aspect of the internet. Theorists have found anonymity one of the most important aspects of the internet because it challenges the social constructs which hold our common life together.[2] Virtual life is forcing us to reconsider the categories of dialogue, debate, and social interaction itself. What such anonymous (really, pseudonymous) comments lack, however, is the accountability one might find in non-virtual settings. One might argue that the threat of embarrassment, shame, or confrontation looms in non-virtual interpersonal and public interactions, and therefore might alter individual choices. I may not say this comment or present that picture, the argument goes, in "real" life for fear of embarrassment. A classic example is the difference between clicking on a pornographic video online and going to buy a pornographic video in person. The primary difference is that in the latter, I have to risk the reaction of other human beings (the shopkeeper, the passersby) that I do not in the former. A more precise description, then, might be "facelessness," although the term is less elegant and has less purchase than "anonymity." Therefore, I retain the term here, fully aware of its imprecision.

This aspect of virtual life is of great interest to theologians, especially from the standpoint of moral theology. If Christian ethics is about how to live well and attain true happiness in the light of revelation, it is no surprise that the internet is quickly becoming an important site for theological reflection.[3] Investigating what it means to "live well" necessarily entails investigating the choices we make and how those choices affect others and ourselves. The anonymity on which so much of virtual life relies—both intentionally and unintentionally—is directly related to the Christian view of the human person. Christian anthropology is incarnational in that it understands the dignity of the human body in the context of the redemption of the body found in Jesus Christ. Theologians seek to maintain the unity and dignity of the human person in the face of virtual activities that would undermine it precisely by means of anonymity.[4]

The claim of Christian anthropology against an individual choice to watch pornography, for example, concerns not only the threat to a person's individual relationship to God but also to his or her relationship to other people. When a person watches pornography, she not only undermines her own dignity but also the dignity of all involved in its production, as well as those around her who may be adversely affected by her formation in watching pornography. Personal exchanges and engagements with mediated content affect our relationships to each other. As the Body of Christ, the community is both particular and universal. In addition, a lack of integrity in its members affects the Body. This makes the question of anonymity pertinent from an ecclesiological perspective as well.

In her work on doing theology online in *Aquinas on the Web?*, Jana Bennett draws on several Christian bloggers to investigate the relationship between the internet and theological discourse. One of the most quoted bloggers in Bennett's work is Susan Bauer, who at one point writes the following: "There are aspects of digital culture that we should fight against, not because they are 'not print' but because they are not godly."[5] Bauer goes on to list these "not godly" aspects, including "the anonymity which allows us to lie and deceive each other."[6] This is the persistent worry about anonymity online, from both Christians and non-Christians alike. The lack of trust that already obtains between strangers in our culture—even between people who live in the same neighborhood—is exacerbated by the ability to conceal or falsify one's identity, appearance, and personality through the medium of the internet. Some Christian theologians, then, have looked at the internet's characteristic anonymity as a symptom of much more serious diseases that plague modern life.

Following Stanley Hauerwas' postliberal project, George Randels uses "narrative, character, and community . . . to analyze cyberspace."[7] He argues that cyberspace is one of the clearest products of the modern condition, as it "involves a conception of the person primarily as an isolated, autonomous, and often anonymous individual rather than as part of a larger community."[8] Anonymity, for Randels, is the high point of the excesses of liberal individualism. Using multiuser domains or MUDs as an illustrative example, Randels contends that "anonymity permits players to be known only by what they explicitly project, and that it encourages some of individualism's excesses."[9] By virtue of its anonymity, then, sociality online is insufficient in light of the fullness of social life one finds in the church. Randels' aim is to set the church over and against the internet by virtue of anonymity reflecting the problems of liberalism: "Atomistic and excessive individualism contrasts sharply with the church, most other forms of community, and most visions of ethics."[10]

Along these lines, Gene Veith and Christopher Stamper write, "The screen name—unlike an actual name—has no social context, presenting no family, with no community ties or obligations."[11] Once again, anonymity precludes traditional social consequences and enables, it would seem, undesirable choices. A "social context" is important for the maintenance of these social consequences, consequences that Veith and Stamper refer to vaguely as "ties or obligations." The "social context" par excellence for Veith and Stamper, as well as Randels, is the local church. The local community is inherently "faceful": an individual physically sees other members, and that seeing alters the choices he makes. This seeing of faces not only provides him with the social consequences to preclude certain behaviors. It also provides a person with examples for living well in light of the gospel. Here, then, the local church becomes the antidote to a digital life veiled in anonymity.

The local church is also "nameful." The Christian church grew and continues to grow by means of witnesses. Named individuals were willing who give their lives, through martyrdom or other means of sainthood, for Christ. They are accountable to their communities, both friendly and oppressive, in a way that challenges the growing preference for anonymity in the social life we find online. Such accountability, the argument goes, relies on an honesty that is undermined by the inherent deception (pseudonymity) of a screenname or avatar.

Having a name is also theologically important because of the Incarnation. Although theologians have tended to focus on the Incarnation while addressing the concern of disembodiment online (treated below), part of Jesus' being fully human is that he had a name that located him as a human being from a particular place: *Jesus of Nazareth* is God Incarnate. Perhaps online anonymity is giving Christian theologians pause because anonymity seems to run against the grain of not only the local church community but also against its picture of both humanity and divinity. Perhaps it is more than just a problem with deception and all of the ways by which we may be enabled to do and say immoral things; it is a problem of the very way we think about who we are and who God is.[12]

VITRIOL

The question of anonymity ushers in a myriad of issues regarding the phenomenon of online nastiness. As a catch-all for the many ways we have found to mistreat each other in virtual space, I refer to this second aspect as *vitriol*. Theologians often focus on how people treat each other online because they are inherently interested in how human beings relate to one another. There is a common implication that online interaction is even worse than the sinfulness we face in ourselves and others offline: people are meaner to one another, practice less patience, and operate with less shame toward their fellow human beings than they do in offline contexts. Although vitriol is often tied to anonymity, people continue to do and say terrible things to each other under their own names and faces. Thus while anonymity and vitriol are related, it is important to treat them separately. More importantly, the theological concern over anonymity is much bigger than the way in which it enables vitriol.

In a short piece in *Word & World*, Adam Copeland considers "each [of the Ten Commandments] as it relates to information communication technologies and digital life."[13] For the second commandment, Copeland argues, "It reminds us that comments should be left with kindness, humility and love. As one Christian blogging site states in its comments policy, 'Blessed are those who refuse to insult or slander others, even if they have been disrespected themselves. They show us all the better way.'"[14] *America*, the Jesuit weekly magazine, once suspended its comment feature on articles for this very concern, though they have since returned them to the website.[15]

Bennett provides perhaps the most sustained account of vitriol by focusing on one particular online discussion. Because of her focus on theological discourse online, she focuses on a discussion over Rob Bell's controversial *Love Wins*, a book that questions common notions of heaven and hell within Christianity. Directly after its publication, *Love Wins* became a hot topic of discussion in online Christian circles, often functioning as a kind of litmus test for various ideological positions. Throughout her treatment of the discussion, Bennett does note the place of anonymity in the conversation, but focuses more extensively on the vitriolic nature of the conversation. She makes the claim that there is something in the very form of the internet that encourages vitriol. She writes, "The internet's architecture makes skimming very easy because of the way web pages tend to be designed. So it would seem that the very nature of the internet forms us to think about others in ways that are dehumanizing."[16] Elsewhere she argues that "our technology does not allow us to view ourselves as created by God, with God as our source, nor does it allow us to understand ourselves as sinners, particularly when it comes to perpetuating evils like racism."[17] Her assertion is that the very form of mediated communication online contributes to or even encourages discourse that does not respect the humanity of our interlocutors. This is especially important for Bennett's focus on theological discourse online. Citing Dyer's piece in *Christianity Today*, she writes, "The medium itself generates rash, hasty responses, compared with the careful, measured reflection that good theology seeks, or at the least, the kinds of virtuous interactions Christians seek to promote."[18]

But Bennett is not keen to give up on theological discourse online. Instead, she points to some ways in which Christians in particular moderate their own discussions. She goes on to cite self-imposed rules and guidelines instituted by online discussion groups. According to Bennett, "Part of what we can see at work in these communal guidelines and checklists is the development of what ethicists call 'practical wisdom' or 'practical reasoning.'"[19] She goes on to argue for the place of the local community in forming individuals by means of moral exemplars.

An appeal to the Incarnation is probably the obvious for the aspect of vitriol. Theologians have made appeals to charity, modeled perfectly by Christ, as a means of combating it within both interpersonal attacks and in remediating questionable content. This appeal to charity is often tied to the importance of the local community, as in the case Bennett draws out of the online discussion over Bell's book wherein one user suggests that one should only say something to another user if he could say it to the person offline as well.

The central question about online vitriol seems to be the one raised by Bennett: Is the "architecture" of the internet, by its very nature, encouraging or even creating such vitriol? Does the internet create more nastiness, either between people or from a moral point of view with regard to the myriad pieces of content which it remediates? In short, it is unclear whether so much theological energy should be put toward the *how* of mediating vitriol and not toward the *what* or *why* of vitriol itself.[20]

AUTHORITY

Thirdly, theologians have focused on the various ways in which the internet disrupts traditional loci of authority. One popular version of this is the worry over how websites have replaced papercraft books as the tools for garnering knowledge on any given topic. Another version is the joke about finding it online so it must be true. The joke works because people are generally suspicious at the content they find online. Of course, one cannot help but notice how these two popular expressions of this attitude toward the internet, when taken together, actually betray a confusion and ambivalence with regard to finding information online: are we too beholden to websites and search engines over more traditional means of research, or are we all pretty sure that online material isn't really that reliable? It seems that we do not know.

Faith communities have particular cause to be concerned about maintaining traditional loci of authority given their already uncomfortable role as choices among many in a marketplace of truth crafted in the modern ideal of pluralism and voluntarism. Real problems arise here. For example, theologian Richard Gaillardetz was already noticing in 2000 the problems of independent "Catholic" websites: "The fact is that however much we may lament over the quality of theological conversation being conducted, it is an exchange being conducted beyond ecclesiastical control. No church office could possibly oversee and credential or approve every Web site that emerges with the word Catholic in its self-description."[21] This gives us insight as to why media and communications are of particular interest to the church. Though we may perceive the sheer number of new loci for "Catholic" information as a new problem, the church has always had to contend with sources of information and knowledge outside its control, which must have relied on some form of mediated communication, however rudimentary it appears to us now. It is at this point where the history of the printing press seems particularly helpful.

Reformation-era historians have long noted the relationship between the Reformers and the pamphlet and other forms of printed materials. Elizabeth Eisenstein takes the example of Martin Luther's *95 Theses* to illustrate the relationship. She argues that schism and debate existed long before Luther's own list of grievances, but that "scribal campaigns had had a shorter wave resonance and produced more transitory effects. When implemented by print, divisions once traced were etched ever more deeply and could not be erased."[22] But in addition to providing the Reformers with a means of vast and efficient dissemination of antipapal materials, the printing press also afforded the church the ability to standardize its liturgy and practices. According to Eisenstein, "One may say that Catholic liturgy *was* standardized and fixed for the first time in a more or less permanent mold—at least one that held good for roughly four hundred years."[23] Thus while technology, specifically technologies which facilitate communications, has proven an integral part of the church's evangelical mission. It has also been the occasion for debate and contention, some of which eventually led to councils whose pronouncements and creeds realign the body back to the truth of the church.[24]

The issue of authority persists in contemporary discussions of the relationship between magisterium and academic theologians. Anthony Godzieba argues that there is an important technological component to present debates over the hierarchy of truth and the authority of magisterial texts. He poses the following questions:

> Does the immediate availability of a wide variety of papal statements via electronic media and the internet change the perceived level of authority that they carry? Even more fundamentally, does this "digital immediacy" influence the reception of these statements, which in turn shapes the statements' truth-value and their influence on the development of the Roman Catholic tradition, the reality of *communion*, and the very character of "teaching authority"?[25]

His answer, in short, is yes: aesthetic differences between online and offline church documents has affected the perceived authority of the documents without regard for traditional levels on the hierarchy of truth within the Catholic Church. Godzieba uses an allocution by Pope John Paul II on assisted nutrition and hydration (ANH) as an example. According to Godzieba, "A one-off papal speech was viewed by some prominent ecclesiastics as a definitive settlement of a contested moral issue."[26] In the debates that ensued over ANH, especially during the case of Terri Schiavo in 2005, theologians attempted to explain how the papal allocution came to have such definitive status. On Godzieba's view, one that was consistently overlooked was the technological.

For Godzieba, the issue was really "the immediate availability of papal and other official Vatican statements through various electronic media—what I am calling 'digital immediacy'—and the precise determination of the form of that availability in our aestheticized culture, a culture saturated with images and constituted by a primacy of the visual."[27] His focus, then, is not as much on the content of the allocution but on its form, which is mediated to most of its readers in electronic form. "Digital immediacy" is the norm of the internet age, according to Godzieba, and "this norm bestows on any official statement an absoluteness."[28] The traditional levels of church teaching that allow theologians and others to negotiate particular texts within the Tradition become collapsed in the digital age. As Godzieba says, "Immediacy equals authenticity equals authority."[29]

In the same volume in which Godzieba's chapter appears, Vincent Miller extends the conversation over authority and the internet into the realm of consumer culture. With regard to Godzieba's claims about the effects of "digital immediacy" on perceptions of magisterial teaching, Miller writes that this immediacy "does not simply free the papacy from the inertia of traditional media structures; it recontextualizes the pope as well."[30] Miller argues that instead of traditional "ecclesial structures" providing the "hermeneutics and pragmatics for interpreting and acting upon magisterial teaching," consumer culture becomes the interpretive framework for such texts.[31] The digital immediacy that Godzieba finds to be a centralizing force for the papacy, reinforcing and exacerbating "managerial" model over and against the *communio*, leaves it susceptible to commodification of religious traditions. Without the thick interpretive tradition which is skirted by such digital immediacy, the papal and magisterial texts that are Godzieba's subject become loosed from their requisite hermeneutical mooring. What is lost, according to Miller, are "tradition-specific interpretive habits" and a connection to "shared community practices."[32]

Miller goes on to argue that there are particular "cultural dynamisms" at work at the intersection of consumer culture and current communications technology. The first is *heterogenization*, an effect of globalization that "allows ever more differentiated communities to flourish."[33] With regard to consumerism, the effect of this for Miller is that it "renders social belonging increasingly a matter of choice."[34] Contemporary media ecology allows for and even encourages communities of choice, based on all kinds of common interests, ideologies, and common goals. "All they need to attract," writes Miller, "is enough participants to maintain a conversation."[35]

The second dynamism Miller names is *deterritorialization*, which he uses to describe the ability of "culture to float free" from the local community, as well as from the nation-state. Speaking elsewhere of deterritorialization, Miller writes, "Globalization arises from and encourages the proliferation of networks, organizations, and operations that escape and erode the national scale."[36] Communications technology is integral to this escape and erosion, which affects the imagination of local communities such as churches as well. This gets at the heart of Miller's understanding of what the internet *does*: as the agent of deterritorialization (or perhaps AN agent, although it seems like the internet is the best example of this), "every group, no matter how much it may be in the demographic majority, can imagine itself a minority with no responsibility for their influence over the status quo."[37]

The effect of both heterogenization and deterritorialization is an emphasis on identity. For the religiously inclined, the problem with identity is that "the complex hermeneutics and casuistry of living traditions with responsibility for putting their beliefs into practice do not fit well in this new identity-focused culture."[38] The effect of globalization—performed, perpetuated, and exacerbated by the internet—is to render magisterial authority inert as it lacks the hermeneutical hierarchical structures, mediated by the local community, necessary for their reception as anything other than another opinion—another consumerist choice among many.

In addition to these issues, theologians are also concerned—primarily as teachers and academics—with the changing loci of authority with regard to all knowledge. According to Bennett, "We cannot see distinctions between ourselves and God when 'attaining knowledge' has been truncated to the phrase 'Let me just Google that.'"[39] This inability to distinguish between ourselves and God, according to Bennett, should help us understand how to name the internet as one of the Powers and Principalities referenced by the New Testament. As a Power, Bennett argues, "the internet is one of many social structures which affects our ability to follow Jesus well."[40] Powers are created and therefore fallen.[41] The fallenness of the internet is primarily in its ability, as a Power, to appear as what it is not. According to Bennett, "We humans are too prone to believing that we make institutions like the internet. But it is exactly in believing this that makes the Powers seem to have autonomy from God; thus they dominate and dehumanize humans by separating us, too, from God."[42] For Bennett, then, the way in which the internet inserts itself as an authority speaks directly to its being a Power, created and fallen, and ultimately set against the true authority of God.

Bennett, Miller, and Godzieba provide different theological perspectives on the relationship between the internet and authority. Bennett argues that as one of the Powers and Principalities, the internet sets up its own authority against the true authority of God, and presumably against truth and knowledge of which God is the source. Miller argues that the internet contributes to the commodification of religion by refocusing culture onto identity, thereby disrupting the traditional structures by which magisterial authority is interpreted. Godzieba argues that "digital immediacy" contributes to a centralization of ecclesial authority by flattening the hierarchy of truth by way of aesthetical form. Their perspectives highlight the dynamic relationship of the sites of authority to consumer culture, as well as the relationship between the church and the culture(s) in which it finds itself throughout history.[43]

The incarnational emphasis of these approaches with regard to authority is not as readily apparent as other aspects of the internet. In fact, the doctrine of the Incarnation offers a critical framework on this aspect only as it pertains to the doctrine of the church. In the discussions of authority above, the church provides the standard of organizational integrity and internal coherence, which it reflects only insofar as it is founded upon and sustained by Christ. An incarnational approach to the question of authority is one that understands the importance of mediating structures, the primary of which is the sacramental life of the church, lived out in local communities. The theological antidote to decentralized, unbounded knowledge proffered by the internet is the joining of oneself to a community with commonly held loci of authority given it by the author of life.

ACCESS

The issue of authority in an online context is closely related to the issue of access. By "access," I mean two distinct but related things. First, there is great concern over how easily we are able to access whatever we want online. Second, there is some concern about discrepancies in access between various groups of people. This is one of the most convincing theological concerns, as one who studies the internet cannot help but notice the degree to which it is centered on the experience of some in the world and ignores or excludes others. Political scientist Pippa Norris is a leading researcher on the so-called digital divide, which she divides into three types: global, social, and democratic.[44] The global digital divide acknowledges differences in access between countries, correlated with differences in development generally. The social digital divide refers to the difference in access between rich and poor within a particular country. Finally, the democratic digital divide refers to differences in utilization of the internet among users.[45]

Bennett addresses the digital divide in its global form, saying, "Third-World peoples may end up feeling coerced by a world in which they cannot fully participate; colonialism emerges once again, this time in the guise of sleek machinery that promises to 'connect us' to a broader world, but in reality disconnects."[46] The problem of access in this respect falls mostly under the topic of development, deserving of a full theological treatment, and thus outside the scope of this project.

The other meaning of access is related Bennett's discussion about attaining knowledge. Drawing on Graham Ward's *Cities of God*, Bennett argues that knowledge and truth become "readily available to us in a variety of convenient interfaces that can be bought."[47] The argument rests in the assumption that the internet is primarily the place of search engines, the magical tools that bring to our eyes and minds whatever it is we call upon. Indeed, for Bennett, perhaps the search engine is best understood as the primary faculty by which the internet behaves as a Power, asserting itself as the locus of all knowledge, a poor substitute for the source of all true knowledge. The anxiety over access under this meaning appears in several other places, including Craig Detweiler's *iGods*. According to Detweiler, "Our machines offer us more access and more computing speed at more affordable prices every day."[48] He assumes throughout his text that "we are inundated by too much information (of our own making)."[49]

Detweiler's argument goes on to be about both information and material goods. With regard to information, his example is, understandably, Google. According to Detweiler, "Google is guided by an ambitious mission statement—organizing the world's information."[50] Like Bennett, Detweiler turns to Genesis for his theological account of this phenomenon. "If the original temptation in the garden was too much knowledge," he writes, "then Google is flirting with ancient lures. The hunger for knowledge can evidently overtake us, taking God out of the center of the world and thereby decentering us."[51]

The worry is over the way in which online habits are forming us as individuals and members of communities. For example, Philip Thompson uses the contemplative project of Thomas Merton "to challenge a technological mentality which is seeking to solve problems at hyper-speed and is justified by the mandates of expediency and efficiency."[52] He recognizes this technological mentality within himself and calls the need to be connected constantly to devices, "compulsive communication anxiety."[53] According to Thompson, "It illustrates how communication technologies can overwhelm our consciousness through an unceasing info-glut that may limit our most important interactions with family and friends."[54] He goes on to list many alarming examples of the negative effects of our "information age": statistics about daily average screentime, the demise of print culture, isolation and the erosion of traditional sites for necessary "social development," the growing number of children and adolescents on psychotropic medications, diminished reading comprehension among younger children, general memory loss after prolonged internet use, lack of sleep due to devices, and more.[55] The list is staggering (if tenuous in terms of causality). All of these problems lead Thompson to conclude, "This communication environment is not particularly hospitable to ancient truths and religious practices."[56]

There is a connection here between access to goods and information, and access to other human beings. The internet affords its users great access to knowledge, but it also provides access to other people. This access to others can take more than one form. It can be friendly communication with strangers or friends, or it can be accessing photos or words of another person within various contexts, most of which they curate themselves. In the latter case, the person can be removed from the moment of access, either consciously or unconsciously. For example, I can access someone else's thoughts through her blog. She need not be present for me to access her words.[57]

Here we see the theological concern over the pernicious effects of a technologized existence. Critics such as Thompson operate with the correct assumption that there is something disturbing about the way in which our time online conditions us not only to desire but to expect things and even people to be readily accessible when we demand them. To put it Bennett's terms of the Powers and Principalities, "Technological life overtakes us and blinds us to the realities in which we live, leaving us powerless to think about how to be and act in the world."[58] Thus enters Miller's concern over the emphasis on identity: we pick and choose our identity markers from the variety of choices to which we have (unprecedented) access online. The internet is a product of consumer mentality as well as a way to reinforce it.

Detweiler picks up this theme in his chapter on Amazon.com. His argument here is that Amazon's voracious appetite to be the single purveyor of all goods perpetuates materialism and our insatiable desire for more and more stuff. His antidote appears to be something like a relational consumerism, wherein our economic behavior is structured not just by price and expediency but by relationships. He writes, "All that time spent online is a step away from human contact. . . . Products used to be created and distributed locally. We knew the cobbler, the tailor, the candlestick maker. . . Shopping became transactional and impersonal."[59] The practical effect of this for Detweiler is the way in which it forms contemporary perceptions of church communities. He argues that Amazon's model of personalized shopping and consumer reviews (anyone is able to leave a review on a product on Amazon) has made its way into how people choose their church homes. Sites such as Yelp allow users to leave reviews of churches and other religious communities, turning communities into commodities.[60]

The theological antidotes to the "info-glut," to use Thompson's phrase, are varied. Thompson's argument throughout his text is that Thomas Merton's contemplative project provides much needed respite from the technologized society in which we live. He applies Merton's reflections on the media of his own time, specifically as they related to advertising, to the technologies with which Thompson finds so many problems. He finds several facets of Merton's own life appealing. First, we must reject the passive subjectivity which many media, especially television, require. Secondly, "we must redevelop our sense of community with neighbors, parishes, civic associations, clubs and families."[61] But the most important antidote to the technological mentality is to cultivate a contemplative prayer life. For Thompson, "The modern technological world and its communication forms have lost the best part of life, the access to a more profound vision that encompasses both temporal and spiritual realities."[62]

Detweiler's suggestion is related, though not as concretely argued. He concludes his work by championing a retreat into the wilderness, "As we hurtle down toward an unknown future with technology, we must plan some conscious pauses and be willing to use a mute button in our lives."[63] He also argues that the abundance of the Garden in Genesis 2 should give us pause, reminding us that true abundance is life with God and not in the "stuff" we fashion by ourselves.

Besides the emphasis on contemplative prayer and silence, two themes persist around this particular theological concern. The first theme is the ecclesiology of the local Christian community. The community functions as the Christian response to an online existence characterized by individualism, fragmentation, and reckless consumption of knowledge, goods, and other people. The Christian community provides the infrastructure and traditions for ways of life that can counter these pernicious behaviors. The second theme is implied in this emphasis on the local Christian community, and it concerns the category of the "real."

Andrew Root frames the unmitigated access afforded by the internet in terms of the question of reality itself. Drawing on Jean Baudrillard, he writes, "Thanks to our screens, we live in an age where symbols and actualities are no longer necessarily connected, where life becomes about consuming images, about correlation to un-real (hyper-real) simulations of beauty, wealth, and celebrity."[64] Although not as explicit as Root, this distinction between the "real" and the not-real or not-as-real symbols and signs of the internet pervades theological discourse about the internet. After all, the salient point of Thompson's cataloguing of culturally detrimental consequences of the internet is to demonstrate how we are being rent from reality itself. In both Root and Thompson, the antidote for the persistent attack on the real is to be rooted in the local community of the church. The church, they argue, offers the truly embodied experience of human life of which the internet can only be a simulacrum. Perhaps the most common evidence for this is the essentially *disembodied* reality of the internet, an aspect that causes great anxiety for theologians and to which we now turn.

DISEMBODIMENT

A common assumption is that when a person is online, her interactions with both content and other people lack "bodily-ness" in a way that offline life does not. This assumption is quickly followed by another, with a more critical edge: "embodied" interactions are more real and therefore better than disembodied ones, meaning that as necessarily "disembodied," online interaction is less real than offline interaction.[65] It is not difficult to see how theologians find cause for concern here, especially in a tradition where materiality and the body play such vital roles in the sacramental and liturgical life of the community.

This notion of disembodiment within online communication appears in both scholarly and popular commentary about the internet. The problem with the internet, we say, is that whatever social interaction takes place there cannot measure up to its offline counterpart precisely because our bodies are somehow not (as) involved. This sentiment appears in explicit or implicit form in nearly every critical account of the internet. It tends to rely on a more general assumption that technology draws people away from the "real," and for theologians and other religiously minded people, being drawn away from the real is being effectively drawn away from source of the real: God.

The editors of *America* magazine provide a summary of the stakes here. They write, "[D]igital isolation will only grow more acute as technology progresses. Imagine being attached to your computer at all times, whether through your watch or your glasses. Genuine human encounters will only be more difficult in a society filled with digital barriers."[66] The editors' use of the word "genuine" here is illustrative. I would argue that what they mean here is that embodied encounter unmediated by digital technology is more *real* than encounters that are.

This assumption runs so deep in critiques of the internet that it is often difficult to separate it from the many other concerns already discussed here. I would argue that disembodiment, by and large, undergirds most of the theological accounts of the internet, if not the nontheological as well. There is a common perception that the increase of the virtual means a decrease of embodied experiences. We are worried that the body will become less relevant to human life. Surely there are some who would argue that human evolution is moving in this direction. So-called "transhumanists" speak of an existence beyond the confines and obstacles of the physical body.[67] This makes theologians (and probably many non-theologians) understandably nervous. The experience of the body is central to how we have thought about what it means to be human since the question was first posed. It is possible that the resistance to transhumanism is at the root of an explosion of scholarship on the "body" from all kinds of academic disciplines.

In reaction to these transhumanist impulses, there has been a tendency to assert the reality of embodied experience over disembodied ones. Therefore, perhaps the most common expression of this particular anxiety over disembodiment is in the real/virtual binary. We saw this in Andrew Root's comments about symbols above. The internet, according to Root, has created a realm of the "hyper-real," which competes with the reality toward which the Christian community is oriented. He writes, "To proclaim the gospel is to speak of the real—most fully, Jesus Christ. But this Christ who is incarnate and crucified can only be found in existence itself, in the realness and fullness of the human experience."[68] But Root never defines "the realness and fullness of the human experience," presumably because he doesn't think he has to. He simply assumes that his words signal, by necessity, a non-digital experience. This is simply what he means when he uses words like "real," "full," and "human."

The effect of this is to separate anything that can be described as "virtual" from being described as "real." What is important is the assumption that genuine or real relies upon a particular version of embodiment, namely that which we perceive to be unmediated. This creates a kind of hierarchy of encounters among the unmediated and the digitally mediated. Should this remain a binary, however, it misses so much of human activity: most of our encounters—with objects, with ideas, and with one another—are mediated by *something*. Language and text are some of the most fundamental that come to mind.

It is not enough, however, to acknowledge the necessary mediation of human encounter. We must also acknowledge that digitally mediated experiences are, in fact, embodied, although perhaps not in the way we mean as we describe it as "disembodied." Pursuing this question of embodiment and online experiences tends to expose the assumptions we carry into discussions of the body. It requires a body to engage with technology. Furthermore, the various mediations of virtual space—photos, sound, text—require sense experiences.

According to Graham Ward, the changes wrought by telecommunications include changes to our conception of space itself. They also include changes in our perceptions of what society is, and, in turn, what the individual is. As predicated on relationships between individuals, society is built upon negotiating trust and doubt. He argues, "With advanced telecommunications, forms of trusting are not only divorced from face-to-face encounter but become founded upon texts, their composition, transmission, and interpretation."[69] Ward is reminiscent of Miller here, arguing that the imagined space has thus become "internationalized." He writes, "The internationalism of space produces international persons who are more diffuse, less embodied, more experimental, and less identifiable."[70] He goes on to argue that this view of the individual, a view in which the disembodied nature of our age plays an integral part, "denigrates being local such that material 'locatedness' is not in vogue."[71]

Thus we have the appearance of one of the theological antidotes to the disembodied realm of the internet: the primacy of the local church community (again). Ward describes the vanishing relevance of the local: "How can an act of local responsibility—being a member of a town council or a volunteer in a regional project for the homeless—escape the sense of being arbitrary or parochial?"[72] One can easily add participation in a church community as "an act of local responsibility." Indeed, he goes on to argue that it is now the church's onus to reassert "the importance of local and particular embodiment and of local and particular relations" in light of the changing technological and social landscape.[73]

Ward also argues that the internet is specifically about the transmission of text. The internet, he argues, "aspires to the pure act of reading, in which the interface between reader and text dissolves."[74] This particular article was written in 2002, before the advent of many of the technologies to which this observation might apply. One need only think of GoogleGlass, a device that places the computer interface into eyeglasses so that as one looks outward to the offline world, one is also peering into the online world. We are moving closer and closer, then, to the disappearing interface of which Ward speaks here. For Ward, this movement is theological. He writes,

> The dreams of fully realistic virtual realities—the kind advertised in *Star Trek*'s holodeck—signal a desire for new textual immediacies. The trajectory of this desire is eschatological. It is a contemporary refiguring, after the various Enlightenment refigurings, of the city of God: a techno-redemption. The euphoria of certain apologists for cyberspace is an expression of a yearning for infinite freedom conceived as infinite light.[75]

The transhumanist impulse to free oneself from the body—to whatever degree it is present in current iterations of online life—is problematic for theologians for several reasons. In addition to the first theological locus of the church, which necessitates a being-together in physical space, a second theological locus emerges here: the Incarnation. The central conviction of the Christian church is that God takes flesh in Jesus Christ, a conviction that influences the Christian perspective on materiality's place in the economy of grace. Thirdly, following from the Incarnation, is the resurrection, both of Jesus Christ and of ourselves. As Graham Ward puts it, "After all, resurrection is resurrection of the body."[76] Theologians have long seen it significant that the risen Christ is risen not in some ethereal, nonphysical form, but in a body, able to be touched by his disciples.

In order to argue for the internet as one of the Powers and Principalities, Bennett argues against the prevailing idea that the internet is primarily a disembodied space. She writes, "It is a body that must use the computer, check the email, navigate the avatar, reflect on how to interact with these people online."[77] But she, and any other theologian, must admit the importance of the local embodied community, especially for the sacramental life of the church. She writes, "The internet is not likely to be a proper site for participating in the sacraments or other physical forms of materiality that signify God's grace."[78] The centrality of the sacraments and the "other physical forms of materiality" which participate in the sacramental order give a rather unavoidable preference to the local church. The centrality of this physically bounded community is incarnational; God's revelation in the person of Jesus Christ changes the way in which Christians see the entirety of the created order. Therefore, both the local church (in its administration of the sacraments) and the Incarnation function as the two main theological loci for theological discussion of disembodiment in virtual life.

CONCLUSION: A WAY FORWARD

Different Christian traditions have negotiated the place of "other physical forms of materiality that signify God's grace" differently. The focus of the next chapter will be the Catholic tradition's insistence upon physical objects and places in the sacramental order by virtue of an incarnational approach to the world.

I have attempted to describe several aspects of the internet that have been of particular concern to theologians. These five aspects are intimately related and often overlapping, and they often appear in nontheological approaches to the internet as well. In short, theologians have relied both implicitly and explicitly on two doctrinal loci to address the concerns of virtual life: the church, specifically in its local form, and the Incarnation. For my part, I am convinced that these are indeed the two most relevant doctrinal loci for analyzing our current technological moment. What I propose, however, is an approach to the internet which attempts to understand its most basic logic, virtuality, as an expansive category that can actually help modern people understand some of the most important aspects of the Catholic imagination.

At the heart of the doctrines of the Incarnation and the church is a necessary dialectic between presence and absence, a dialectic upon which both interpersonal communication and mediation rely in virtual space. Although I will not return precisely to these five aspects of the internet, together they describe the "virtual" and in some cases are integrally important to religious modes of thought that sustain the life of the church and the Catholic imagination in particular.

The very category of "virtual" under which exists all of the activity and content theologians have found to be interesting and troubling is a constitutive part of the sacramental and ecclesial theology of the Catholic tradition. By focusing on what we mean by "virtual" in different contexts, I argue that we can come to see mediation as more than just a function of the internet. Mediation is, in a sense, the very practice that sustains the sacramental imagination. The church needs a "virtual logic" in order to understand both the sacraments and all of the physical-material entities which participate in the larger sacramentality of creation itself. In addition, in order for the church to be understood fully in both its universal and local iterations, one needs both presence and absence. This church has its own virtuality at the heart of its self-understanding as transcendent of both space and time.

Such virtuality necessarily entails attributes such as disembodiment and anonymity, and the necessity of these modes of social interaction and religiosity in the church should alert us to the fact that much of what is making theologians uncomfortable or worried about the internet is not about the form of mediation but in its referent. It is virtual space cultivated not for a community oriented toward God but often oriented toward themselves. While much attention has been given to mediation itself, I propose we instead focus on what or whom is being mediated and to what end. We have begun our theological discourse about the internet by focusing on its form and assuming that its mediating logic is necessarily antithetical to the sacramental and ecclesial convictions of the church. I contend, however, that we must expand our understanding of "virtual," using it as a hermeneutic for the church's long history of mediation. This will enable us to return to the internet with a more productive and honest theological evaluation.

NOTES

1. The technologically adept will be quick to point out that it is possible to discover someone's identity through IP addresses or extensive research.

2. See Hua Qian and Craig R. Scott, "Anonymity and Self-Disclosure On Weblogs," *Journal of Computer Mediated-Communication* 12, no. 4 (July 2007): 1428–1451; Erin E. Hollenbaugh and Marcia K. Everett, "The Effects of Anonymity On Self-Disclosure in Blogs: An Application of the Online Disinhibition Effect," *Journal of Computer Mediated-Communication* 18, no. 3 (April 2013): 283–302.

3. Servais Pinckaers, *The Sources of Christian Ethics*, trans. Sr. Mary Thomas Noble, O.P. (Washington, DC: The Catholic University of America Press, 1995), 8.

4. Here one could point to alarming accounts of "virtual" rape through avatars in games, for example.

5. Quoted in Jana Marguerite Bennett, *Aquinas on the Web? Doing Theology in an Internet Age* (New York: T & T Clark, 2012), 57.

6. Bennett, *Aquinas on the Web?*

7. George Randels, "Cyberspace and Christian Ethics: The Virtuous and/in/of the Virtual," *Annual of the Society of Christian Ethics* 20 (2008): 165.

8. Randels, "Cyberspace and Christian Ethics," 167.

9. Ibid., 169.

10. Ibid.

11. Rob Haskell, "eVangelism: The Gospel and the World of the Internet," *Evangelical Review of Theology* 34, no. 3 (2010): 280.

12. The sacredness of God's name in the Jewish tradition contributes to this desire for namefulness as well. The God of Israel is particular and personal, although in Christ, the ineffable God of Abraham, Isaac, and Jacob—described in terms of the people whom He has chosen—takes on a name so as to take on humanity. The veil of the sanctuary rips in two, no longer dividing those who can speak God's name and those who cannot.

13. Adam Copeland, "The Ten Commandments 2.0," *Word & World* 32, no. 3 (Summer 2012): 218.

14. Copeland, "The Ten Commandments 2.0," 220.

15. National Public Radio has become the latest organization to struggle with online comments. In 2016, they published an article with the following statement: "After much experimentation and discussion, we've concluded that the comment sections on NPR.org stories are not providing a useful experience for the vast majority of our users." Scott Montgomery, "Beyond Comments: Finding Better Ways To Connect With You," NPR.org (August 17, 2016).

16. Bennett, *Aquinas on the Web?* 145.

17. Ibid., 71.

18. Ibid., 147.

19. Ibid., 151.

20. I return to the issue of vitriol when discussing Pope Francis' 2017 and 2018 Communications Day addresses.

21. Richard R. Gaillardetz, "The New E-Magisterium," *America* 182, no. 16 (May 6, 2000): 9.

22. Elizabeth Eisenstein, *The Printing Revolution in Early Modern Europe* (New York: Cambridge, 1983), 151–152.

23. Eisenstein, *The Printing Revolution in Early Modern Europe*, 153.

24. Although the Reformation provides a clear example of the role of media in the church, earlier examples exist. Even as early as 325 CE, the positions of Arius at the Council of Nicaea and others involved in the Christological controversies were mediated by means of sermons, a kind of early "mass medium."

25. Anthony Godzieba, "Quaestio Disputata: The Magisterium in an Age of Digital Reproduction," in *When the Magisterium Intervenes: The Magisterium and Theologians in Today's Church*, ed. Richard Gaillardetz (Collegeville, MN: Liturgical Press, 2012), 140. Godzieba's worries here could easily be placed under "Access" below as well. At the heart of his concern, however, are the ways in which the internet affects perceptions of authority.

26. Ibid., 143–144.

27. Ibid., 146.

28. Ibid., 147.

29. Ibid. There are related concerns in other ecclesial contexts over communities or individuals online who are promulgating noncanonical texts as Sacred Scripture. Michael Legaspi argues that the shift from understanding the Bible as Scripture to understanding it as "text" can be understood as a shift to "opacity." The reformers "contributed to what I have called scriptural opacity, with the authority, meaning, and location of the Bible all becoming contested questions" (Legaspi 25). The fixed type of the printing press is clearly an important factor in this opacity reliant on the fixity of the text. In the digital age, however, text has, in some ways, regained its transparency. Text can be altered with a few key strokes, ideas, and images deleted and added at will. It should come as no surprise, then, that there is a small but real consideration of the canon from communities who have been established on the very opacity of the text itself. Our interactions with technology may have affected our views of text itself, including the central text of Christian communities.

30. Vincent Miller, "When Mediating Structures Change: The Magisterium, the Media, and the Culture Wars," in *When the Magisterium Intervenes: The Magisterium*

and Theologians in Today's Church, ed. Richard Gaillardetz (Collegeville, MN: Liturgical Press, 2012), 157.

31. Miller, "When Mediating Structures Change."
32. Ibid., 159.
33. Ibid.
34. Ibid., 162.
35. Ibid.
36. Vincent Miller, "Media Constructions of Space, the Disciplining of Religious Traditions, and the Hidden Threat of the Post-Secular," in *At the Limits of the Secular: Reflections on Faith and Public Life*, ed. William A. Barbieri, Jr. (Grand Rapids, MI: Eerdmans, 2014), 178–179.
37. Miller, "When Mediating Structures Intervene," 164.
38. Ibid., 165.
39. Bennett, *Aquinas on the Web?* 47.
40. Ibid., 103.
41. Col. 1:16–17.
42. Bennett, *Aquinas on the Web?* 105.
43. As George Randels writes, "This technology may require the church to reinterpret itself and its sources, re-emphasize or de-emphasize parts of its tradition, or adopt new points of view, even as the church also influences the use of computer technology."
44. Pippa Norris, *Digital Divide? Civic Engagement, Information Poverty and the Internet in the Democratic Societies* (New York, NY: Cambridge University Press, 2001), 4.
45. Norris, *Digital Divide?* 5. Theologians have begun to deal with the first two kinds of divide, but have been largely silent on the third.
46. Bennett, *Aquinas on the Web?* 18.
47. Ibid.
48. Craig Detweiler, *iGods: How Technology Shapes Our Spiritual and Social Lives* (Grand Rapids, MI: Brazos Press, 2013), 15.
49. Detweiler, *iGods*.
50. Ibid., 115.
51. Ibid.
52. Phillip M. Thompson, *Returning to Reality: Thomas Merton's Wisdom for a Technological World* (Eugene, Oregon: Cascade Books, 2012), xx.
53. Thompson, *Returning to Reality*, 36.
54. Ibid.
55. Ibid., 39.
56. Ibid., 46.
57. Access in this way also applies to the various unsavory aspects of the internet, such as pornography or erotic literature.
58. Bennett, *Aquinas on the Web?* 105.
59. Detweiler, *iGods*, 89.
60. Ibid., 92.
61. Thompson, *Returning to Reality*, 48.

62. Ibid., 50.

63. Detweiler, *iGods*, 219. But Detweiler parts ways with Thompson in offering as his final reflection the image of the city as a crucial aspect of the eschatological vision.

64. Andrew Root, "A Screen-Based World: Finding the Real in the Hyper-Real," *Word & World* 32, no. 3 (Summer 2012): 241.

65. I will assume, for the purposes of reviewing this literature, that online interaction is "disembodied." Later, I argue that the category is complicated, if not ultimately unhelpful.

66. "Our Digital Future," Editorial, *America* (February 17, 2014), accessed online, http://americamagazine.org/issue/our-digital-future.

67. One of the most well-known authors on transhumanism is Ray Kurzweil, who proposed singularity as humankind's telos in *The Singularity Is Near: When Humans Transcend Biology* (New York: Penguin Books, 2005).

68. Root, "A Screen-Based World," 242.

69. Graham Ward, "Between Virtue and Virtuality," *Theology Today* 59, no. 1 (2002): 58. I find the use of "face-to-face" to be more specific and more helpful than "disembodied," though it too has problems.

70. Ibid., 59.

71. Ibid.

72. Ibid., 61.

73. Ibid., 62.

74. Ibid., 64.

75. Ibid., 65. Here Ward is drawing on Sean Cubitt's *Digital Aesthetics* (London: Sage Publications, 1998).

76. Ibid.

77. Bennett, *Aquinas on the Web?* 79.

78. Ibid., 49.

Chapter 2

Ecclesial Perspectives on Media and Communications

The Magisterium of the Catholic Church is no stranger to the questions posed in the preceding chapter. The church has long had an interest with the modes and effects of human communication, as well as with the consequences of technology. In general, magisterial documents have taken a cautiously optimistic approach toward the progress of communications and media. According to *Gaudium et Spes*, part of "reading the signs of the times and interpreting them in the light of the gospel" is being honest about the obvious shortcomings and problems of modern life. The document balances its enthusiasm with statements like the following:

> [T]he modern world shows itself at once powerful and weak, capable of the noblest deeds or the foulest; before it lies the path to freedom or to slavery, to progress or retreat, to brotherhood or hatred. Moreover, man is becoming aware that it is his responsibility to guide aright the forces which he has unleashed and which can enslave him or minister to him. That is why he is putting questions to himself.[1]

The guiding vision for the church's official commentary on media and communications, then, is a realistic vision of both its possibilities and its pitfalls. What follows is a review of ecclesial perspectives on three interrelated questions: technology, media, and communications. The least amount of attention is given to technology in explicit terms in the ecclesial documents. The church has been more explicit about addressing the questions of media and communications, questions they have tended to consider together under the category of "social communications" following the Second Vatican Council.

The question of "where to begin" on these topics is especially difficult. In 1766, Pope Clement XIII promulgated the encyclical *Christianae Reipublicae* in which he dealt primarily with the dangers of anti-Christian publications. He wrote that the Holy See is required to see that "the unaccustomed and offensive licentiousness of books which has emerged from hiding to cause ruin and desolation does not become more destructive as it triumphantly spreads abroad."[2] Already in 1766 we have a document about the effects of technological progress (printed text and global travel) in the realm of communications on social relationships and personal morality. By mentioning this eighteenth-century document, I mean to promote a broader notion of media than one usually finds in both informal and formal discourses on the subject. It is a perspective that I believe is not only faithful to the church's approach to media for the last century or so but also more helpful than somewhat popular but narrow approaches for understanding our current media environment.

Each of the texts reviewed in this chapter has its own historical context and any number of other important contextual factors (debates over true authorship, ecclesial politics, implicit audiences, etc.) that are beyond the scope of the current project. While I present these texts chronologically, it is by no means a sufficiently rich account of their historical contexts.[3] Instead, the aim of this chapter is to discern the major themes in this body of church teaching, so as to elucidate, in a general way, the approach the church has taken toward issues of media and communications.

Taken as a whole, these ecclesial perspectives have variously focused on the church and the Incarnation as the theological loci for the question of media. To be sure, the former has been the most pronounced in these texts, while the latter has been more implicit and only emphasized in the latter part of the twentieth century. At its heart, this body of church teaching is about communion. Magisterial interest in communications revolves around a desire for true human community by virtue of shared *imago Dei* and salvation in the incarnate Word. Before the Second Vatican Council, the church focuses on communion within the context of the church alone, while after the council this communion extends outward to include the "whole human family." Even the renewed focus on evangelization in the papacies of John Paul II and Benedict XVI can be understood in the context of this outward-looking desire for communion.

For the church, social communications, media, and their necessary technologies are always to be understood in terms of communion. Various means of communications are measured against the standard of the communion found in the sacramental life of the church. They are also judged for the degree to which they contribute to this communion. There are many characteristics of this communion, including virtue (Pius XI); art that is "subjected to the sweet yoke of the law of Christ" (Pius XII); building the common good (Second Vatican Council); self-communication in love (Pontifical Council for Social Communications); human freedom (John Paul II); upholding marriage and family (Benedict XVI); and engendering an encounter with Christ (Francis). As they draw on the Incarnation and the church to understand human communication, church leaders have had as their standard and their end "relationships among human beings with God through Christ and the Holy Spirit."[4] To consider communications technology is to enter into much larger conversations about culture, politics, and economics. Therefore, although the most relevant texts come at the end of the twentieth century, this review thus includes sources that span the century as well as precede it.

PRE-CONCILIAR ECCLESIAL PERSPECTIVES

Ecclesial sources from the early twentieth century written on communications and technology focus primarily on the cinema and radio. Since its inception, film has garnered the attention of various religious authorities, including the Catholic Church. During the 1930s and 1940s, the church exercised its influence in this area through the Catholic Legion of Decency. As Anthony Burke Smith notes, "The Legion represents perhaps the most successful endeavor undertaken by the church to influence American culture."[5] It was a massive effort not only for censoring objectionable film but also for creating a culture of "decency" with regard to film within communities through the use of the Pledge in parishes.

The impetus for the Legion of Decency in the United States came from a more universal effort within the church to combat the moral evils of film, radio, and even books. In 1936, Pope Pius XI promulgated the encyclical *Vigilanti Cura*. The primary focus of *Vigilanti Cura* is the moral hazard of films. Objectionable films "are occasions of sin; they seduce young people along the ways of evil by glorifying the passions; they show life under a false light; they cloud ideals; they destroy pure love, respect for marriage, affection for the family."[6] The Incarnation (any mention of Jesus, really) is noticeably absent from the text. The church, however, looms large. Bolstered by the success of the Legion of Decency in the United States, and owing to a historical context of the Catholic subculture (at least in the American Catholic Church), Pope Pius XI insisted that the church is obligated to protect people from the evils of cinema, even as he acknowledged its ability to be a "bearer of light and a positive guide to what is good."[7] As the century progressed, the church expanded its reflections on the possibilities of media without losing its concerns over the ways in which they can be employed for malicious ends.

The church comes to the fore in the section entitled "Concrete Proposals." Pius XI began, notably, with the role of local pastors. He praised the Legion of Decency and its Pledge throughout the encyclical. Thus he proposed that "all Pastors will undertake to obtain each year from their people a pledge similar to the one already alluded to which is given by their American brothers and in which they promise to stay away from motion picture plays which are offensive to truth and to Christian morality."[8] He also suggested that each diocese employ the "Catholic press" to bolster this effort, specifically by "the prompt, regular and frequent publication of classified lists of motion picture plays."[9] Bishops should also set up an office for monitoring these lists, the administering of the Pledge, and the "existing motion picture theatres belonging to parishes."[10]

At the center of each of these "concrete proposals" is confidence in the efficacy of the local community upon the cultural engagement of its members. To the twenty-first-century reader, such faith in this efficacy carries an air of nostalgia for Christendom. We rarely if ever have sustained experiences of the kind of local communities that would make such an effort feasible or even coherent. This is the standard of human communion for the church: relationships centered on Christ and in the sacramental life of the church embodied locally in parishes and extra-ecclesial social structures.[11]

In his 1929 encyclical, Pope Pius XI made familiar comments about the moral effects of various media in the context of education. According to *Divini illius Magistri*, books provided unprecedented access due to their low prices, the cinema was the realm of unmitigated and often immoral display, and radio had immense and unequaled power of communication.[12] He wrote, "These most powerful means of publicity, which can be of great utility for instruction and education when directed by sound principles, are only too often used as an incentive to evil passions and greed for gain."[13] Media appeared in this encyclical for obvious reasons, as education involves necessarily the formation of young people and the use of particular media therein.

While the Incarnation is absent from the explicit argument of *Vigilanti Cura*, Pius XI referenced Christ generally throughout *Divini illius Magistri*. He named Christ as the ultimate teacher, beginning the encyclical by noting Jesus' "tenderness and affection for children."[14] Jesus also commands the church, "Teach ye all nations," which extends to all of the faithful and even those "outside the Fold."[15] Here he implied the image of the Good Shepherd, placing Christ at the center of the church's educational mission, a mission that is particularly focused on steering young people away from objectionable media. Christ is also the image of virtue into which young people are to be formed: "By His example He is at the same time the universal model accessible to all, especially to the young in the period of His hidden life, a life of labor and obedience, adorned with all virtues, personal, domestic and social, before God and men."[16] Although Pius XI did not discuss the relationship of Christ as God made flesh, as God incarnate, explicitly, he did include Christ throughout the encyclical as his theological grounding for the church's educational mission.

As in *Vigilanti Cura*, the efficacy of the church looms large in *Divini illius Magistri*. Somewhat more familiar to contemporary readers, Catholic education is presented as divinely mandated and especially urgent for the salvation of souls. Education, as well as the means of communication that participate in and aid it, is a matter of cultivating true communion, sustained by the sacramental life of the church. *Divini illius Magistri* picked up on the social structure envisioned by Pope Leo XIII in *Rerum Novarum*, emphasizing the different levels of society, or more properly, the three interrelated kinds of society: "Education is essentially a social and not a mere individual activity. Now there are three necessary societies, distinct from one another and yet harmoniously combined by God, into which man is born: two, namely the family and civil society, belong to the natural order; the third, the church, to the supernatural order."[17] The family is central to Christian education and has right to educate its children: "The family therefore holds directly from the Creator the mission and hence the right to educate the offspring, a right inalienable because inseparably joined to the strict obligation, a right anterior to any right whatever of civil society and of the State, and therefore inviolable on the part of any power on earth."[18]

The encyclical then connects the rights of the family and the church in terms of education, emphasizing that civil authority has a role in education but only as it befits the mission of education established by God within the church and family. Between church and family is the fabric of the local community. Early in the encyclical, Pius XI writes, "We implore pastors of souls, by every means in their power, by instructions and catechisms, by word of mouth and written articles widely distributed, to warn Christian parents of their grave obligations."[19] Coupled with the "concrete proposals" of *Vigilanti Cura*, this warning to pastors is all set against the backdrop of "the dangers of moral and religious shipwreck" found in books, radio programs and film. To steer young Catholics—all Catholics—away from such perilous content one needs the church, instantiated in the thick matrix of local pastors, the local parish, and the family.

Near the middle of the twentieth century, television coupled the intimacy of the family radio with the visual elements of film, bringing the moral dangers of the earlier media into the very heart of the home. In 1957, Pope Pius XII addressed film, radio, and even television in *Miranda Prorsus*. Pius XII extended his predecessor's comments about motion pictures into various forms of electronic media. He conveyed the persistent worry from the Holy See to extol the virtues of such media and enumerate their dangers: "From the time when these arts first came into use, the church welcomed them, not only with great joy but also with a motherly care and watchfulness, having in mind to protect her children from every danger as they set out on this new path of progress."[20] *Miranda Prorsus* continued the project of *Vigilanti Cura* insofar as it pays close attention to the ways in which these media shape the morals of media consumers. The church, therefore, has the solemn duty of ensuring that those entrusted to its care do not find themselves in the near occasion of sin by virtue of any given film, radio, or television program.

In assessing the situation before him, Pius XII understood the possibilities and promises of media technology to go beyond education and formation, the foci of his predecessor. He connected the media to the mission of the church itself: "Much more easily than by printed books these technical arts can assuredly provide opportunities for men to meet and unite in common effort."[21] While *Miranda Prorsus* continued to assert the role of bishops and priests in steering the community toward proper use of the media, the emphasis on each medium considered—television, film, and radio—was broader and more universal in its ecclesial vision. Pius XII went on, "Since this purpose is essentially connected with the advancement of the civilization of all peoples the Catholic Church—which, by the charge committed to it, embraces the whole human race—desires to turn it to the extension and furthering of benefits worthy of the name."[22]

Miranda Prorsus also placed more emphasis on the responsibility of individual media consumers. This seems like a natural evolution in emphasis, given the shift from film to television as the medium of central concern. The difference, according to *Miranda Prorsus*, is that "Television shares, in a sense, in the nature and special power of sound broadcasting, for it is directed towards men in their own homes rather than in theatres."[23] As essentially public, film lends itself to a more communal effort, introduced and encouraged by the parish priest. Television, on the other hand, concerns the daily choices of individuals and families, free from the accountability of publicly entering a theatre.

On the surface, these relatively early encyclicals on media appear to sacrifice any theological account of media or technology itself for an intense insistence on the morality of particular products. That is, most of both *Miranda Prorsus* and *Vigilanti Cura* addressed how pastors (bishops and priests) should work toward encouraging (or insisting upon) responsible and moral media consumption. One is tempted to characterize these texts as antiquated moral pronouncements that reflect a nostalgic yearning for a time when the church was a cultural and political force which could insist upon the "objective moral order" as the standard for all media production. But within these texts emerges a distinctly theological account of these media and their concomitant technologies, especially in *Miranda Prorsus*. Before attending to the moral questions of any particular medium, Pius XII writes, "From the drawings and inscriptions of the most ancient times down to the latest technical devices, all instruments of human communication inevitably have as their aim, the lofty purpose of revealing men as in some way the assistants of God."[24] One can see the germ of this theological understanding of media technologies in Pius XI, who writes that "the essential purpose of art, its *raison d'etre*, is to assist in the perfection of the moral personality."[25] While Pius XII continued this emphasis on the relationship between media and morality, he furthered the theological basis for it by including a more detailed account of how the media actually work and of their relationship to a theological anthropology:

> Among the various technical arts which transmit the ideas of men those occupy a special place today, as We said, which communicate as widely as possible news of all kinds to ears and eyes by means of sounds and pictures. This manner of spreading pictures and sounds, so far as the spirit is concerned is supremely adapted to the nature of men, as Aquinas says: 'But it is natural to man to come to things of the understanding through things of sense; for all our knowledge has its origin in a sense.' Indeed, the sense of sight, as being more noble and honorable than other sense, more easily leads to a knowledge of spiritual things.[26]

What this captures, even at such an early date in the influence of these various media, is the degree to which communications technology are part of the economy of grace. The wisdom of these papal statements is that while they understand such media to be "instruments," they do not argue for their inherent neutrality. Instead, they recognized the way in which their existence actually tells us something about what it means to be human, specifically what it means to be made in the image of God. This emphasis is hard to find in contemporary theological engagements with the internet. There is an implicit and sometimes explicit assumption that the internet and its culture is somewhat of an aberration, something separate from what we might call "religious" or "Christian." Consequently, the practical recommendations from a Christian perspective seek to *add to* online life, searching for ways to carve out a distinctly Christian space within cyberspace. In contrast, these ecclesial perspectives challenge us to engage in discourse that situates media—presumably to include the internet—within the very fabric of the created universe, as a vital part of human history and culture, and even a mediator of "spiritual things."

Therefore, one can argue that a deeply incarnational theology, while not explicit, undergirds these early ecclesial perspectives on media. By taking on human flesh, God has redeemed the world and made it possible for even the most banal aspects of creation to participate in the economy of grace. This is the incarnational theology on which the sacramental life is based. These documents are more explicit in explaining the place of the church in their particular cultural situations with regard to media. On the level of the church universal, the documents reflect an optimism about the relationship between the church and the rest of society that is difficult to maintain in our hyper-pluralistic culture today. On the level of the local church community, much emphasis is placed on the roles of bishops and priests to affect the media consumption of average Catholics. An example of this local effort would be the Pledge to stay away from immoral films. At the time of their writing, these documents could insist upon such cultural influence on the part of the church precisely because of the thick parish communities in which people lived. As the century progressed, ecclesial perspectives on media and communications would continue to point out both the positives and negatives of media. They would also more explicitly draw upon an incarnational perspective for their understanding of communications itself. With regard to church, they would continue to make suggestions for the diocesan and parish levels, but would extend the ecclesial vision of *Miranda Prorsus* by emphasizing the role of the media in the themes of the common good and solidarity.

CONCILIAR AND POST-CONCILIAR ECCLESIAL PERSPECTIVES

A mere six years after *Miranda Prorsus*, the Second Vatican Council produced *Inter Mirifica*, the Decree on the Means of Social Communication. This document is important for several reasons. First, it introduces the phrase "social communications," which is an acknowledgment of the relative insufficiency of "media" or "mass media." This is immensely helpful for applying its ideas to current technologies like the internet.[27] Secondly, it establishes a World Day of Communications,[28] which becomes an annual occasion for the current pope to give some commentary, however brief, on the issue of communications technology. Thirdly, it ensures that social communications will remain a focus for the church by proposing a "special office of the Holy See" on the topic. This will later become the Pontifical Commission for Social Communications, responsible for some of the most important (and theologically rich) ecclesial commentary on media and communications to date.

Despite these developments, *Inter Mirifica* remains, in the words of John O'Malley, "virtually forgotten."[29] Discussion of the decree was remarkably short and "many felt that the council was wasting its time discussing mass communications."[30] Even by those who did not share this view, the final document was not entirely well received. Three American journalists—John Cogley (*Commonweal*), Robert Kaiser (*Time* and *Life*), and Michael Novak (*The New Republic*)—released a statement calling the document "hopelessly abstract" and one "that may be cited as a classic example of how the Second Vatican Council failed to come to grips with the world around it."[31] One way to interpret the place of the decree in the context of the council as a whole is that it is an early product of the council and as such, does not reflect the characteristic "voice" of later documents.[32] Specifically, while the title of the document reflects an "openness and wonder," the document itself "seems at times more like a laying down of rules."[33]

Admitting obvious differences in tone from later conciliar documents, it is important to note that *Inter Mirifica* begins with an optimistic statement not unlike those found in the other documents produced by the Second Vatican Council: "Man's genius has, with God's help, produced marvelous technical inventions from creation, especially in our times."[34] What follows is a sort of "updated" version of the cautious tone of *Miranda Prorsus* and *Vigilanti Cura*. The church is aware of the possibilities of social communications, "but the Church also knows that man can use them in ways that are contrary to the Creator's design and damaging to himself."[35] Unlike *Miranda Prorsus*, which is organized by type of media, *Inter Mirifica* focuses on what the drafters have deemed to be the most relevant aspects of these media for social communications: information, art and the moral law, public opinion, and the role of civil authorities. The document continues the focus of its predecessors on morality to the media that are its subject, but does more to outline the creative possibilities of the media in question. The document expresses great confidence in the role of information in the modern world: "If news or facts and happenings is communicated publicly and without delay, every individual will have permanent access to sufficient information and thus will be enabled to contribute effectively to the common good."[36]

The document goes on to establish the absolute primacy of the objective moral order, which is "superior to and is capable of harmonizing all forms of human activity, not excepting art, no matter how noble in themselves."[37] Once again, we might be tempted to move quickly past such pronouncements as woefully nostalgic of a time and place when and where the church had social capital to exercise such authority; pluralism, among other cultural dynamisms, has long precluded such influence. However, there is an interesting assumption at work in this section of the document. Instead of sequestering media to a realm of neutrality from which the church can then pull for its own uses, it is quite clear here that the church sees all of human activity within the purview of its moral care. The language that *Inter Mirifica* uses here is notably stronger than earlier ecclesial statements. The council fathers write, "It is the Church's birthright to use and own any of these media which are necessary or useful for the formation of Christians and for pastoral activity."[38] Thus even in a tone that reflected previous approaches to the pastoral uses of media, *Inter Mirifica* moved toward a more integrated view of the relationship between the church and media.[39]

Once again, the implication is that media are neither neutral tools nor essentially evil spaces into which the church must interject itself. Instead, *Inter Mirifica* and the earlier papal encyclicals present a view of these media as constitutive of both creation and of human activity. This is an immensely important assumption for any theologically informed commentary on modern media and technology. Theologians and pastors would do well to remember the church's position here, developing steadily in these documents from *Vigilanti Cura* onward.

While *Inter Mirifica* is important for establishing the terms for the ecclesial discussion of social communications, the discussion is taken up more fully by the Pontifical Commission for Social Communications' Pastoral Instruction, *Communio et Progressio* in 1971. This document details the various topics introduced by *Inter Mirifica*, specifically public opinion, freedom of information, and the relationship between and roles of "communicators" and "recipients." In some ways, public opinion foregrounds the entire discussion of social communications in *Communio et Progressio*. The document understands "the means of social communications" as "a public forum where every man may exchange ideas."[40] Public opinion is a reflection of the exercise of various freedoms, including freedom of speech and freedom of information. One cannot form an opinion without access to accurate and timely information: "Freedom of opinion and the right to be informed go hand in hand."[41] This right carries the *duty* of being well-informed. According to the text, a person "can freely choose whatever means best suit his needs both personal and social."[42] Such freedoms, however, are not "limitless" and must be seen in the context of other rights, namely "the right of truth," "the right of privacy," and "the right of secrecy which obtains if necessity or professional duty or the common good itself requires it."[43] Consequently, the various actors within the means of social communications have particular freedoms and duties associated with their roles, be they "communicators" or "recipients."

If any aspect of these two documents is problematic for the application of ecclesial sources to the contemporary technological moment, it is these categories of "communicators" and "recipients." They are particularly illustrative of a view of media that understands them as the conduits of products (news pieces, programs, texts, etc.) by one group of people (communicators) to be consumed or received by the other (recipients). Such is the standard understanding of "mass media": media that is intended for and distributed to large masses of people. The concept of "social communications" provided by *Inter Mirifica* and expanded by *Communio et Progressio* is somewhat able to capture the dynamism of communications technologies beyond mass media. The communicator/recipient binary, however, is less helpful given the fluidity of such roles in the internet age. User behavior online does not fall neatly into either of these categories. At one moment, I am a communicator, and the next, I am a recipient. Even more complicated is the fact that in one act, I can be both. Commenting on an online article is difficult to classify along the communicator/recipient binary. I am a communicator because I am producing text to be read by others, yet by commenting, I am displaying an interaction with the original article, performing my role as recipient. The inherent interactivity of online life, especially with the advent and growth of "social media," betrays a problem with these categories as we move beyond "mass media." A choice presents itself: do we simply apply the duties and responsibilities of both categories to all internet users? Or are these categories too beholden to a perspective of media technologies as part of what we call "mass media"?

In addition to understanding media as primarily "mass media," another important assumption of the ecclesial perspectives comes to light in *Communio et Progressio*. The latter half of the document outlines the responsibilities of the "civil authorities," as well as Catholics and other religious people who find themselves in a position to affect media. Coupled with the earlier discussion of "public opinion," the implication here is that the spheres of the church and the civil authority meet each other in a public space capable of negotiating the interests and values of each party. The insistence on public opinion is particularly telling. What good is a well-informed opinion if there is no place to express that opinion? Such expression seems reserved for an as yet undefined "public." This comes to light when the Commission describes the role of the so-called recipients:

> Recipients can be described as active when they know how to interpret communications accurately and so can judge them in the light of their origin, background and total context. They will be active when they make their selection judiciously and critically, when they fill out incomplete information that comes their way with more news which they themselves have obtained from other sources, and finally, when they are ready to make their view heard in public, whether they agree, or partly agree or totally disagree.[44]

What exactly defines the social space in which these recipients are "to make their view heard in public"? In addition to complicating the communicator/recipient binary, the internet has also complicated the public/private binary on which so much of the ecclesial commentary on society and culture has relied. *Communio et Progressio* is often considered one of the most optimistic ecclesial perspectives on communications technology. It is also idealistic when it comes to the structure of society, specifically because of its perception of a neutral "public" or "civil" space in which the church can express its position toward the various media of concern.

Communio et Progressio is a detailed discussion of social communications which flows from not only *Inter Mirifica* but also from "*Gaudium et Spes*: Pastoral Constitution on the Church in the Modern World." The document takes its primary task from *Inter Mirifica*, attempting to provide theological and ecclesial commentary on topics related to social communications that are only briefly introduced at the Council through *Inter Mirifica*. In at least two ways, however, *Communio et Progressio* is also a product of the church-world relationship envisioned by *Gaudium et Spes*. According to the Council fathers as expressed in the Pastoral Constitution, the church "must therefore recognize and understand the world in which we live, its expectations, its longings, and its often dramatic characteristics."[45] *Gaudium et Spes* addresses many aspects of the modern world, and in so doing, provides an example for subsequent ecclesial texts of creative engagement with the "dramatic characteristics" of the modern world. When the Pontifical Commission drafts *Communio et Progressio* in 1971, then, they do so in the shadow of both *Inter Mirifica* and *Gaudium et Spes*. The effect of the latter is to encourage and even demand of the Pontifical Commission a perspective on this important aspect of culture and human history—the media—that is well informed on its lived realities, both positive and negative.

Communio et Progressio insists that social communications be employed for furthering the common good, specifically through education and informing the public opinion. When read as a particular application of the theological project of *Gaudium et Spes*, the eschatological implications of the ecclesial perspective on social communications from this period come to light. Chapter 3 of *Gaudium et Spes*, "Man's Activity Throughout the World," argues for the place of all of this "feverish activity" of humanity in salvation history. This section of the document is theologically rich and pertinent to the current project:

> [F]ar from thinking that works produced by man's own talent and energy are in opposition to God's power, and that the rational creature exists as a kind of rival to the Creator, Christians are convinced that the triumphs of the human race are a sign of God's greatness and the flowering of his own mysterious design. For the greater man's power becomes, the farther his individual and community responsibility extends.[46]

This perspective applies to any number of human activities; *Gaudium et Spes* is not referring just to art or labor or technology, but appears to put the entirety of human activity within the "realization in history of the divine plan."[47] When taking on the specific activity of social communications, then, *Communio et Progressio* applies this perspective to the various and increasing number of media in the twentieth century. In addition to the relative optimism of *Gaudium et Spes*, *Communio et Progressio* also adopts the language of rights and responsibilities, a persistent theme in Catholic social thought since *Rerum Novarum*. *Gaudium et Spes* discusses the rights of humans in the modern world; *Communio et Progressio* asserts the particular rights to information and expression. *Gaudium et Spes* argues that the common good and the absolute inviolability of human dignity should guide all of human activity, even and especially in light of such rapid change and progress; *Communio et Progressio*, as noted above, maintains that "the right to information is not limitless," and that these limits are dictated by a respect for the common good and for the dignity of all human life.

Here the document reflects the aforementioned emphasis on communion. The documents from the Second Vatican Council from which *Communio et Progressio* takes its cues include human solidarity and the global common good as a way of extending the standard of true communion to the whole world. While the sacramental life of the church instituted by Christ is the performative means of communion for the baptized, all human beings share the image of God, which gives each person an inherent dignity as well as the innate desire for true relationships with other people and with the divine. Again, as social communications become the focus of these mid-century- and late-twentieth-century documents, they are discussed within the context of building communion both within and outside of the church that is grounded in the relationship to the divine which all human beings share in Christ's redemption.[48]

As a Pastoral Instruction, *Communio et Progessio* has several proposals for better incorporating social communications into the church itself. It adds the consultation of media experts to the activities of priests, bishops, and other "ecclesiastical authorities."[49] The document has a range of specific proposals, including reinforcing the need to establish World Communications Day, the nurturing of an apostolate of social communications at the diocesan level, establishing national offices for communications media, appointing a press officer in each of the episcopal conferences, and making better and more frequent use of press releases.[50] In the conciliar spirit of the Second Vatican Council, then, the Pontifical Commission focuses on nurturing a better engagement with the world of social communications on the level of national episcopal conferences, while continuing to gesture to the role of the local community.

The earnest attempt to understand social communications found in *Communio et Progressio* is instructive for theological discussions of contemporary iterations of such technologies and institutions. All of the pastoral suggestions found in the latter half of the document and listed above are undergirded by the document's theological assumptions. These assumptions inform the ecclesial perspective as expressed by the Pontifical Commission for Social Communications in both this document and beyond. The theological assumptions of *Communio et Progressio* are primarily incarnational in focus: "While he was on earth, *Christ revealed himself as the Perfect Communicator.*"[51] This frames the document's definition of communication itself in theological terms from the start. The Commission writes, "Communication is more than the expression of ideas and the indication of emotion. At its most profound level, it is the giving of self in love."[52] This *kenotic* perspective moves the theological discussion in a necessarily more optimistic direction than some of the accounts above. It allows for a moral complex discussion of what the church might mean by "moral" with regard to particular products of media. One can take a given program or film and ask, *To what degree does this reflect the giving of the self, the highest example of which is the* kenosis *of Christ, God incarnate?*

As incarnational, the project of *Communio et Progressio* undertakes the pressing questions of media technologies with the assumption that doing so is not just a matter of dealing with the newest version of humanity's hubristic production. Indeed, to discuss social communications is to discuss the human participation in the ultimate self-communication of God made flesh in Jesus Christ. Incarnational perspective colors not only their approach to media technologies but to the very relationship between church and world: "The People of God walk in history. As they, who are, essentially, both communicators and recipients, advance with their times, they look forward with confidence and even with enthusiasm to whatever the development of communications in a space-age may have to offer."[53]

What the "space-age" had to offer, it seems, was a world in which social communications are mediated by computers. The occasion of the twentieth anniversary of *Communio et Progressio*, then, saw the (belated) publication of *Aetatis Novae*, a Pastoral Instruction on Social Communications from the Pontifical Commission (1992). The document reasserts the key themes of *Communio et Progressio* and includes an extensive set of guidelines for better incorporating the means of social communications on the parish and diocesan levels. It does so, however, in light of new developments in social communications, specifically computer-mediated communication: "Taking for granted the continued validity of the principles and insights of these conciliar and postconciliar documents, we wish to apply them to new and emerging realities."[54]

The document also begins with an acknowledgment of the pervasiveness of media in the twenty-first century, such that "to a considerable extent, human experience itself is an experience of media."[55] *Aetatis Novae* goes on to assert that "today's revolution in social communications involves a fundamental reshaping of the elements by which people comprehend the world about them, and verify and express what they comprehend."[56] This perspective is incredibly helpful for figuring out the theological stakes of both technology and media. Technology, especially that which contributes to our means of communicating with each other, changes the way we see the world, including the way we see other people. This is also the business of religious communities. One approach to this reality is to understand communications technologies as competitive means of formation against which the church must reassert its claims on individuals and communities. Another approach, the one seemingly undertaken by *Aetatis Novae* and the approach for which I would argue, is to see these means of social communications as possibly (but not always) contributive to the *communio* of the church itself.

According to *Aetatis Novae*, social communications must be a part of the church's life in order to foster the very relationships which sustain it, particularly the relationships between lay people and ecclesial authorities. This exchange, necessarily facilitated and influenced by the various means of communications, "is one of the ways of realizing in a concrete manner the church's character as *communio,* rooted in and mirroring the intimate communion of the Trinity."[57] The pastoral plan offered by *Aetatis Novae*, then, is not simply a list of suggestions at the end of an abstract text. According to Angela Ann Zukowski, "The idea of an integrated pastoral plan for social communications is the heart of *Aetatis Novae*. Even though found in an appendix, it does not stand as an afterthought but as the key for implementing the vision of the document."[58]

Reflecting the other theological locus of interest here, *Aetatis Novae* picks up the incarnational focus of the preceding document, explaining the implications of communications-as-kenosis: "*Communication mirrors the Church's own community* and is capable of contributing to it."[59] Because of God's own self-communication, the Commission writes, "the communication of truth can have a redemptive power, which comes from the person of Christ."[60] This is again related to the eschatological vision of *Gaudium et Spes* Chapter 3, wherein the "feverish activity" of humankind is understood at part of and not antithetical to God's action in the world. *Aetatis Novae* makes this more plain in saying, "History itself is ordered toward becoming a kind of word of God, and it is part of the human vocation to contribute to bringing this about by living out the ongoing, unlimited communication of God's reconciling love in creative ways."[61]

On February 28, 2002, the Pontifical Council for Social Communications (PCSC) released two documents: *The Church and Internet* and *Ethics in Internet*. The PCSC intended the documents to be read in tandem, although they felt that the topics of each document deserved their own treatment. *Ethics in Internet* proposed a "Catholic view of the Internet" and an "ethical evaluation of social communications" within the context of the continued development of internet technology.[62] The Pontifical Council here provided the single most astute description of online life from the church:

> It is instantaneous, immediate, worldwide, decentralized, interactive, endlessly expandable in contents and outreach, flexible and adaptable to a remarkable degree. It is egalitarian, in the sense that anyone with the necessary equipment

and modest technical skill can be an active presence in cyberspace, declare his or her message to the world, and demand a hearing. It allows individuals to indulge in anonymity, role-playing, and fantasizing and also to enter into community with others and engage in sharing. . . . It can be used to break down the isolation of individuals and groups or to deepen it.[63]

This statement solidifies the PCSC as the most attuned to technological issues within church leadership. Despite their acumen on the subject, however, the Pontifical Council remains relatively unknown to lay people within the church, whereas attention to the papal office has only increased, especially with the reign of Francis. To close, then, I outline the pontifical statements on social communications from the pontiffs after the Second Vatican Council.

PONTIFICAL PERSPECTIVES ON SOCIAL COMMUNICATIONS

In addition to establishing the Pontifical Commission for Social Communications, *Inter Mirifica* established the World Communications Day (WCD) as an annual event for the church to reflect upon these issues. According to *Inter Mirifica*, the WCD is meant "to make the Church's multiple apostolates in the field of social communication more effective."[64] It is a day on which "the faithful will be reminded of their duties in this domain."[65] The degree to which the goals of this day are accomplished is hard to adjudicate. What it has produced is a substantial body of speeches from popes Paul VI, John Paul II, Benedict XVI, and Francis on the topics of media, communications, and technology. Each pontiff reiterates the themes and concerns of many of the ecclesial perspectives detailed above, adding his own inflection and focus to the topic of social communications. Some years, the pope has chosen to discuss media in general, while in others he has focused on a particular medium, a particular demographic (i.e., youth), or a particular theological idea (see table 2.1 for a complete list of topics). In lieu of detailing each year's message, I will discuss the messages of each pontiff more generally, giving the most attention to Pope John Paul II, whose pontificate included the most number of WCD messages, and whose employment of mass media was a central feature of his papacy.

Paul VI

Pope Paul VI issued a message for World Communications Day annually from 1967 to 1978. By and large, his messages continue many of the themes found in both *Inter Mirifica* and *Gaudium et Spes*. The Pontifical Commission

Table 2.1 World Communications Day Speeches and Topics 1967–2018

Pontiff	Year	Topic
Paul VI	1967	First WCD
	1968	Development
	1969	Family
	1970	Youth
	1971	Unity
	1972	Truth
	1973	Spiritual Values
	1974	Evangelization
	1975	Reconciliation
	1976	Rights and Duties
	1977	Advertising
John Paul II	1978	Recipients: Rights/Duties
	1979	Childhood
	1980	Family
	1981	Human Freedom
	1982	Elderly
	1983	Peace
	1984	Faith and Culture
	1985	Youth
	1986	Public Opinion
	1987	Justice and Peace
	1988	Religion in Mass Media
	1989	Solidarity and Fraternity
	1990	Computer Culture
	1991	Unity
	1992	Evangelization
	1993	Video/Audio Cassettes
	1994	Television
	1995	Film
	1996	Media and Women
	1997	Evangelization
	1998	Holy Spirit
	1999	"In Search of a Father"
	2000	Evangelization (Millennium)
	2001	Evangelization
	2002	Evangelization (Internet)
	2003	Peace
	2004	Family
	2005	Solidarity
Benedict XVI	2006	Media
	2007	Education
	2008	Truth
	2009	Relationships
	2010	Priests
	2011	Truth/Authenticity
	2012	Evangelization/Silence
	2013	Networks

(Continued)

Table 2.1 World Communications Day Speeches and Topics 1967–2018 *(Continued)*

Pontiff	Year	Topic
Francis	2014	Encounter
	2015	(Encounter and) Love
	2016	(Encounter and) Mercy
	2017	Hope and Trust
	2018	Fake News

was doing its work on *Communio et Progressio* during the early years of his pontificate, and most of the "heavy lifting" with regard to social communication fell under (and continues to fall under) their purview. For his first message, Paul VI gives a succinct and lucid account of what modern communication technologies do: "Time and space have been conquered, and man has become aware as it were a citizen of the world, sharing in and witnessing the most remote events and vicissitudes of the whole human race."[66] As the first of its kind, this speech is broad in its message, and continues the cautious optimism of the other ecclesial documents reviewed here. He speaks, like the Council and like his papal predecessors, of the responsibility to keep communications media in "conformity with the objective moral order."[67] This language is reminiscent if not mimetic of the words of *Vigilanti Cura* and *Miranda Prorsus* from before the Council.

But Pope Paul VI also uses notably optimistic language to describe communications technology of his time. He says of the "transformation" of social communications, "In all this We see the unfolding and the realization of a wonderful plan of God's providence, which opens to man's genius ever new ways of achieving his perfection and of attaining his final end."[68] When he turns to the relationship between social communications and young people in 1970, Paul VI says that they "provide new sources of knowledge and culture."[69] In a message from 1975, he calls the means of social communications "wonderful extensions of His creation which have been brought to such perfection in our time."[70] It is not enough to say that his approach in several of these messages was optimistic; it was also notably theological. Media are not simply tools that are ambivalent to the eschatological pilgrimage of humanity; they are providential, they are inherently part of the created order, and they are an integral piece of human culture, not just as a reflection or conveyor of culture but also as a producer of it.

Pope Paul VI also continues the Council's emphasis on the role of communications in working toward the common good and cultivating solidarity. The focus on global common good is particularly important for Paul VI's second message for WCD, wherein he takes up the topic of "Social Communications and the Development of Nations." He claims that there is a great temptation to put communications media only to selfish purposes, especially ones related to consumerism and the fostering of frivolous desires for economic gain. "Once this temptation is overcome," says the pontiff, "a great enterprise lies before them: they can do so much to voice the appeals of humanity in distress, to put in bold relief the efforts at cooperation, the initiatives and strivings for peace."[71] In addition to giving voice to the many problems of the modern world, the means of social communications should also be employed for evangelization. The topic of evangelization will become of great concern to his successor, Pope John Paul II.

John Paul II

The media played an important role in the pontificate of John Paul II. He traveled more than any pope in history, travels that were well documented by the media. These travels, especially in their ability to be mediated to people all around the world, played a significant part in the perception of the pope, especially by young people. Both Anthony Godzieba and Vincent Miller cite these aspects of John Paul II's pontificate as part of their arguments for the relationship between magisterial authority and the communications media, specifically the internet. Before proposing his own aforementioned theory about the digital immediacy of the pope's statements, Godzieba writes that "John Paul II's personal charisma (which led commentators to note his 'rock star' status among youth), his role as an uncompromising moral icon (at least until the mishandling of certain scandals late in his papacy), and his uncanny use of the media" all contributed to the "absolutizing" of some of the pope's statements, regardless of their actual magisterial weight.[72] For his part, Miller relays the story of a boy in Colombia who "called out to John Paul, 'I know you, you're the pope. You're the same one I saw on television.'"[73] Instead of interpreting this moment, as the director of the Vatican Press office did, as part of the ministerial power of John Paul II, Miller writes, "For the boy, John Paul would share the company of the Colombian equivalents of Barney and Spongebob Squarepants; for his parents, Oprah and Dr. Phil."[74]

This is all to say that John Paul II's relationship to the mass media is not neutral or without its complications. Nevertheless, the very time frame of his papacy makes his speeches for World Communication Day particularly interesting: he was pope during the climax of mass media and the turn toward new media that is the concern of this project. His papacy is on the very cusp of what he calls "computer culture."

John Paul II's papacy presents us with a large body of reflection on the topic of social communications. He covers many different topics from several different angles. His first message for WCD relies on the aforementioned distinction, found first in *Inter Mirifica*, between "communicators" and "recipients." Very much in line with the claims of *Communio et Progressio*, the message aims to present "recipients" as agents within communication, not simply objects of communication itself. He says, "Responsible collaboration is required from the 'recipient' himself, who ought to take an active part in the formative process of communication."[75] John Paul sees the possibility in social communications for what he terms a "round table of society," referencing the importance of public opinion and public expression of that opinion from *Inter Mirifica* and *Communio et Progressio*. This "round table" and the dialogue it requires is another facet of the true communion of human beings envisioned in the ecclesial perspectives.

For Pope John Paul II, communication is about formation, which places the family at the center of his second message, "Social Communications for the Protection and Development of Childhood in Family and Society." Families have both the right and duty to ensure that children are protected from evils in media, and communicators themselves are responsible for "offering [the child] recreational and cultural programs that will help in its search for identity and gradual entry into the human community."[76] The following year, the family is taken up again, this time with even more critical language from John Paul. He says of the media that they "frequently present a distorted picture of what a family is," and that the family has the freedom and responsibility to maintain the integrity of family life, especially in the education of their children.

Human freedom is central to John Paul II's entire theological vision, and it comes to light in these statements as well. In fact, he devotes an entire WCD message to human freedom, saying, "Man, even in the presence of the mass media, is called to be himself: that is, free and responsible, a user and not an object, critical and not passive."[77] The pope sees human freedom as central to communications because of its ability to expose those places where human freedom is not being realized. This is a concrete expression of the emphasis on the common good and solidarity from Paul VI and the Commission. A specific example of his thinking on this matter is his WCD message from 1982 on the elderly. He contends, "The media instruments . . . can quickly and eloquently concentrate general attention and excite general reflection on the elderly and on their conditions of life," conditions that may be standing in the way of their human dignity and exercise of human freedom.[78]

From 1978 to 1989, John Paul II's WCD messages focused on all of the traditional media that had been the focus in ecclesial texts from *Vigilanti Cura* to *Communio et Progressio*. In 1990, he turned his attention to computers. In his message for the twenty-fourth WCD, John Paul writes, "One no longer thinks or speaks of social communications as mere instruments or technologies. Rather they are now seen as part of a still unfolding culture whose full implications are as yet imperfectly understood and whose potentialities remain for the moment only partly exploited."[79] The ecclesial perspectives on media and social communications expressed throughout the twentieth century have variously described them as "instruments" or "technologies." And surely they are both of these things. But John Paul II knew that he must say something different about computers. There are many ways what is said about film or radio or television can be applied to computer-mediated communication, yet he recognized the emergence of something new in "computer culture."

In the same message, John Paul II goes so far as to claim that the vision of the global common good and unity which he envisioned in other places, and which he inherited from Paul VI and the Second Vatican Council, was showing signs of fruition in computer culture:

> With each day that passes the vision of earlier years becomes ever more a reality. It was a vision which foresaw the possibility of real dialogue between widely-separated peoples, of a worldwide sharing of ideas and aspirations, of growth in mutual knowledge and understanding, of a strengthening of brotherhood across many hitherto insurmountable barriers.[80] (cfr. *Communio et Progressio*, 181, 182)

The pope sees in computers the real possibility for the "round table of society" he envisioned in his first message for WCD. Specifically, it has the ability to give "recipients" the means of critical agency, and to give "communicators" a better sense of their responsibility to the human community.

But John Paul II does not return to computers explicitly until 2002, continuing in the intervening years to conceive of social communications in terms of the traditional media of "books, newspapers and periodicals, radio, television, and other means."[81] This time, he takes on the internet specifically, after a full twelve years of rapid expansion and development of the internet as a means for social communications as well as a "culture" unto itself. He discusses the internet as it relates to evangelization, comparing it to a Roman forum: "It was a crowded and bustling urban space, which both reflected the surrounding culture and created a culture of its own."[82] John Paul describes the internet as pastorally helpful to the follow-up required by evangelization. He affirms the necessarily embodied character of both conversion and participation in the life of the church but offers the internet as a "supplemental" new element to this ancient process. "The Internet can never replace that profound experience of God which only the living, liturgical and sacramental life of the church can offer," says John Paul, "[but] it can certainly provide a unique supplement and support in both preparing for the encounter with Christ in community, and sustaining the new believer in the journey which then begins."[83]

Like the many ecclesial perspectives before his, John Paul II tempers his optimism about the internet as a forum for human unity and evangelization with concerns about possibilities for misuse: "An almost unending flood of information," keeping people from necessary "inner quiet," and the limits of disembodied human communication, especially in the context of evangelization. Curiously, in outlining these concerns, John Paul II returns to the language of "instrument" to describe the internet. The internet is an instrument for evangelization (like other means of social communications) in John Paul's view, but he goes on to describes it, echoing his description of computers from 1990, as a "forum" and a "culture" in the same text. Surely these aspects of the internet need not be mutually exclusive but one wonders what exactly he means by "culture" with regard to the internet. Unfortunately, he never takes the idea of "internet-as-culture" up again before his death in 2005. For the most part, John Paul II's contribution through these speeches was to cover a wide array of topics as they relate to traditional forms of "mass media," and to begin the conversation about the advent and expansion of the "computer culture" at the turn of the century.

John Paul II's final comments on the internet returned to the measured openness to understanding technological culture that we find in his message from 1990. In the final year of his pontificate, John Paul II penned his last apostolic letter entitled *The Rapid Development*, addressed to "Those Responsible for Communications." In the letter, John Paul II directly addressed the internet, describing it as part of the "current phenomenon of communications."[84] Echoing the words and spirit of *Gaudium et Spes*, John Paul II goes on to say that this phenomenon "impels the Church towards a sort of pastoral and cultural revision *so as to deal adequately with the times in which we live.*"[85] As internet technology continues to evolve, so too must theological and pastoral reflection on social communications.

Benedict XVI

Pope John Paul II's ability in the world of media relations was a hard act to follow. Pope Benedict XVI assumed office in 2005, and was noticeably less adept to wielding the media than his predecessor. But Benedict had much to say about the media and social communications, and he borrowed heavily from John Paul II in the process. His concerns throughout the speeches fall into three major themes: family and sexuality, truth, and evangelization. For the most part, these themes represent the first-, second-, and third-thirds of his WCD speeches, with some overlap.

The first theme of note from the WCD of Benedict XVI is his persistent mention of sexuality, marriage, and the family. Each of his first four WCD speeches mentions the effects of the media on perceptions of the family. For his first WCD, Benedict says, "The need to uphold and support marriage and family life is of particular importance, precisely because it pertains to the foundation of every culture and society."[86] When he turns to education for the topic of 2007's message, the topic of the family makes up the majority of his statement. Sexuality also comes to the fore in that year: "Any trend to produce programmes [sic] and products—including animated films and video games—which in the name of entertainment exalt violence and portray anti-social behavior or the trivialization of human sexuality is a perversion, all the more repulsive when these programmes are directed at children and adolescents."[87] This message ostensibly has education as its topic but it is really about the negative effect of various media on the formation of children in general. Benedict's 2008 message echoes his worries from 2007, wherein he says that communication "can tend to legitimize or impose distorted models of personal, family or social life."[88] In 2009, Benedict suggests ways for Christians to promote the gospel online, saying that "all users will avoid the sharing of words and images that are degrading of human beings, that promote hatred and intolerance, that debase the goodness and intimacy of human sexuality or that exploit the weak and vulnerable."[89]

Pope Benedict XVI is simply articulating in greater detail what the many documents reviewed above were worried about with regard to media and the family all along. But the documents from the early twentieth century were focused on the family as the site for formation for the proper Christian engagement with culture. With the exception of the 2007 message on education, issues of the family are coupled with sexuality and violence in Benedict's speeches, in order to demonstrate the pervasively negative effects of the media on the family. This is not to argue with Pope Benedict that the media can negatively affect families insofar as they portray violence and debased sexuality. It is simply to demonstrate one of the primary lenses through which Benedict tended to view the media: as a threat to the Christian view of family and sexuality, a theme which he appears to have inherited from John Paul II but sharpened in focus.

A second theme begins to appear in the WCD message from 2008. He worries about the distortion of reality that occurs in social communication: "Today, communication seems increasingly to claim not simply to represent reality, but to determine it, owing to the power and the force of suggestion that it possesses."[90] In addition, new networks of communication engendered by "the global reach and penetration of the internet" have begun to change human relationships themselves, even raising the question of what constitutes "true" relationship in the digital age. More than once, Benedict states that online relationships should not replace offline relationships. His language on this point is telling, and reminiscent of the theological work from chapter 1 on disembodiment online: "If the desire for virtual connectedness becomes obsessive, it may in face function to isolate individuals from real social interaction."[91] Once again the adjective "real" is used in contradistinction to the "virtual."

For his last four messages, Benedict focuses primarily on evangelization but continues this reflection on "real" relationships in that context. In 2012, he says once again that virtual engagement and relationships must not replace "direct human contact."[92] The reassertion of embodiment in the church becomes particularly acute in this message: "Even when it is proclaimed in the virtual space of the west, the Gospel demands to be incarnated in the real world and linked to the real faces of our brothers and sisters, those with whom we share our daily lives. Direct human relations always remain fundamental for the transmission of the faith!"[93]

Perhaps the most theological aspect of Benedict XVI's approach to media and communications is his reiteration of *communion*. He sees in modern communications technology the possibility for true human community and communion, although his optimism on this point is much more cautious than the Second Vatican Council's, Paul VI's, or the Pontifical Commission's. The reason for this could be one of temperament, or it could just be a function of the time period. Perhaps *Gaudium et Spes* and *Communio et Progressio* would appear more measured in a world where people can buy and sell human beings for sex with the click of a mouse, or where people can virtually rape one another in the pretext of a video game. Perhaps Benedict is more measured in his assessment because the internet has far exceeded the categories with which the church had been operating to understand and utilize mass media. The world of new media, perhaps, is a different enough animal to warrant renewed explanation of its ill effects. As with John Paul II, Benedict XVI sensed that the internet raises all kinds of new questions which are related to but ultimately beyond those of "mass media," and his pontificate ended in the midst of transition into new media as the predominant cultural paradigm for the church.

THE INTERNET'S POPE

Pope Francis' first official message to representatives of the media reflects his much larger emphasis on the negative effects of globalization and his desire for "a Church which is poor and for the poor!"[94] The theme of his message is "encounter," a theme that has extended to other speeches and his encyclical, *Lumen Fidei*.[95] In a style somewhat simpler than his predecessors, Francis reflects on the internet in his first message for WCD in this way: "The internet, in particular, offers immense possibilities for encounter and solidarity."[96] Like the previous ecclesial statements, his message includes an acknowledgment that not everything about the "world of communications" is good. It can be isolating, it can perpetuate wealth disparity, and it can cause confusion due to sheer amount of opinions and data. "While these drawbacks are real," says Francis, "they do not justify rejecting social media; rather, they remind us that communication is ultimately a human rather than technological achievement."[97]

Despite his personal luddite propensities, Francis is perfectly suited to virtual space. His simple style, genuine nature, spontaneity, and humility translate perfectly to an online context. Stories, videos, and pictures of the pontiff proliferate in ways that would make any social media consultant jealous. Moreover, he is not just a pope well suited to the internet. If Francis-focused content such as memes are any indication, he is better understood as the internet's pope. This is, of course, a ridiculous thought, given the general distaste for religious institutions one easily finds online, a mere reflection of the growing disaffiliation from religion among younger people in the West.[98] It is somewhat remarkable, however, that at the same time that young people are leaving traditional religious communities (especially young white Catholics) Francis holds a special place within internet culture.

His name and face are everywhere online, and stories about him appear even in the most unlikely of places. It is somewhat unlikely that Francis himself crafts stories, images, quotes, and other Francis-phernalia into easily postable,[99] shareable, and spreadable online content. Nevertheless, his very image and words appear to facilitate a new encounter among all kinds of people not only with the Catholic Church but with those who occupy so much of the pope's attention: the poor and marginalized.

Francis is not convinced in *Laudato Si* that internet media are truly capable of fostering the kind of encounter that he has in mind. A long passage in Chapter One, "What Is Happening to Our Common Home," deals explicitly with the issue of social interaction in modern media:

> True wisdom, as the fruit of self-examination, dialogue and generous encounter between persons, is not acquired by a mere accumulation of data which eventually leads to overload and confusion, a sort of mental pollution. Real relationships with others, with all the challenges they entail, now tend to be replaced by a type of internet communication which enables us to choose or eliminate

relationships at whim, thus giving rise to a new type of contrived emotion which has more to do with devices and displays than with other people and with nature. Today's media do enable us to communicate and to share our knowledge and affections. Yet at times they also shield us from direct contact with the pain, the fears and the joys of others and the complexity of their personal experiences. For this reason, we should be concerned that, alongside the exciting possibilities offered by these media, a deep and melancholic dissatisfaction with interpersonal relations, or a harmful sense of isolation, can also arise.[100]

But Francis' pontificate is not so easily summed up with this relatively pessimistic understanding of the internet.

Despite his own reservations and personal choices with regard to technology,[101] his pastoral sensibilities mean that he is keenly aware of the world in which he and the church he leads exist. In his 2016 message for WCD, Francis gives a beautiful treatise on the relationship of communication and mercy, as was fitting the Jubilee Year of Mercy. The message does not mention any particular media or technology until the very end, where Francis focuses specifically on the internet.[102] In the English translation at least, this section is the least elegant of the message. One gets the sense that Francis knows he must mention the internet, but that he does not, as is somewhat typical, know exactly what to say.

In the message's most provocative image, Francis offers that the internet is another version of the "streets" into which Christians are called to bring others into encounter with the living God: "The digital highway is one of [those streets], a street teeming with people who are often hurting, men and women looking for salvation or hope."[103] In this message, Francis emphasizes the internet's role in the Christian mission to bring the world into a genuine encounter with Christ, an encounter often inhibited by present economic situations. His concerns about technology and media vis-à-vis their role in the destructive effects of globalization fully acknowledge a more complex role of all members of the church within contemporary social communications.

Francis calls the internet a "digital world" that is "a public square, a meeting-place where we can either encourage or demean one another, engage in a meaningful discussion or unfair attacks."[104] It is not clear whether this image is an extension of Francis' earlier image of the "streets," or if it represents a change in his thinking. On the one hand, both images speak to the key to Francis' pontificate as a whole: encounter. In lifting up "encounter" as the main theological category of his pontificate, Francis is calling for new spaces whereby all members of the Body discover each other anew, spaces that are always fragile and imperfect. On the other, the "public square" is less provocative than "streets." One wonders if Pope Francis' time on the floor of United States Congress has in some way reoriented his focus on fostering an encounter with the merciful love of God from the world's least powerful to its most powerful. Nevertheless, we have in Francis' most recent attempt at the topic of the internet another call for dialogue and mercy, and a cautious optimism about its ability to cultivate communion.

The 2017 and 2018 WCD messages from Francis reiterate common themes like encounter, hope, and peace. The context for these messages, however, is a growing right-wing populist movement in Europe and the United States, deeply influenced and inflected by racist ideologies. These movements have relied heavily on virtual spaces for their fomentation, driven largely by dubitable news sources whose authors indirectly (if not directly) influenced the democratic processes of both Great Britain (Brexit) and the United States (Donald Trump). The 2018 message for WCD addresses these news outlets directly: "In today's fast-changing world of communications and digital systems, we are witnessing the spread of what has become 'fake news.'"[105] Francis juxtaposes "fake news" with journalism for peace. Fake news, he says, "can serve to advance specific goals, influence political decisions, and serve economic interests."[106] Journalism for peace, on the other hand, "flows from free relationships between persons, from listening to one another."[107] Fake news, in other words, is the very opposite of encounter.

Near the end of the 2018 address, Francis describes journalism as a "mission," and calls journalists "protectors of news." He speaks of the vocation with great respect and reverence, as many of the pontiffs above do. In this section of the address, however, one hears Francis speaking to people with whom he has developed quite a relationship over the past five years. This section of the address brings to mind one of the defining characteristics of Francis' pontificate vis-à-vis media: the mid-air press conference.

On his many trips, Francis has given press conferences while standing in the aisle of the airplane, facing the press corps in their coach seats. These press conferences have provided some of the most memorable moments of Francis' pontificate, including his famous "Who am I to judge?" (in reference to homosexuality) and his marrying of two flight attendants. These moments demonstrate his straightforward and more relaxed style, and his willingness to practice the encounter he argues is so crucial for the modern world. The press conferences also demonstrate the profound way in which Francis—his image, his words, his presence—is so perfectly suited for the media moment in which he became pope.

Parallel to his formal pronouncements about "encounter," Francis has become the pope we can daily encounter online. I see his Tweets every morning and his Instagram posts every afternoon. These, of course, are carefully curated by people who are not Pope Francis. His Instagram, for example, is copyrighted by *L'Osservatore Romano*. And one could argue that no matter who had been elected in 2013, the pope would still have opened an Instagram account in 2015, as Francis (or those working for Francis) did, and taken over the Twitter account started in 2012 during the pontificate of Benedict XVI.

Nevertheless, in both cases, we are seeing new spaces opened for laity around the world to encounter not only the leader of their church but each other as well. Each post on both Instagram and Twitter elicits thousands of responses, some of which are vile, to be sure. But many—and I would say most for the Instagram posts—are simply the word "Amen" or "Amen" and an emoji or little picture to go with the text, usually praying hands. In addition to these papal social media accounts, Francis has inspired new hope for many both inside and outside of the church. This hope often finds its expression in virtual space. The Francis effect is surely evident in local parishes, but it is overwhelmingly present online. Many lay Catholics the world over are finding the internet an important additional if not preferable space to their local, geographically bounded faith communities for sharing their joys, frustrations, hopes, and disappointments.

For many different reasons, maybe as individual as each user, these platforms—often deemed frivolous at best and destructive at worst—are providing space for lay participation, especially nonliturgical participation. I propose that we ask why these spaces are growing and thriving. First, I submit that digital life is not a separate or added space to non-digital life. Rather, these two spaces enjoy a complex, interwoven relationship that is constantly changing and difficult to ascertain. Secondly, I propose that these spaces—of which there are thousands online—are highlighting a desperate need in the church. There is a deep need for spaces of formation and fellowship due in large part to changes in traditional spaces, the primary of which is the local parish. Despite a popular and persistent narrative that new media and technologies are in fact causes of the sociological crises of traditional spaces, we do well to remember that this is a complex historical and sociological story. One important aspect of that story is economic: industrialization and later, globalization, drastically altered social life long before we got online.

Before expressing our righteous frustrations with such new social spaces, especially in their relationship to the church, let us first open ourselves to an honest consideration of the following: Where in the contemporary church are there spaces for dialogue, debate, or just plain friendship? Where can Catholics, especially lay Catholics, ask hard questions or raise deeply personal topics without fear of reproach or responses that will cause a crisis of conscience that might usher them out of the church? What has replaced, especially for young Catholics, the union halls, the bowling leagues, and CYO sports teams that functioned as liminal spaces—that is, as thresholds or doorways through which the Eucharistic way of life goes into the world and the life of the world pours in to be transformed and find its purpose and meaning? Without these spaces, the church finds itself at the mercy of the marketplace, reduced often to an ideology all too easy to reject. It is only when the church exists as interconnected spaces for truly shared social life centered on but extending beyond the Eucharist that it will fulfill its mission as the space of encountering God and one another in God.

The theological loci of Incarnation and church are not as pronounced in the short messages for WCD across the pontificates of Paul VI, John Paul II, Benedict XVI, and Francis as they are in the theological work surveyed in chapter 1. Paul VI focuses most of his comments on the matter around the themes of common good and solidarity coming out of the Second Vatican Council. John Paul II focuses on any number of issues surrounding "mass media" and its various agents and audiences, as well as acting as a transitional ecclesial perspective with regard to computer-mediated communication and the internet. Evangelization comes to the fore in both his and Benedict XVI's messages, along with the family and sexuality. It is too early to say much about Francis' perspective, but it seems that his reflections on social communications will be expressed in the context of a globalized economy that, in his own words, "is unjust at its root."[108]

But all of their messages have one thing in common: they all reflect on social communications in the context of communion. As I argued in chapter 1, communion is the nexus of Incarnation and the church. What is really at stake in any discussion of communication, computer-mediated, or otherwise is communion. For Christians, true communion is not just connection, and it can be damaged by communication structures as much as it can be nurtured. This is the wisdom of the church about media since *Vigilanti Cura*. True communion is rooted in the *imago Dei*, the shared image of God in which all people are created, and the baptism to which all are called to join themselves to Christ in the church.

NOTES

1. Second Vatican Council, *Gaudium et Spes:* Pastoral Constitution on the Church in the Modern World (December 7, 1965), accessed via http://www.vatican.va, §9. Unless otherwise noted, all magisterial documents are accessed from the Vatican's website.

2. Clement XIII, *Christianae Republicae: On the Dangers of Anti-Christian Writings* (November 25, 1766), §1.

3. For such an account, see Warren A. Kappeler, *Communications Habits for the Pilgrim Church* (New York: Peter Lang Publishing, 2009).

4. Dennis Doyle, "Henri de Lubac and the Roots of Communion Ecclesiology," *Theological Studies* 60 (1999): 211.

5. Anthony Burke Smith, *The Look of Catholics: Portrayals of Catholics in Popular Culture from the Great Depression to the Cold War* (Lawrence, Kansas: University of Kansas Press, 2010), 11. Smith goes on to argue that too much emphasis

on the Legion can obscure the contribution of Catholics to film itself, as both subjects and agents.

6. Pius XI, *Vigilanti Cura* (June 29, 1936), §24, in *Church and Social Communication: Basic Documents*, ed. Franz-Josef Eilers, SVD (Manila: Logos Publications, 1997), 13–22.

7. *Vigilanti Cura*, §43.

8. Ibid., §44.

9. Ibid., §45.

10. Ibid., §50.

11. This emphasis on the local community persists through the ecclesial perspectives on media and communications. It continues to be an important locus for ecclesial engagements with media and communications throughout the twentieth century, and, as we have seen above, persists through contemporary theological discussions of the internet.

12. It is worth noting that taken together, these three represent persistent anxieties about the internet in our present time. See especially "Access" and "Vitriol" above.

13. *Vigilanti Cura*, §90.

14. Pius XI, *Divini illius Magistri: On Christian Education* (December 31, 1929), §1. Also: "But nothing discloses to us the supernatural beauty and excellence of the work of Christian education better than the sublime expression of love of our Blessed Lord, identifying Himself with children, 'Whosoever shall receive one such child as this in my name, receiveth me'" §9.

15. *Divini illius Magistri*, §25–26, passim.

16. Ibid., §100.

17. Ibid., §11.

18. Ibid., §32.

19. Ibid., §7.

20. Ibid., §4.

21. Pius XII, *Miranda Prorsus* (September 8, 1957), §43, in Eilers, 27–54.

22. *Miranda Prorsus*.

23. Ibid., §135.

24. Ibid., §24.

25. *Vigilanti Cura*, §4.

26. *Miranda Prorsus*, §41.

27. The category of "mass media" will be more fully addressed in chapter 4.

28. The documents from these days will be treated more fully below, after a review of the major statements on communications.

29. John W. O'Malley, *What Happened at Vatican II* (Cambridge, MA: Harvard University Press, 2010), 3.

30. Robert P. Waznak, "The Church's Response to the Media: Twenty-Five Years after *Inter Mirifica*," *America* (January 21, 1989), 37.

31. Franz-Josef Eilers, SVD, "'Inter Mirifica' after 50 Years: Origins, Directions, Challenges," *SEDOS Bulletin* [online] 45, no. 11/12 (November/December 2013): n.p.

32. Richard John Neuhaus, "The Decree on the Instruments of Social Communication, *Inter Mirifica*," in *Vatican II: Renewal within Tradition*, eds. Matthew Lamb and Matthew Levering (New York: Oxford, 2008), 353.

33. Ibid.

34. Second Vatican Council, *Inter Mirifica: Decree on the Means of Social Communication* (December 4, 1963), §1, in Eilers, *Church*, 60–66.

35. *Inter Mirifica*, §2.

36. Ibid., §5.

37. Ibid., §6.

38. Ibid., §3.

39. I am in disagreement here with Waznak, who writes that "the decree is filled with presumptions about the power of the Church to control and influence the mass media. Its authors failed to understand that unlike previous times, the Church was now entwined and dependent on a channel of communication, which was outside its control." Robert P. Waznak, S. S., "Preaching the Gospel in a Video Culture," in *Media, Culture and Catholicism*, ed. Paul Soukup (Kansas City: Sheed and Ward, 1996), 138. I agree with Waznak that *Inter Mirifica* retains the strong presumption about the Church's ability to influence media ecology. Nevertheless, I discern in the document a movement away from strictly delineated spheres of "church" and "media," and an openness toward investigating the Church's *theological* relationship to media and communication. It is this theological relationship that I explore in chapter 3, and one that appears in the documents *Communio et Progressio* (1971) and *Aetatis Novae* (1991).

40. Pontifical Commission for the Means of Social Communication, *Communio et Progressio: Pastoral Instruction for the Application of the Decree of the Second Vatican Council on the Means of Social Communication* (May 23, 1971), §24, in Eilers, 74–115.

41. *Communio et Progressio*, §33.

42. Ibid., §34.

43. Ibid., §42.

44. Ibid., §82.

45. *Gaudium et Spes*, §4.

46. Ibid., §34.

47. Ibid.

48. See Second Vatican Council, *Unitatis Redintegratio: Decree on Ecumenism* (December 21, 1964), §2.

49. *Communio et Progressio*, §165.

50. See ibid., §162–180.

51. Ibid., §11. Italics in text.

52. Ibid., italics in text.

53. Ibid., §187.

54. Pontifical Council for Social Communications, *Aetatis Novae: Pastoral Instruction on Social Communications on the 20th Anniversary of Communio et Progressio* (February 22, 1992), §1, in Eilers, 121–136.

55. *Aetatis Novae*, §2.

56. Ibid., §4.

57. Ibid., §10.

58. Angela Ann Zukowski, MHSH, "Formation of Church Leaders for Ministering in the Technological Age," in *Media, Culture and Catholicism*, ed. by Paul A. Soukop (Kansas City, MO: Sheed and Ward, 1996), 173.

59. *Aetatis Novae*, §6. Pope John Paul II includes this particular claim in his 2005 Apostolic Letter *The Rapid Development*. He extends it, however, by including the sacramental element of God's self-communication: "In the Word made flesh communication itself takes on its most profound saving meaning. . . . There is . . . a culminating moment in which communication becomes full communion: the Eucharistic encounter," §5.

60. Ibid.

61. Ibid.

62. Pontifical Council for Social Communications, *Ethics in Internet* (February 28, 2002), §2–3.

63. *Ethics in Internet*, §7.

64. *Inter Mirifica*, §18.

65. Ibid.

66. Paul VI, "Church and Social Communication: First World Communication Day," 1967.

67. Ibid.

68. Ibid.

69. Paul VI, "Social Communications and Youth," 1970.

70. Paul VI, "The Mass Media and Reconciliation," 1975.

71. Paul VI, "Social Communications and the Development of Nations," 1968.

72. Godzieba, "Quaestio Disputata," 145.

73. Miller, "When Mediating Structures Change," 157.

74. Ibid.

75. John Paul II, "Rights and Duties of the Recipients in Social Communication," 1978.

76. John Paul II, "Social Communications for the Protection and Development of Childhood in Family and Society," 1979.

77. John Paul II, "Social Communications and Responsible Human Freedom," 1981.

78. John Paul II, "Social Communications and the Problems of the Elderly," 1982.

79. John Paul II, "The Christian Message in a Computer Culture," 1990.

80. Ibid.

81. John Paul II, "Proclaiming Christ in the Media at the Dawn of the New Millennium," 2000.

82. John Paul II, "Internet: A New Forum for Proclaiming the Gospel," 2002.

83. Ibid.

84. John Paul II, *The Rapid Development* (January 24, 2005), §9.

85. Ibid. Italics mine.

86. Benedict XVI, "The Media: A Network for Communication, Communion and Cooperation," 2006.

87. Benedict XVI, "Children and the Media: A Challenge for Education," 2007.

88. Benedict XVI, "The Media: At the Crossroads between Self-Promotion and Service. Searching for the Truth in order to Share it with Others," 2008.

89. Benedict XVI, "New Technologies, New Relationships: Promoting a Culture of Respect, Dialogue and Friendship," 2009.

90. Ibid.
91. Ibid.
92. Benedict XVI, "Silence and Word: Path of Evangelization," 2012.
93. Ibid.
94. Pope Francis, "Audience to Members of Communications Media," March 16, 2013.
95. See Pope Francis, *Lumen Fidei*: "Faith is born of an encounter with the living God who calls us and reveals his love, a love which precedes us and upon which we can lean for security and for building our lives" (§4).
96. Pope Francis, "Communication at the Service of an Authentic Culture of Encounter," 2014.
97. Ibid.
98. See *Putnam and Campbell, American Grace: How Religion United and Divides Us*, 2010.
99. Easy to post to various social media platforms such as Facebook or Twitter. "Posting" and "sharing" are essentially the same act online.
100. *Laudato Si*, §47.
101. I am referring here to the oft-reported fact that Francis does not own a television and says that he has not watched television in over twenty years. See Nick Squires, "Pope Francis Has Not Watched Television since 1990," *The Telegraph* (May 25, 2015), http://www.telegraph.co.uk/news/worldnews/the-pope/11628348/Pope-Francis-has-not-watched-television-since-1990.html.
102. This is not entirely precise, given the list that Francis provides: "Emails, text messages, social networks, and chats can also be fully human forms of communication."
103. Pope Francis, "Communication and Mercy: A Fruitful Encounter," 2016.
104. Ibid.
105. Pope Francis, "'The Truth Will Set You Free' (Jn 8:32): Fake News and Journalism for Peace," 2018.
106. Ibid.
107. Ibid.
108. Pope Francis, *Evangelii Gaudium* (November 24, 2013), §59.

Chapter 3

Incarnation, Virtuality, and the Church

Life seems to have become virtual. So many of the activities that used to occur in physical space (or through media such as telephones or letters) have gone virtual. Consider what it means to begin college now, in a virtual world. It is possible and even preferable for many college freshmen to apply for college, receive their acceptance letters, shop for clothes, books, and dorm stuff, meet their new roommates, register for their classes, and even take some of those classes . . . virtually. In many cases, there is no other option—no nonvirtual alternative—for the various steps of the process. In short order, we begin to ask what this shift means and what it is doing to us. Indeed, this is the impetus for so much of the theological work described in chapter 1. What does it mean that our lives are now so *virtual*?

The word itself has become an important cultural symbol and its connotation includes a range of social and personal modes of existence and behavior. It has become possible to use "virtual" as a ready-to-hand category under which all of the aspects explored in chapter 1 fall. When one utters the word "virtual," one is able to conjure images and memories of disembodied, anonymous/pseudononymous access to other people and content of various degrees of authority, sometimes (often?) enabling personal engagement vitriolic in nature.

Virtuality seems like a shiny new thing, as that which belongs properly to a world dominated by computer-mediation. "Virtual reality" (VR) and "virtual" are words used by the young, the affluent, and the otherwise technologically adept. It might even be one of those words that marks identity; perhaps the world can soon be divided into those who use it—who know it intimately and know the world by it—and those who don't. If this is true at all, then "virtual" is a very important word. We should be clear about what it means. It does not mean (only) the new and the shiny. In fact, I argue that virtuality as a mode of cultural production and participation is very, very old. Although it is still helpful to acknowledge a turn to the virtual with regard to its computer-mediated version, I want to suggest that the virtual is a constitutive part of what it means to be human from the perspective of Christian anthropology. I extend the category of virtuality beyond its common usage in order to interrogate the importance of mediation within the economy of grace generally and within the sacramental economy of the Catholic tradition more specifically.

What follows is an historical argument about this increasingly important category. But this historical argument is in service to a much more important theological argument. I suggest that virtuality is a possible hermeneutic for the sacramentality of the church. A broader and more inclusive definition of "virtual" allows us to read different moments of Christian history as performances of mediation that are, essentially, *virtual*.

Contemporary usage of "virtual" to describe digital environments, especially when coupled with "reality," is often credited to Jaron Lanier, computer scientist and philosopher of technology. Lanier's understanding of virtual is somewhat circumscribed, as he coined the term during his work with technologies that helped bring a more bodily experience to computing. "You can think of an ideal virtual reality setup," Lanier writes in a recurring column, "as a sensory-motor mirror opposite of the human body."[1] Although now in common usage to refer to computer-mediated environments, "virtual" retains its pre-computer usage in its adverbial form, "virtually." Thus while often paired with "reality" within the context of technology, "virtual" retains its meaning as very nearly but not fully real. Indeed, it's a common practice to offer "real life" as the opposite of life that is lived in the "virtual" world.

My understanding of "virtual" is broader than Lanier's. I take its current cultural meaning to refer to a variety of computer-mediated contexts, including everyday computing that required no "sensory-motor" apparatuses beyond those of the average users such as screens and keyboards. The aim of this chapter is to take the category of the virtual in a retrospective direction, using it to describe the cultivation of imaginative space within the Catholic tradition. The chapter proceeds as follows: first, I explore the idea of mediation by interpreting the work of computer scientists theologically. Second, I provide a representative project of what I advance here, namely a hermeneutic of virtuality that illustrates the productive dialectic of presence and absence in the church's sacramental imagination. Third, I provide two examples of this broadened notion of virtual space in Catholicism: Paul's letters as virtual space and the virtual logic of replica grottoes of Lourdes. Although the particularities of these two examples are important in their demonstration of Catholic virtuality, I hope they provide representative examples for further interpretation of the Christian tradition within the framework of the "virtual."

REMEDIATION

The internet has the capacity to present and re-present various kinds of content over space and time. I refer to any given piece of content as a "third object," and have in mind all kinds of mediated objects. These include pictures, film/videos, sounds/music, and text.[2] Since the 1970s, theorists have described computers as a "meta-medium." By this they mean that the computer (and even more so, the internet) functions as a translucent medium through which users encounter other kinds of media. The computer, they argue, "viewed as a medium itself, can be *all other media* if the embedding and viewing methods are sufficiently well provided. Moreover, this new 'metamedium' is *active*—it can respond to queries and experiments—so that the messages may involve the learner in a two-way conversation."[3] This description of the computer is helpful for understanding the hypermediacy—the proliferation of all kinds of other media—on the medium of the internet (by means of a computer or computer-like device). It is particularly helpful for advancing the concept of the "third object" I have suggested above, specifically in its recognition that this "meta-mediation" serves to draw users into an active relationship with media and with other people who engage the same media.

Ultimately, however, I find the description of the computer as a meta-medium to be incomplete. As a supplement, Jay David Bolter and Robert Grusin, authors of *Remediation: Understanding New Media*, provide a more robust description of what the internet is "doing" in terms of mediation. For Bolter and Grusin, the mediating process of the internet must be understood in a larger historical and cultural context. They argue that all media engages in *remediation*, the act of "presenting themselves as refashioned and improved versions of other media."[4] Remediation relies on the "twin logics" of immediacy and hypermediacy. "Immediacy" refers not so much to a reality as to a desire, one that Bolter and Grusin argue to be at least as old as the Renaissance. Since the advent of perspectival painting, they argue, Western civilization has desired immediacy. This desire is persistent and insatiable. It drives the production of more and more media, with the goal of creating a direct experience with some third object—nature, another person, an inanimate thing. Thus modern society lives within what Bolter and Grusin term an "ambivalent and contradictory" space when it comes to media. The paradox of remediation is that the desire for immediacy results in the continuous production and engagement with more and more mediating forms.

With regard to computers, we can understand this in terms of the interface: "A transparent interface would be one that erases itself, so that the user is no longer aware of confronting a medium, but instead stands in an immediate relationship to the contents of the medium."[5] Somewhat ironically, this desire for immediacy actually cultivates the logic of "hypermediacy." The desire for immediacy is precisely the impetus for all kinds of media. This mediation, in turn, gestures back toward the desire for immediacy: "In every manifestation, hypermediacy makes us aware of the medium or media and (in sometimes subtle and sometimes obvious ways) reminds us of our desire for immediacy."[6]

This understanding of the "twin logics" of immediacy and hypermediacy is helpful for analyzing the digital: "New digital media oscillate between immediacy and hypermediacy, between transparency and opacity."[7] One of the primary functions of the internet is to present "third objects" like pictures and sounds, the very mediation of which speaks to their absence. The diffuse technologies of the music recording, the printed film, and the written text are all gathered and re-mediated by means of digital technologies because of the persistent desire for immediacy with these objects (and often with the subjects who produce them).

Bolter and Grusin place the genesis of this collective desire for immediacy and its resultant hypermediating activity at the Renaissance in order to highlight the effects of applying mathematics to nature and all of reality. I appreciate their genealogy for the way in which it describes the mathematizing mentality of the modern period. However, I am concerned that their narrative does not sufficiently attend to the immediacy/hypermediacy dialectic in premodern contexts. They do mention that the "European cathedral with its stained glass, relief statuary, and inscriptions was a collection of hypermediated spaces, both physical and representational."[8] In what follows, I hope to present an argument for extending their narrative even further back into history. In fact, this desire for immediacy is not simply historical; it is anthropological. Theologically speaking, the desire for immediacy at the heart of our hypermediating tendencies reflects the ultimate desire for communion with God and with one another.

In addition, I present a theological account of these spatial imaginations by suggesting that the "third objects" of Catholicism which exist in the sacramental imagination are always oscillating between the immediacy and hypermediacy—the proliferation of media meant to bring us into contact with others or other realities—of other Christians, biblical narratives, holy sites, and even of God himself. That is, our desire for immediacy is essentially a desire for unmediated presence. This desire, ironically, results in effort after effort to bring that which is absent into presence. It is simply inherent to Catholic Christianity that the desire for immediacy results in the production of hypermediated spaces that testify to both the presence and the absence of that which they are mediating.

The theological implications of these "twin logics" come to the fore at different moments in Bolter and Grusin's analysis of digital technologies. Ultimately, "Hypermedia and transparent media are opposite manifestations of the same desire: the desire to get past the limits of representation and to achieve the real."[9] The Stations of the Cross can function as a helpful example of this. The imaginative space of Good Friday is the context for a Friday afternoon Stations of the Cross procession, wherein Christians physically travel from one place to another, stopping in front of visual representations of Christ's passion. The Stations re-mediate the Passion: the desire for immediacy, to join with the suffering of Christ, results in the proliferation of hypermediated spaces like the Stations themselves, carved and painted to draw the onlooker into the Passion. This oscillation between immediacy and hypermediacy is the movement of the life of the church, especially in its sacramental imagination. In what follows, therefore, I argue that all of the material, textual, and spatial elements that constitute the church's rich sacramental life are examples of re-mediation. In this way, we can come to understand the virtual as an appropriate if not preferable category for understanding this sacramentality. Bearing in mind the logic of re-mediation, I turn now to defining the "virtual," in order to argue for a "virtual logic" at the center of the Catholic imagination.

BEYOND VR: THEOLOGY OF THE VIRTUAL

Media studies scholarship from the 1980s and 1990s focused heavily on the possibilities and challenges of VR. Bolter and Grusin argue that VR replaces artificial intelligence as the new paradigm for the computer. This paradigm shift means that "the graphical interface replaced the command-line interface, which was wholly textual."[10] Although text remains an important feature in both programming and user interface, Bolter and Grusin are simply directing our attention toward image-production being the primary function of the computer. Therefore, despite the relative decline in enthusiasm for traditional headset style VR, VR persists as the underlying motif of the internet: it is still primarily about presenting third objects as immediately as possible, resulting, as Bolter and Grusin demonstrate, in a hypermediated interface which strives for transparency while simultaneously betraying its opacity.

Our concern here is with the various definitions for VR in order to propose an expanded definition that can help us understand analogously mediated forms, especially in the Catholic tradition. The enthusiasm for VR, especially in the 1990s, produced many reflections on its definition, promises, and challenges. In 1991, Michael Spring wrote that VR "might be paraphrased as 'a fact or real event that is such in essence, but not in fact.'"[11] VR in this sense is defined by representation, which is defined completely in terms of a computer's ability to mimic objects through visual experience. Indeed, this is how we still think about "virtual" in terms of the internet: the internet presents to users, in a variety of contexts, objects (sometimes things, sometimes places, many times, people) in a way that gives them their "essence" but not their "fact."[12] Therefore, when my friend sends me a video of my godson over an email, I am confronted with the child in his essence but not in fact. This is because my godson is not actually in the room with me, although he is with me on some level because of the mediating presence of the video, and more specifically, because I can *see* him. This is the understanding of "virtual" that obtains in most computer science conversations.

This distinction between "essence" and "fact" underlies the work of Woolley, who prefers to understand VR in terms of "artificialization." He defines VR as "the technology used to provide a more intimate 'interface' between humans and computer imagery."[13] Again, VR depends on computers' ability for representation, which Woolley describes as "simulating the full ensemble of sense data that make up 'real' experience."[14] What is particularly curious about these rather commonly accepted definitions for VR is that while they focus specifically on computers, they also present concepts that are widely applicable to all kinds of mediation. If Bolter and Grusin are right about the collective desire for immediacy (and its subsequent hypermediating activity in response to that desire), speaking of "sense data" probably applies to far more than the computer interface.

When we imagine VR, we too often limit ourselves with vision being the primary or sometimes only sense whereby we are drawn into an experience of an object (thing, place, person) being "real." Sometimes VR is even defined as that which you can see but cannot touch. The limiting factor, the reason why vision remains the primary sense for mediating the virtual, appears to be the ability of the computer. A computer can give you a picture—an incredibly detailed and three-dimensional picture—of a box of chocolates, but you will never be able to feel the smoothness of the "real" chocolate through a VR interface, be it a computer screen or VR headset/glove system. Incidentally, if you cannot touch the chocolate, it goes without saying that you surely could not taste it either. And while VR enthusiasts of the last century may have envisioned interfaces whereby tastes, sounds, and even smells might be simulated, vision remains the primary sense through which the real is mediated.

As Bolter and Grusin demonstrate, however, mediation is always about the real because it is always about the desire for immediacy. They prefer to talk about the "twin logics" of re-mediation in terms of transparency and opacity, but there are other ways to understand the immediacy/hypermediacy dialectic. Mediation is also about presence and absence simultaneously. The mediation of a particular third object is a re-presentation of that object. The object is made present over space and time. For example, my godson is re-presented to me by means of a video. However, by virtue of the fact that it is a mediation at all, the object is necessarily absent. Essentially, mediation is the movement between presence and absence. The VR box of chocolates is both present to me and absent from me by means for the visual mediation of a computer graphic.

The language of remediation and the twin logics of immediacy/hypermediacy are helpful for understanding the relationship between media. By introducing presence and absence into this framework, I mean to connect the discourse of religion to this theory of media. There is a compelling reason to understand religious traditions primarily through the category of mediation. As Birgit Meyer writes, "After all, the relation between religion and media is neither as new nor as weird as was suggested by the initial excited attention devoted to electronic mass media such as television and film. Upon deeper reflection, media were found to be intrinsic to religion."[15] The addition of presence and absence, however, evokes the long tradition of religious sensibilities which acknowledge the ability to experience the presence of God (cataphatic) as well as the utter ineffability and inaccessibility of the divine (apophatic). These twin logics at the heart of so many religious traditions are analogous to the twin logics of immediacy and hypermediacy.

Put in these terms, VR can thus be understood as an interface (broadly construed) that attempts to evoke the most immediate experience possible by means of a mediation. It is not enough, in the logic of VR—*and* in the logic of re-mediation that has driven our technological advances from painting to photography to film to computer graphics—to read a description or stare at a picture of a box of chocolates; we strive for more and more immediate experiences of it. Once again, I argue that this desire for immediacy is not simply an effect of the modern view of nature but is a constitutive part of what it means to be human. This anthropological claim is theological in nature. For Christians, the desire for immediacy is the longing for communion with God, the source of all truth and reality itself. In fact, the very dialectic of immediacy and hypermediacy is essential to the Christian imagination. When God takes flesh in Jesus Christ, God becomes at once immediate and hypermediate to the human condition. This incarnational perspective necessarily affects the Christian perspective of all of creation, and contributes to the hypermediating demonstration of the human desire for immediacy with the Creator.

The central claim of Christianity is that God took flesh in the person of Jesus Christ. In a sense, all of Christian theology is about figuring out what this means in itself, as well as what this means for all of human existence. The Incarnation is an important doctrinal locus for theology being done about the internet, including this book, because it is at the very heart of what Christians are compelled to say about embodiment. The issue of embodiment, it seems, continues to come to the fore in the digital age. But Christian theologians are not "using" the Incarnation because it's handy for talking about the internet; Christian theologians cannot help but read the whole world through the

Incarnation. All of human existence must be read through the person of Jesus Christ.

So what is the relationship between the Incarnation and this new sense of virtuality? First, it is important to understand the relationship between the Incarnation and the sacramentality of the church itself. We will save the sacramental life of the church in its formal aspects for chapter 5 where I will discuss the Eucharist and its relationship to ecclesiology. The concerns of this chapter, however, are all of the physical mediations of the Christian tradition that correspond to but are not circumscribed by any one of the seven sacraments. Such physical mediations are not exclusively Catholic, but they are inherent to Catholicism in a way that they often are not in other Christian traditions. Non-Catholic Christian traditions place a great emphasis on the writings of Paul, for example, but I contend that a Catholic perspective on scripture necessarily understands it as intimately related to the sacraments and that this relationship cultivates an understanding of the text as part of the sacramental order. To this end, the text functions like so many media in the church, remediating stories, people, and doctrine to individuals and the community. Such remediation, as noted above, relies on the dialectic of presence and absence. The third object signifies its referent (a person or group of people, an idea, an original image, etc.), presenting it to the individual or community while simultaneously standing as evidence of the absence of the referent. This remediation is at the heart of the Catholic imagination. This is the mode of icons, statues, rosaries, Stations of the Cross, paintings, and music. Theologically speaking, the point of grace is that the presence of the remediated is not swallowed up by its absence. Grace upholds the suspension between presence and absence, inviting a person into the tension but never resolving it one way or the other.

This tension between presence and absence is how we have to understand God in the world in light of the Incarnation. It is the creative space in which God invites the church into the mystery of the God-human. It seems to presume that we know what both are: that we know what God is, and that we know what it means to be human. But the mystery ramifies, then, when we realize the impossibility of defining either one. Born out of the liturgical life of the church, the Christological Councils of the fourth and fifth centuries may give us language for the content of the apostolic witness. According to the Council Fathers at Chalcedon, Jesus is "one and the same Christ, Son, Lord, only begotten, acknowledged in two natures which undergo no confusion, no change, no division, no separation; at no point was the difference between the natures taken away through the union, but rather the property of both natures is preserved and comes together into a single person and a single subsistent being."[16]

The Christological Councils, ancient in their logic and definitive in their teaching, continue to remind us of our own tendency to collapse the mystery of the Incarnation. The creedal doctrine draws us into the tension between presence and absence (or between humanity and divinity) but we are always tempted to try to resolve the contradiction. Sometimes, we are tempted to emphasize Christ in his divinity, carving a space for the divine in a world that no longer has eyes to see it. Other times, we are tempted to emphasize Jesus in his humanity, joining our sufferings and our other distinctly human experiences to his. The teachings of the Councils function as the boundary lines for theological reflection. This allows us to see the tension between humanity and divinity, between God being present to us and utterly absent and ineffable, as a space of creativity. This tension functions as a kind of necessary logic for understanding both God and the world.

Michel de Certeau understands this logic as a "structuring discourse" for the Christian tradition. In *The Mystic Fable,* his analysis of what he calls *mystics* (understood as a field or discipline, not simply a group of people), de Certeau begins his genealogy of "the mystical science" with the Incarnation. He recounts Henri de Lubac's argument in *Corpus Mysticum* that the "mystical" moved from the Eucharist to the community. Before recounting this critical narrative, however, de Certeau makes a few observations about the church that are helpful for seeing presence and absence at the heart of the Christian imagination. He writes, "Christianity was founded upon the loss of a body—the loss of the body of Jesus Christ, compounded with the loss of the 'body' of Israel, of a 'nation' and its genealogy."[17] De Certeau is concerned with the loss of the body because of his focus on mystics in the early modern period. He argues that mystical discourse is essentially about the ongoing "disappearance" of the mystic's body. But de Certeau also understands the role of absence in the doctrine of the Incarnation. One can then understand mystical practices that appear to be a rejection of the body. He writes, "What is termed a rejection of 'the body' or of 'the world'—ascetic struggle, prophetic rupture—is but the necessary and preliminary elucidation of a historical state of affairs; it constitutes the point of departure for the task of offering a body to the spirit, of 'incarnating' discourse, giving truth a space in which to make itself manifest."[18] Mystics (in the more traditional sense of the word) highlight the absence of the divine, denying their own bodies and thereby the ways in which they *presently* experience the world. But in so doing, their spiritual experiences also become tied to human embodiment. De Certeau appropriately situates the rise of "the mystical science" in the early modern period and its seismic shifts in the paradigm of the body, understood personally, socially, and ecclesially. However, he also argues that this dialectic of presence and absence so clearly demonstrated by mystical discourse is present at the very earliest moment in church history.

De Certeau understands the absence of Christ's body as a defining characteristic in the life of the early church. He writes, "In the Christian tradition, an initial privation of body goes on producing institutions and discourses that are the effects of and substitutes for that absence: multiple ecclesiastical bodies, doctrinal bodies, and so on."[19] But de Certeau's tone on this point can be read too cynically if we understand "substitutes" as simulacra. Indeed, what he reminds us is that the Christian tradition is always on pilgrimage, variously experiencing the profundity of moments of *present* grace on the journey and the longing for the still *absent* destination. He provides a helpful biblical reflection on this point: "Before the empty tomb stood Mary Magdalene, that eponymous figure of the modern mystic: 'I do not know where they have put him.' She questioned a passerby: 'If you are the one who carried him off, tell me where you have laid him.'" Mary Magdalene articulates, at the very moment of the Resurrection, the absence at the heart of Christianity. But absence is, of course, not the end of the story, and the liturgical community cannot help but hear Mary's question and feel a sense of dramatic irony. Her pleading has as its backdrop the glory of the resurrected Christ. That glory is, at the very moment of Mary's profound sense of absence, already present to the world, and soon will be present to her and all of the other apostles.

But the risen Christ does not remain present to them forever. Narratively, the Gospel alternates between the themes of Christ's presence and absence. After spending time with the risen Christ, so present as to eat breakfast with them, Christ ascends. The apostles stare dumbfounded at the sky after Jesus' ascension, and one can only read their refusal to lower their eyes as a refusal to enter into the reality of his absence. But then comes the Holy Spirit, God's fiery presence among them, to compel them into the streets of Jerusalem. Therefore, Mary Magdalene's desperate questioning, "articulated by the entire primitive community, was not limited to one circumstance. It structured the apostolic discourse."[20] Christ's body "is structured by dissemination, like a text. Since that time, the believers have continued to wonder: 'Where art thou?' And from century to century they ask history as it passes: 'Where have you put him?'"

NOTES

1. Jaron Lanier, "Jaron's World: Virtual Horizon," *Discover* (May 11, 2007).

2. It can also be understood, however, in a more dynamic way as a particular image, text, or idea that changes as it moves throughout virtual space. These more dynamic third objects are commonly known as "memes" for their mutative character.

3. Alan Kay and Adele Goldberg, "Personal Dynamic Media," *Computer Media and Communication: A Reader* (Oxford: Oxford University Press, 1977, 1999), 112.

4. Jay David Bolter and Robert Grusin, *Remediation: Understanding New Media* (Cambridge, MA: MIT Press, 1999), 15.

5. Ibid., 23–24.
6. Ibid., 34.
7. Ibid., 20.
8. Ibid., 34–35.
9. Ibid., 53.
10. Ibid., 32.

11. Michael B. Spring, "Informating with Virtual Reality," in *Virtual Reality: Theory, Practice, and Promise*, ed. Helsel and Roth (London: Meckler, 1991), 6.

12. While I attempt to follow this distinction here, I ultimately find it to be imprecise and not very helpful.

13. Benjamin Woolley, *Virtual Worlds: A Journey in Hope and Hyper-Reality* (Cambridge: Blackwell, 1992), 5.

14. Ibid.

15. Birgit Meyer, "Media and the Senses in the Making of Religious Experience: An Introduction," *Material Religion* 4, no. 2 (July 2008): 127 (124–135).

16. Quoted in Norman Tanner, *The Councils of the Church: A Short History* (New York: The Crossroad Publishing Company, 2001), 28.

17. Michel de Certeau, *The Mystic Fable: The Sixteenth and Seventeenth Centuries*, trans. Michael B. Smith (Chicago: University of Chicago Press, 1992), 81.

18. De Certeau, *The Mystic Fable*, 80.
19. Ibid., 81.
20. Ibid., 82.

Chapter 4

Virtuality and Sacramentality

If we understand absence to be at the center of Christianity, we can understand sacramentality to be the mediating activity that takes place between presence and absence. I am using sacramentality in this chapter to mean the imagination of the created world (including human beings and their products) which flows from the practices and theology of the seven sacraments of the Catholic Church. These sacraments, of course, are predicated on an incarnational view of the world itself, which understands the presence of God analogically. The concern of this chapter is not these seven sacraments themselves, then, but the sacramentality that gets extended to the rest of the created world because of them. This has resulted in centuries of art, music, and texts which mediate God's presence in the world without overtaking the place of the sacraments themselves. This is all of the extra "stuff" of Catholicism: the rosary beads, the candles, the icons, the sacred music, the texts of prayers and poems, the incense, and the crucifixes. These *things* are understood as participating in the larger sacramental order, which ultimately includes all of creation.

There are countless examples of sacramentality in present-day Catholicism. The argument of this chapter is that virtuality is the primary logic for sacramentality across the centuries of Christian thought. Art historian Kathryn Rudy demonstrates how we might employ this hermeneutic of virtuality for understanding the sacramental imagination. Her work *Virtual Pilgrimages in the Convent* explores how religious women in the late Middle Ages were able to go on pilgrimages—primarily to Jerusalem, but to other sites as well—*virtually*. She sums up the findings of her extensive research when she writes, "Virtual travelers obtained and copied real pilgrimage diaries, which came in a variety of texts and textual circumstances. There were souvenirs, maps, physical and metric relics from local shrines and beyond, all reused, recycled, and recontextualized into devotional handbooks and new forms of imagery that mediated pilgrimage to be imagined."[1] Rudy divides the findings of her research into three main parts: (1) souvenirs of pilgrimage, including travelogues and various types of relics; (2) interior devotional practices with the souvenirs; and (3) exterior (somatic) devotional practices with the souvenirs. Rudy contextualizes the practices of religious women within larger devotional practices apparent in lay communities as well, but focuses primarily on cloistered sisters.

Cloistered religious women could not make the journey to Jerusalem themselves given not only the nature of their religious vows but also because of the dangers of travel. However, they were able to experience holy sites and "even obtain the indulgences, without exposing themselves to danger and expense" through the efforts of male pilgrims.[2] Journals, complete with both text and images, were especially important for devotional practices that centered on the pilgrimage in cloistered women's communities. These journals became the mediating texts for the creation of replica pilgrimages, pilgrimage experiences which Rudy describes throughout her work as "virtual."

For example, Felix Fabri's *Die Sionpilger* from 1492 was intended to aid in the pastoral care of Dominican sisters with which he had been charged. According to Rudy, "The text describes how the brother from the Dominican Monastery at Ulm told the sisters of his travels so that they might travel to Jerusalem and kiss the footsteps of Christ."[3] Texts like *Die Sionpilger* offered a "mental exercise" meant to conform the devotee's mind to that of Christ. It does so by means of evocative imagery meant to transport the reader to the pilgrimage on which she could not physically go.

Die Sionpilger represents one kind of text meant for mostly interior practices of religious devotion. Rudy also refers to these as "stationary pilgrimage devotions." These virtual pilgrimages took place primarily within the interior person. Such stationary virtual pilgrimages relied upon two different kinds of texts: the more descriptive pilgrim journal (e.g., Fabri's *Die Sionpilger*) and more prescriptive devotional texts, often penned by the sisters themselves. The cloistered religious women "copied and put to use texts containing instructions for taking vicarious pilgrimages. These texts were designed to simulate *in the minds of readers* the experience of walking in Christ's footsteps."[4]

According to Rudy, interior pilgrimages are made possible by inheriting the method of *memoria technica* from antiquity. Cicero's *Rhetorica ad Herennium* makes a distinction between natural and artificial memory, the latter with which the rhetorician must concern himself in order to make an effective argument. Artificial memory, says Cicero, includes two parts: backgrounds and images.[5] Backgrounds provide the setting against which images are remembered. For the pilgrims in Rudy's study, the cultivation of the artificial memory—which Cicero says is the subject of discipline—is at the heart of the virtual pilgrimage: "The rememberer builds an imaginary 'memory house,' in which each room contains an event such as the Flagellation, or an object such as the column of the Flagellation, which is meant to trigger the memory, in this case the intricate narrative of the Passion of Christ."[6] In Cicero's terms, the rooms and house make up the backgrounds and the Flagellation and column of Flagellation make up the images.

Although such devotions were primarily interior to the devotee, these virtual pilgrimages had important exterior and physical components.[7] Of particular note is how the religious women would interact physically with the documents. Images especially became incredibly important for re-presenting holy sites and experiences for the women. For example, "the user rubbed several images, smearing the ink and obscuring the faces of the soldier who throws dice for Christ's garment."[8] One cannot help but be struck here by the action of smearing or rubbing as an experience of both the absence of the site itself but its presence to whom Rudy calls the "user." We too feel compelled to engage with our virtual environments physically, a compulsion that is all too clear in the movement of communications technology to primarily tactile engagement in phones, tablets, and computers. The desire to touch our mediating images and texts does not seem to be all that new.[9]

In addition to travelogues, pilgrims would provide special kinds of relics for those who could not make the pilgrimage to Jerusalem. In addition to journals, these pilgrims also took back for the religious women so-called metric relics, measurements of significant objects that would then be displayed prominently and venerated as a particular kind of relic. For example, measurements of the True Cross of Christ would be brought back to Europe and "remapped onto the local environment"[10] of the cloister. The measurement would be etched into the wall for veneration and contemplation. Christ's tomb was another object for measurement. One cloister still bears the inscription of the metric relic of the tomb of Christ, including the following words: "Look at this fissure / And do not scorn what you read / The depth of this is that / Which the sepulcher of Christ had."[11] The purpose of these measurements was to engender the most "real" experience possible, precisely through an essentially virtual mediation. Metric relics function in a complex system of details in order to bring the religious women along in pilgrimage: "These details aim to supply the most believable ersatz experience possible. . . . All of these specificities enhance the 'reality effect' of the account and transport the experience home."[12]

Some measurements were not etched into the local environment but remained in the text for another kind of virtual experience. Such was the case for measurements of the "Measured Wound of Christ."[13] These wounds, stunning in their deep red color, were purportedly the true measurements of Christ's wounds and were often provided along with the true measurement of the nails themselves. According to Rudy, "The impulse to know the size of Christ's wound was related to the impulse to know the size of his cross, his grave, the nails driven through his hands and even the size of the titulus that hung over his cross. Such measurements made Christ's suffering tangible and immediate."[14] Such desire for immediacy was, of course, met through an intensely mediated experience. These wounds and nails were presented to the women virtually, through the use of texts and images. One's physical engagement with these mediations was also an important part of its function in the virtual pilgrimage. For example, one of the pages bearing a wound of Christ includes the following directions: "To read the text, the viewer/reader has to turn the entire codex 360 degrees, thereby turning around in his/her mind the veracity of the wound, made plain by the text that traces the gash."[15] This "turning around," both physically and spiritually, was not only a matter of reading but a matter of touch and movement as the virtual pilgrim would read the words around the wound by means of turning the book in which it had been recorded.

The practices surrounding the Measured Wound of Christ fall into Rudy's second category of virtual pilgrimages: the exterior practices or "somatic pilgrimage devotions." Another kind of metric relic is especially helpful for understanding somatic devotions. The women of these cloistered religious communities were compelled to engage both mentally and physically in replica pilgrimages. According to Rudy, "Virtual pilgrimage was often not sedentary, but involved a physical component in order to approximate the motions of pilgrimage, especially of walking along Christ's side as he travelled through Jerusalem to reach Calvary." This physical component sometimes took the form of assuming different bodily positions associated with the pilgrimage, such as laying one's head with John or carrying the cross with Simon. More frequently, however, precise numbers of footsteps provided the pilgrim with a physical activity to engage her body in the virtual pilgrimage:

> [She] carried her book to places she had selected in her convent to represent events from the Passion. Before stopping at each one to pray on her knees, she peregrinated around the cloister a counted number of times so that she could cover the same physical distance that Christ had traversed on the *via crucis*. She imitated Christ with the greatest degree of verisimilitude she could muster as he stumbled and caromed through his Passion under the weight of the Cross.[16]

Virtual pilgrimages were mediated by a complex system of text, images, and physical movement. It is tempting to describe the objects of Rudy's study as historically obscure devotional practices by a particular set of Christians during a very particular moment in the church's history. I submit, however, that these virtual pilgrimages participate in a tradition of Catholic virtuality that existed before and continues to exist after them.

Rudy never offers a definition for "virtual." One can infer from her text that she uses it to describe replicated but intensely real experiences that are mediated by text and images. The "intensely real" aspect of these virtual pilgrimages is evidenced by evaluations of them from both the religious women themselves and ecclesial authorities. These pilgrimages were understood by the sisters to be just as efficacious as the pilgrimages on which they were based.

One text contains the life of Sister Truyde Schutten, including details of a virtual pilgrimage undertaken on January 7, 1417. In this text, we can see an answer from the sisters to the question of whether or not such pilgrimages were "real": "Sister Truyde states that she had been to Rome once before, by which she means that she had been there virtually. Indeed, no physical pilgrimage to Rome is recorded in her *vita*."[17] In addition, a story from the *Golden Legend* tells of a nun whose gout prevented her from physical pilgrimage. She decided to undertake the pilgrimage in her mind, however, and "devised her own strategy for virtual travel," by which she was cured at the end of the pilgrimage.[18]

One of the primary motivations for pilgrimage during this period was the acquisition of indulgences. This economy of indulgences would, of course, become contentious in the subsequent period of Reformation. It is quite easy to see why, as one could amass great indulgences not only for oneself but also for others, to be doled out to both living and dead. This economy, however, also formed the background for the efficacy of the virtual pilgrimage. The transference of indulgences from living to dead translated into the transference of indulgences from physical pilgrimage to virtual pilgrimage: "In their fungibility, [indulgences] could also be transferred from real experience to bird's-eye experience, and from there to internal vision or to one gained through the medium of a painted proxy."[19]

The kinds of objects that facilitate virtual pilgrimages in the fourteenth and fifteenth centuries would also become part of the Protestant Reformation's scorn. Such documents, relics, and other souvenirs would come to be understood as part and parcel of the larger economy of indulgences. Indeed, such physical manifestations of devotional life represent the symptoms of the disease that the Reformers understood to have corrupted the body of the church. But the logic at the heart of these practices is one that stems from the central doctrine of the Incarnation itself. As noted above, the created world is, especially after Christ, understood to have the potential to manifest the divine. All of the banalities (oil, water, bread, etc.) of the Catholic Church's seven sacraments testify to this analogical perspective. By virtue of its doctrinal roots, a kind of virtual logic persists in the Catholic sacramental imagination.

Although modern Catholics might not recognize all aspects of the sisters' pilgrimage practices, there is something about these practices that simply makes sense to the Catholic imagination. The thing that "makes sense" is the ability for texts, images, and objects to make gracious realities present, while at the same time speaking to their absence.

Perhaps Rudy never defines "virtual" in her work because she does not think she needs to. It is quite clear what she's getting at throughout the text. It is important, however, that we define it here as the mediating space between presence and absence. To be virtual, an experience is both re-presenting a reality and speaking to its absence. Applying the category of virtual to Catholic sensibilities is not only possible; it is a preferable new way of talking about the church's rich sacramental tradition.

PAULINE ECCLESIAL-VIRTUAL SPACE

It is the vein of Rudy's guiding assumption—namely, that the category of virtual has not only an appropriate but indeed continuous application to religious sensibilities—that I turn now to two other examples of virtuality in the Catholic tradition. The first of these examples is important for Catholic and non-Catholic Christians alike. I operate with the assumption, however, that the Catholic view of scripture is theologically related to the Catholic perspective on all kinds of created realities which participate in the sacramental order of creation. Scripture is, as *Dei Verbum* conveys, the written account of God's revelation. The Christian scriptures are intimately related to the tradition of the church, the witness of the apostles that has been handed on through the centuries. The Council Fathers write,

> The words of the holy fathers witness to the presence of this living tradition, whose wealth is poured into the practice and life of the believing and praying Church. Through the same tradition the Church's full canon of the sacred books is known, and the sacred writings themselves are more profoundly understood and unceasingly made active in her; and thus God, who spoke of old, uninterruptedly converses with the bride of His beloved Son; and the Holy Spirit, through whom the living voice of the Gospel resounds in the Church, and through her, in the world, leads unto all truth those who believe and makes the word of Christ dwell abundantly in them.[20]

Both tradition and scripture have God as their origin, and both testify to the truth of God in Jesus Christ. Scripture is incarnational insofar as the church is confident in the ability of words, which are merely human expressions, to manifest God to the world. If God can be revealed in the God-Man Jesus Christ, God can also be found within creation itself, including its simplest materials. We often think of this in physical terms, that the Incarnation allows us to see the material world as having the potential to manifest the divine. However, words are an important part of the sacramental imagination as a necessary part of the created order. Speech itself is owing to the discursive thought we bear as marks of our creatureliness. Letters, words, grammars, and entire systems of language are thus part of the created order. It is this assumption which underlies the confidence both Jews and Christians have in the ability of scriptures to facilitate an encounter with the divine. That facilitation is what we might call "inspiration," the very breath of God being present in the text.

This sacramental approach to words, both spoken and written, is crucial to understanding the place of Paul's epistles in the canon. As a little girl, I was always baffled by the second reading in the Liturgy of the Word. I could not figure out why these letters from one person to another group of people who no longer existed were considered scripture. I always felt like I was eavesdropping on a very strange conversation. Every once in a while, Paul would have written something that made sense to me and my life. Mostly, however, it seemed very esoteric, even if I could never have described it that way with my elementary school vocabulary. The questions I have about Paul's letters now are not as centered on their canonical status, although they are not unrelated to those issues either. I am more concerned with the following question: to what extent can we consider Paul's letters to various Christian communities—both in their written and spoken (read) forms—a virtual space?

Paul's letters create and maintain a virtual space for the early church by means of three things: (1) Paul's role as a traveler, (2) the substitutionary function of the letters, and (3) the liturgical use of the epistles. Paul's letters were necessitated by his constant travels around the Mediterranean. We must understand the context for travel in first-century Mediterranean culture in order to best understand Paul's self-understanding of the physical aspect of his mission and its effects on local communities. We must also understand how the texts themselves functioned in the life of the communities. Here I will draw on the work of scholars who have discerned liturgical functions in Paul's letters. From an ecclesial perspective, the relative similarity in the liturgical aspects of this text serves to create an early universality for the first-century church. Finally, the most virtual aspect of the Pauline corpus is the way in which the text functions as a substitution for Paul himself. It is significant that Paul relies on texts to sustain the local communities with whom he has relationships, belying a long-standing confidence in the persistence of personal presence over the absence engendered by both space and time. It is in this dialectic of presence and absence—the essence of the virtual—that present-day Christians are able to enter into the virtual space of Paul's letters.

Paul's ministry was characterized by travel. The Acts of the Apostles, which carries a later date than Paul's own letters, provides a more detailed account of his travels than the Pauline corpus. It also provides an account of his conversion, which took place in the midst of travel as well: "*On his journey*, as he was nearing Damascus, a light from the sky suddenly flashed all around him" (Acts 9:4). Today, travel often connotes luxury and privilege. This was not the case, however, for many centuries.[21] Rudy's account of virtual pilgrimages above takes the danger of travel as an important historical starting point: the pilgrimages were performed virtually because for most people, physically traveling to holy sites was incredibly dangerous. The dangers of travels were not, of course, limited to the Middle Ages. Travel in the ancient world was incredibly dangerous and its perils were understood by everyone to such a degree that it factors heavily in ancient literature and poetry.

Timothy Marquis argues that travel is the central motif of Paul's leadership of the new Christian community. Paul's travel, however, was understood in the context of the Roman Empire: "For Romans in particular, travel encapsulated all the dangers and necessities of newness. Even though the most revered heroes of Rome's mythic history were regaled for bracing stupendous adventures as they traversed the earth, audiences and authors alike understood these epic journeys as conveying both glory and curse."[22] For Marquis, Paul's constant traveling provided the perfect example for the sacrifices he was willing to undertake for Christ. Paul connected his own suffering, undergone primarily because of travel itself, to Christ's suffering on the cross.

The Acts of the Apostles is a more detailed account of Paul's life than his own letters. As such, they provide a more complete account of his travels around the Mediterranean, outlining the traditional three journeys of Paul. It is on the second journey wherein Paul encounters most of the communities to whom he writes the now-canonical epistles.[23] This journey is dated to approximately AD 49–50, dated relative to the Claudius Edict of 49.[24]

But how does travel function in the creation and maintenance of virtual space? In the imagination of the first-century Christian communities with whom Paul had a relationship, Paul was more absent than present. Even in his arrival, his identity as a traveler precluded any claims that any particular community might want to make on Paul's person. In addition, one of the primary features of an itinerant missionary was his financial independence. Paul himself makes this clear in 1 Thessalonians 2:9: "You recall, brothers, our toil and drudgery. Working night and day in order not to burden any of you, we proclaimed to you the gospel of God."[25] According to Eva Ebel, "Financial dependence upon his churches would have called into question Paul's apostolic freedom and authority."[26] Local communities that Paul visited on his many travels had no claim on him materially or temporally. Paul was always in the process of moving on, bound only to the communities by means of Christ himself. Even when present, then, Paul's absence loomed large because of his constant travels.

If Paul was always moving about the Mediterranean, he had to find a way to maintain the life of the communities which he established and visited. He maintained these communities primarily by means of epistles. Letters provided the best way to continue Paul's relationship to these communities but also for facilitating some sort of relationship between various communities. N. T. Wright argues that the form of Paul's writings is dictated by the cultural milieu of the first-century church. Wright says that the church "formed (in Paul's view) a world of its own, standing in a unique relation to the other three worlds" of Judaism, Hellenism, and the Roman Empire.[27] In relation to these three contexts, Wright argues, the first-century church required media such as letters for "the creation of cells, and networks, which would be regarded as suspicious or even downright subversive within the world of his day. . . . Content determined form; belief shaped the mode of address . . . the same redefined monotheism generated communities of a particular shape, demanding a particular kind of pastoral supervision."[28]

Wright describes Paul's letter as "pastoral supervision," a point against which few would argue. If this is true, there is a real sense in which these letters functioned as mediations of Paul himself. In lieu of his persistent absence, the epistolary corpus of St. Paul functioned for early Christians as a virtual space in which they could encounter an apostle. This encounter was the basis for their existence as a Christian community, and it speaks as well to the inclusion of Paul's letters into the canon of scripture itself.

The medium of Paul's virtual presence was textual. Text has come to factor heavily in the historical accounts of the Reformation, but the physical realities of textual mediation have played an important role in the theological and ecclesial life of Christianity long before the sixteenth century. Elizabeth Eisenstein notes that the printing press spurred a dramatic increase in literacy in Europe.[29] But as scriptural communities of faith, ancient Judaism and Christianity both had to contend with the issue of literacy. According to Gamble, the Jewish historian Josephus documented that "in first-century Judaism it was a duty, indeed a religious commandment, that Jewish children be taught to read."[30] We should pause here to admit the relatively complicated situation of referring to "first-century Judaism" in the singular, given its diversity and the problems of generalizing over class and region. It seems safe to conclude, however, that the centrality of Torah in a least some Jewish communities necessitated some level of literacy.

For early Christians, whatever discernible tradition of literacy that could be inherited from Judaism obtained but did not necessarily result in widespread literacy among Christians. According to Gamble, it is necessary to expand the notion of literacy from whether or not individuals can read or write to a complex communal reality in which an illiterate person could still participate: "It may seem paradoxical to say both that Christianity placed a high value on texts and that most Christians were unable to read, but in the ancient world this was no contradiction."[31] Gamble goes on to explain the highly communal nature of Christian scripture, meaning that the many illiterate among early Christians encountered texts regularly in their hearing of it during liturgy. "Christians who could not read," he writes, "nevertheless became conversant with the substance of scriptural literature and also with other texts that were occasionally read in the setting of worship."[32] It is possible to see in this history the dynamic relationship between cultural factors such as education and literacy and assumptions about scripture. While text has been a major part of Christianity since the letters of Saint Paul became important features of local Christian communities, scripture was understood as essentially communal. This invites a different kind of reflection on the spatial dynamics of the Bible. The cultural and material realities of early Christianity reflect their commitment to the liturgical and communal assumptions about the text.

A more properly technological development in ancient Christianity can help further demonstrate the relationship I am trying to highlight here. Gamble explains that unlike the Greco-Roman and Jewish preference for the scroll as the primary scriptural vehicle, Christians preferred the codex: "Almost without exception, the earliest Christian books known have the form not of the papyrus roll but of the papyrus codex, or leaf book, which is the model of the modern book."[33] It is relatively unclear why this is so, but Gamble's hypothesis on this count is particularly telling for the argument I am advancing here. He proposes that because of its compact size, the codex would have been preferred by "people who traveled with books, as early Christian missionaries probably did."[34] This is particularly pertinent when thinking about the ultimate traveling Christian missionary, Paul.

As Gamble points out, many Christians' engagement with text took place in communal, liturgical settings, which is the focus of John Paul Heil's work. Heil argues that Paul's letters were "originally performed publicly in a liturgical assembly."[35] He provides an analysis of all thirteen canonical, Pauline texts, focusing on their liturgical function and largely bypassing the debates over authorship. To the degree that all of the texts, whether written by Paul's own hand or simply in the tradition of Paul, functioned as liturgical texts, this approach makes sense. Indeed, my own argument here is about the function of the texts and tradition of Paul, and I am less concerned with which of the letters were authentically Paul's own.

Paul's letters, in their textual form both visually and orally, functioned as a virtual space in which the local community encountered Paul. Heil writes that "as substitutes for his personal presence, the letters of Paul make him present to his various audiences in and through his words of worship considered as ritual 'speech acts,' that is, words that actually do what they say, words that communicate by not only informing but performing."[36] These letters, then, were aggressively present mediations of an absent Paul. Heil's language in describing the liturgical elements of Pauline letters is especially helpful here. Throughout his study, Heil uses present tense verbs to describe what Paul is doing in the text, which continues to mediate Paul to the community in an active sense despite his physical absence: "Paul *leads* the Corinthians, gathered as a liturgical assembly, in an act of worship that celebrates the significance of what God has done in raising Jesus from the dead."[37]

Also absent from the local community were the other local communities to which they are connected. Paul's witness to the gospel is the primary means of connection for these communities and his efforts to bring them into conformity on whatever level was possible at the time. According to Heil, for example, a "concern of Paul [in 1 Corinthians] is that the church at Corinth conforms with all of the other churches (4:12; 7:17) and that they avoid giving offense to the church of God (10:32)."[38] To the extent that Paul was successful in these efforts, he achieved conformity by means of a mediated presence in his texts, read within the context of the community in a liturgical mode. His letters provided not only a focal point for a local community but a point of connection to other communities as well. Thus whenever Paul was textually present to a given community, they are drawn into an imaginative space beyond local confines to the whole of the burgeoning church.

It is not, however, just the liturgical character of Paul's letters that facilitates the space into which early Christians could imagine themselves participating and coming into communion with one another. Paul's identification with Christ himself frames the efficacy of the worship. Throughout his letters, Paul presents himself as the mediating figure between the worshipping community and Christ. In 1 Corinthians, for example, Paul presents himself more than once as the model for Christian discipleship: "Therefore, I urge you, be imitators of me," (4:16) and "Be imitators of me, as I am of Christ" (11:1). According to Bailey's study on 1 Corinthians, "'be imitators of me' is not an ego trip for Paul. Students of a rabbi were expected to live with the rabbi. They could learn from him in two ways. His teachings provided one method of learning. Watching him live in observance of the law provided the other."[39] But we know that for most early Christian communities, the opportunities to observe Paul in their midst were few. His letters themselves testify to this fact. If they are meant to imitate Paul, therefore, they did so primarily by means of collective memory and his textual presence. This is extremely important theologically, given that their Christian discipleship rested in imitating Paul in order to imitate Christ. One does not "imitate" text; one imitates a certain person. There had to be a way in which, at least for Paul's part, that his letters were understood as making Paul *really* present to others. We would not say that the letters are the same as Paul standing in the midst of the community, but they do *real* work in the community.

The very mode of Paul's mediating presence demonstrates the constitutive place of *absence* in his mediation of the gospel. The fact that Paul wrote letters in order to sustain and minister to communities throughout the Mediterranean places movement, specifically movement away, at the center of the epistolary project. It is difficult for us to understand text as virtual, as we too often set written texts—especially ancient ones—over against electronic mediation. Text, however, is essentially a presentation that implies the absence of its author and to any other individuals or communities that contribute to the text. Paul's letters can be understood as a virtual space in which communities across the Mediterranean participated. I have thus far attempted to demonstrate how the contextual and textual aspects of the letters serve to operate in the mediating space between presence and absence. However, we must also consider the reception of these letters in order to advance the understanding of Pauline letters as virtual.

Heil's guiding assumption in his project on the liturgical function of Pauline letters is that they are (1) communal and (2) often aurally received. He writes, "The original setting for the public performance of these letters was communal worship that was most likely connected to the celebration of the Eucharist. . . . Even the letters addressed to individual delegates of Paul—Titus and Timothy—were not purely personal letters but were also addressed to the worshipping community as a whole."[40] The primary context for receiving these letters in the "worshipping community" would have been in public recitation, meaning that very few members of the community would have read the text themselves. Moreover, Christianity attracted slaves, poor, women, and other groups who would have been illiterate, and thus unable to read them even if given the opportunity to read Paul's letters for themselves. In terms of the virtual character of the text I have been advancing here, this aural reception of Paul's letters is incredibly important for cultivating a space into which the early Christian *listener* imaginatively entered.

According to Walter Ong's seminal work, *Orality and Literacy*, modern technologies raise new questions about earlier paradigm shifts in knowledge production and reception. Specifically, Ong describes the important changes from oral cultures to literate cultures. Ong is interested in "primary orality," in the thought and speech structures of people who are "totally unfamiliar with writing."[41] According to Ong, "the culture that produced the Bible" retained what he calls a "high oral residue."[42] This "residue" of oral culture has many characteristics, and there are a few who speak directly to the experience of Paul's communities. Ong describes oral culture as that which has no visual imagination for language: "Without writing, words as such have no visual presence, even when the objects they represent are visual. They are sounds."[43] The lack of visual presence means that a person's relationship with knowledge is different than it is in literate (visual) culture. Borrowing from Eric Havelock's work, Ong writes, "For an oral culture learning or knowing means achieving close, empathetic, communal identification with the known."[44] Objectivity is a result of the distance created by the written text. Oral cultures are "objective" to the extent that the speaker makes use of "formulaic expressions" which are "encased in the communal reaction, the communal 'soul.'"[45]

For the hearers of Paul's letters—that is, for the majority of the early Christians who encountered Paul's letters—Paul is re-presented with each reading. If these communities retained, as Ong argues, a "high oral residue," they would not imagine the content of Paul's letters as existing outside of the context of worship and communal recitation. As demonstrated above, the "content" of Paul's letters were not just theological ideas but the salvific worship of Christ and the mediating presence of Paul. In this way, the text—read aloud to individuals from an oral culture—functions as virtual to the degree it presents an absent Paul in their midst with each reading. Furthermore, this "high oral residue" would, according to Ong, mean a less objective approach to Paul's words than those of us from a high literate culture could imagine. When Paul tells his listeners to "imitate" him, therefore, they are better suited to a subjective response. Paul does rely upon "formulaic expressions" that tap into a "collective 'soul.'"

These expressions further the notion of his letters as virtual in that they present images from the Hebrew Bible that serve to unite communities across space and time. For example, 1 Corinthians contains a theology of the new Temple of Jesus Christ. According to Bailey, "The struggling, newly born, deeply flawed congregations that he was founding were, in his eyes, the *restored land* and the *glorious temple* promised by the prophets. He was not de-Zionizing the tradition; rather he was *transforming it into a new form of Zionism* that needed no particular geography and no special building!"[46] If we understand Paul's letters as oral presentations to a culture with "high oral residue," we are able to see them functioning *virtually* as a means by which early Christians came to understand both Paul and the rest of the Christian community as present, despite their glaring absence.

By focusing on these New Testament texts, I hope to have demonstrated the way in which text can function as virtual spaces that mediate between presence and absence. From a theological perspective, it is not appropriate to set these mediations against "real" immediacy, for it is clear that in the cases of both Paul's letters and the various objects of virtual pilgrimages that they are both *virtual* and *real*. In fact, the real often relies upon the mediation facilitated by the virtual for its religious economy. That is, the sisters in the convent would not have been afforded indulgences were it not for the mediation by pilgrimage objects, nor would the various communities of Paul's letters have been drawn into worship as the church Paul envisioned were it not for the absence but presence of Paul in his letters. My argument is that this logic of the virtual pervades the Catholic imagination. The sacramental life of the church, which both flows out of and sustains the sacraments themselves, relies upon mediation—of places, of other people, of historical moments, and most of all, of God himself. The virtual can function as a kind of hermeneutic by which we can understand all of the material and spatial aspects of the church's life, even in the modern world. The pervasiveness of virtuality in our daily lives can then actually function to bring new understanding of the church's sacramental mysteries. As an example of the way virtual logic persists for the Catholic imagination, even and perhaps especially in the modern world, I turn now to the example of replica grottoes of Lourdes, extending the argument with regard to texts advanced above into spatially-mediated spiritual experiences.

LOURDES AND VIRTUAL SPACE

In February of 1858, a French girl named Bernadette Soubirous went out with a few other children to the outskirts of Lourdes. While gathering wood, Bernadette encountered the figure of a woman whom she called *Aquero*, or "that one," in a grotto. The woman appeared to her a total of eighteen times, with different messages and instructions. On February 25, *Aquero* told Bernadette to drink from the spring and eat the herb growing there. On March 25, the woman finally told Bernadette who she was, saying "I am the Immaculate Conception."[47] Four years earlier, the Catholic Church had promulgated the Immaculate Conception, the dogmatic confirmation of Mary's own sinless conception. The dogma both reflected and exacerbated popular piety surrounding the Virgin Mary. Coupled with the new, seemingly miraculous spring waters, Lourdes quickly became a place of pilgrimage for Catholics.

Millions of pilgrims travel to Lourdes every year.[48] Many of them suffer from physical ailments, and they travel to Lourdes in hope of physical and spiritual healing. Scholars are quick to point out that these pilgrimages have turned the tiny town of Lourdes into one of the most visited tourist destinations in the world, complete with the shops, hotels, and restaurants of other destinations. Many more people can go on pilgrimage to Lourdes now than in the nineteenth century. Colleen McDannell's chapter on Lourdes water in *Material Christianity* describes how American Catholics in the late nineteenth century participated in the spiritual economy of the holy site. For the most part, devotees sought after water from Lourdes for their various ailments. A system of importing and distributing water from Lourdes sprung up as a result. This system was maintained predominantly by the Holy Cross community, whose aim was to cultivate "a national Marian piety" among the various Catholic immigrant groups now living in America.[49]

According to McDannell, "Widely distributed Lourdes water and constructed grotto replicas became material reminders of the power and influence of Mary."[50] In lieu of undertaking the dangerous and expensive trip to Lourdes itself, American Catholics wrote letters to Edward Sorin, the founder of Notre Dame in Indiana, in order to obtain water from Lourdes. They would also write letters after receiving the water, telling of the great miracles and healings caused by using it. The water itself formed a connection between the individual in America and the miraculous events of the grotto at Lourdes.

McDannell goes on to discuss the replica grotto of Lourdes constructed at Notre Dame. According to McDannell, such replication at Notre Dame and elsewhere is related to the logic behind the importation and distribution of water. This "logic" is that of *translation*: "The holy did not reside in a fixed place. It could be de-localized, moved from place to place, and still retain its ability to heal or work other miracles."[51] This is especially clear in the case of relics, which are moved around and to which people move by means of pilgrimage. The Catholic logic of translation is how we might understand the movement of relics and other objects from the Holy Land to the cloistered communities of Rudy's study above.

Replication of the grotto, therefore, is another means of this translation. It is a way for people in a different locale to experience the holy object or locale. The oldest replica grotto of Lourdes in the United States is in Emmitsburg, Maryland. Its official title is the National Shrine Grotto of Our Lady of Lourdes. Emmitsburg is in the Catoctin Mountains in western Maryland. Its mountainous topography lends itself to replicating the holy site in Lourdes. It also has a mountain spring which flows into the site of the replica grotto. According to the National Shrine's own history, the grotto existed as a site for Marian devotion even before Bernadette's apparitions. It was only later that it was turned explicitly into a replica grotto of Lourdes. As a result, the site is not only a replica of Lourdes, but also includes expansive Stations of the Cross, a reflecting pool with a statue of Mary, various devotions to saints like Our Lady of Guadalupe and Jude, and a small chapel called St. Mary's. The primary focus of the campus, however, is the replica grotto.

As a student at Mount St. Mary's University, the college and seminary that maintains the National Shrine, I witnessed many pilgrims visiting the grotto every year. Many of these pilgrims were from other countries, both as visitors and immigrants to the United States. One example of these pilgrim groups is the Vietnamese community, which has been making an annual pilgrimage from Philadelphia for over thirty years. My own experience was that every weekend, if not every day, a new group of pilgrims poured into the replica grotto of Lourdes. One of the primary foci of the pilgrimage for both groups and individuals was the mountain spring, which had been narrowed to flow into a spout for filling containers or using directly. On every visit to the grotto, I would dip my hand into the spring and sometimes take a drink.

When pilgrims fill jugs of water from the Catoctin mountain stream, do they really think that water is from Lourdes? Of course not. For the Catholic imagination, however, there is a way in which the water *is* from Lourdes, for in Catholic sacramentality the distinction between sign and signified is never too sharp. For McDannell, this replication of the holy falls neatly into the category of *translation*, a way to understand the movement of the holy from one place to another. She writes, "Like the water, duplicate grottoes were translations: they permitted the sacred to be de-localized and moved about. The construction of facsimiles of the Lourdes grotto was completely an exercise in creating authenticity."[52] The National Shrine Grotto of Lourdes in Emmitsburg is a quintessentially Catholic space. It is not really Lourdes, but it is really real. I contend that an appropriate way to understand a space like Lourdes—and any Catholic space which operates with a similar logic of replication and translation—is through the category of the virtual.

For McDannell, the connection between replica grottoes to Lourdes in France is narrative: "Catholics did not ship rocks and dirt from Lourdes to be used in the building of new grottoes. Duplicate shrines became sacred because they participated in the story of Lourdes and allowed Catholics to express dramatically their sentiments about the miraculous and the supernatural."[53] But this sense of Catholic spaces is too thin.[54] These spaces do not simply tell stories; they form the imagination in important ways. Moreover, this formation of the imagination is done primarily through sensory data like images, smells, textures, and even tastes.

There is a way to understand the grotto of Lourdes in the mountains of Maryland as a virtual space, a mediation which provides "sensory data" in order to create an experience of the holy site in France. But this sensory data need not be that which you can see but not touch. Indeed, touch and smell are incredibly important parts of the Catholic sacramental experience. Therefore, I can see Our Lady of Lourdes and St. Bernadette in statuary in the National Shrine, but I can also touch the rocks, smell the candles people light for prayers, and drink the water. These experiences are highly sensory but also highly virtual: they express simultaneously the endless desire for immediacy as well as the hypermediated spiritual economy of the church. As a response to an apparent moment of the divine presence at Lourdes, Catholics around the world took various steps to bring that moment into their own spaces and time by erecting replica grottoes and importing Lourdes water. Objects, people, and places mediated by icons, spaces, and replica grottoes are at once present and absent from us. Ultimately, this is what it means to be humans out of perfect communion with God. We sense in our hypermediating religious landscape the inescapable and unquenchable desire for immediacy, envisaged so perfectly as the first human walking in the Garden with God. But our mediations, especially sacred spaces like grottoes and churches, remind us of God's presence, even as much as they remind us of God's absence.

I have argued in this chapter for a broader understanding of "virtual" that can be used to describe the sacramental imagination of the Catholic tradition. This requires a broader understanding of virtual than currently exists in most discourse about the internet. I have argued that virtuality is essentially about the tension between "presence and absence," a tension that is not only familiar to but is necessary for the Catholic imagination. The dialectic between presence and absence is another way of describing the dialectic of immediacy and hypermediacy, which I contend is part of what it means to be human. The desire for immediacy produces hypermediation, a process seen clearly in Catholic sacramentality.

This sacramental imagination applies not only to the many objects and spaces of Catholicism but also to texts. In particular, St. Paul's letters function as a sort of virtual space in which Paul presents himself and the rest of the Christian community to early Christians. This relies heavily on Walter Ong's contention that early Christians operated with "high oral residue." Oral cultures imagine concepts differently than literate ones, and as a result of the largely oral culture of the New Testament, Paul's letters could function as an imaginative space in which listeners encountered both Paul and each other.

One can extend this understanding of virtual into the hypermediated space of replica grottoes of Lourdes. By way of example, the National Shrine Grotto of Our Lady of Lourdes in Emmitsburg, Maryland, demonstrates how Catholic spaces function as replications while at the same time presenting the "real." The Catholic imagination has never relied on "simple presence," and therefore, absence is fundamental to the Catholic view of both creation and Creator.

Any theological commentary on virtuality must contend with the unavoidably virtual nature of Christian sacramental and ecclesial life, mediated by texts, spaces, and art. The aim here is to recover absence as an important theological category so as to make space for thinking about virtuality in a constructive way. More often than not, virtual spaces are about bringing people into contact with one another. The virtual is thus not simply about the mediation of objects and places but about the mediation of human life. In the next chapter, I explore the dynamics of social life online and begin the task of the final chapter: proposing a renewed understanding of the relationship of the church and online social life.

NOTES

1. Kathryn M. Rudy, *Virtual Pilgrimages in the Convent: Imagining Jerusalem in the Late Middle Ages* (Turnhout, Belgium: Brepols, 2011), 255.
2. Rudy, *Virtual Pilgrimages in the Convent*, 47.
3. Ibid.
4. Ibid., 119. Emphasis mine.
5. See Cicero, *Rhetorica ad Herennium*. Book III. Loeb Classical Library (Harvard University Press, 1954), 208.
6. Rudy, *Virtual Pilgrimages in the Convent*, 150.
7. Rudy also presents complex dioramas found in these religious communities as objects of virtual mediation. These scenes, known as *bestolen hofjes*, were meant to "suggest that Paradise is visibly available while at the same time physically removed." In the terms suggested above, paradise is both present and absent by virtue of the mediation. The mediating space functions as a representation as well as a sign of its absence from the subject. Rudy describes it, quite helpfully, through the metaphor of travel: "The *hofje* is a vehicle that transports the beholder to Paradise, to a walled garden far from the walled garden in which she dwells" (115).
8. Rudy, *Virtual Pilgrimages in the Convent*, 68–72.
9. One might also think of a statue like that of Saint Peter in the Basilica of St. Peter at the Vatican. Peter's foot has been worn down to a smooth, rounded surface because so many pilgrims have touched and kissed it over the centuries.
10. Rudy, *Virtual Pilgrimages in the Convent*, 97.
11. Ibid., 102.
12. Ibid., 104.
13. Ibid., 103.
14. Ibid., 104.
15. Ibid., 103.
16. Ibid., 259.
17. Ibid., 123.
18. Ibid.
19. Ibid., 150.
20. Second Vatican Council, *Dei Verbum* (November 18, 1965), §8.
21. And is, indeed, not the case for the growing numbers of migrants and refugees in the world today.
22. Timothy Marquis, *Transient Apostle: Paul, Travel, and the Rhetoric of Empire* (New Haven: Yale University, 2013), 6. Paul seems to acknowledge this by placing "strangers and sojourners" together in Ephesians 2. He assures the community in this chapter that they participate in the promises of God made to Israel. "Strangers and sojourners" is evocative of the "widows, orphans and aliens" of the Hebrew Bible's prophetic tradition.
23. Eva Ebel, "Paul's Missionary Activity," in *Paul: Life, Setting, Work, Letters*, ed. Oda Wischmeyer, trans. Helen S. Heron (New York: Continuum, 2012), 115.
24. Eva Ebel, "The Life of Paul," in *Paul: Life, Setting, Work, Letters*, ed. Oda Wischmeyer, trans. Helen S. Heron (New York: Continuum, 2012), 99.

25. cf. 1 Cor 4:12, 9:3–18; 2 Thes 3:7–9.

26. Ebel, "Paul's Missionary Activity," 119.

27. N. T. Wright, *Paul in Fresh Perspective* (Minneapolis: Fortress Press, 2005), 4–5.

28. Wright, *Paul in Fresh Perspective*, 106.

29. See Eisenstein, *The Printing Revolution in Early Modern Europe*, 151–152.

30. Harry Gamble, *Books and Readers in the Early Church* (New Haven, CT: Yale University, 1995), 7.

31. Gamble, *Books and Readers in the Early Church*, 8.

32. Ibid.

33. Ibid., 49.

34. Ibid., 55.

35. Paul Heil, *The Letters of Paul as Rituals of Worship* (Eugene, OR: Cascade Books, 2011), 1.

36. Heil, *The Letters of Paul as Rituals of Worship*, 3.

37. Ibid., 41. See also page 42: "Paul's proclamation of this scriptural prophecy thus *leads* the Corinthians in a hymnic praise of the grace of God."

38. Ibid., 37.

39. Kenneth Bailey, *Paul Through Mediterranean Eyes: Cultural Studies in 1 Corinthians* (Downers Grove, IL: InterVarsity Press, 2011), 152.

40. Heil, *The Letters of Paul as Rituals of Worship*, 2.

41. Walter J. Ong, *Orality and Literacy: The Technologizing of the Word*, 30th Anniversary Edition (New York: Routledge, 1982, 2012), 11.

42. Ong, *Orality and Literacy*, 38.

43. Ibid., 31.

44. Ibid., 45.

45. Ibid., 45–46.

46. Bailey, *Paul Through Mediterranean Eyes*, 127–128.

47. Rene Laurentin, Bernadette Speaks: *A Life of Saint Bernadette Soubirous in Her Own Words*, trans. John W. Lynch and Ronald DesRosiers (New York: Pauline Books and Media, 1999).

48. According to McDannell, "Currently Lourdes Authorities Estimate that Each Year 5 Million People Visit the Shrine" (135).

49. McDannell, "Currently Lourdes Authorities Estimate," 133.

50. Ibid.

51. Ibid., 136.

52. Ibid., 155.

53. Ibid.

54. McDannell comes closer when she says the following: "While an outsider might not see the resemblance between the original and the replica, for the devout even the barest hint provides an imaginative orientation toward the sacred. The site or object becomes authentic in the desire of the spectator, not in the precision of the details" (161).

Chapter 5

The Social Dynamics of Life Online

The argument of the previous chapter was that virtually mediated objects are, at least on some level, *really real*. They are also categorically similar to forms of cultural production that are central to the sacramental imagination of the Catholic Church. This similarity presents virtuality as a hermeneutic for understanding sacramentality in the twenty-first century. This argument focused consciously on the Incarnation in its discussion of mediation as a way of engaging one of the two most common doctrinal loci found in theologies of technology. This chapter investigates the nature of social life online, turning from more general questions about mediated content online to the ways in which people actually communicate in virtual spaces. It draws from media and internet studies for guidance on the basic social aspects of digital life. Ultimately, the chapter approaches the question of community from a particularly Christian perspective, focusing on the other prominent doctrinal loci of the local church community.

Since the 1980s and 1990s, many people have been interested in the social aspects of the internet. Greater connectivity and access online led, quite naturally, to broader communities. These communities shared information and interests. Indeed, these interests were often esoteric and specific enough to give the internet a niche feeling. The web or the net (to use late-twentieth-century parlance) was a place for otherwise dispersed and sometimes socially marginalized individuals to engage social interaction. The internet afforded community to those looking for others who shared obscure hobbies, such as woodworking or collecting comic books. Perhaps the most iconic of these hobbies is gaming in its various formats and contexts. If such games did rely on computers, they were predisposed to encouraging computer-based community, facilitated efficiently by an internet connection. These early kinds of communities gave the internet its stereotypically "nerdy" reputation.

According to this stereotype, the kind of person whose social life takes place mostly through a screen is the kind of person whose personality or proclivities prevent an offline social life. In the first decades of the twenty-first century, however, characterizing the internet in this way no longer makes much sense—if it ever did.

This project finds part of its impetus in the "becoming ordinary" of the internet: internet-facilitated communication is no longer only the domain of hobbyists looking for the friends they cannot find in their own neighborhoods. Based on both sociological data and our own experience of the culture, it is easy to see that many of our daily interactions with others—be they perfunctory or meaningful—are mediated by what we can simply call the internet. Speaking at least for the Global North, the internet has become an almost indispensable facet of daily life.

The internet has become indispensable because it now mediates much if not most of business, both personal and professional. The impact of the internet in the American workplace over the past twenty years is self-evident: emails have replaced memos, companies have expanded on the promise of wireless connections overseas and continents, and companies, large and small, maintain websites crucial to their business model. The internet has also become ordinary in personal business, by which I mean the errand-like activities of participating in civil society. Although offline alternatives remain, the internet dominates as the preferred mediating space for a wide variety of tasks such as changing one's address, applying to college and jobs, and even applying for food stamps and subsidized healthcare.[1] In these various ways, the internet has become ordinary insofar as it has become the primary mediating space of these kinds of communication.

This chapter focuses on communication and community, but these are not interchangeable. The internet functions as a space for communication, but that communication is not always the grounds for community. Community does, however, require communication between its members. The internet has become a space for all kinds of communication, including that which contributes to community and that which does not. Sociological and psychological research about the internet has been focused almost exclusively on the former. What remains to be described in sufficient depth, however, is the relationship between these kinds of communication, and how that relationship might change, challenge, or otherwise affect our perspective on the very notion of "community" itself. For now, I follow the work of social scientists by focusing on the notion of "social life" as a broad category for capturing the various forms of communication that contribute to the building of communities, varied as they are in character, purpose, and depth.

What follows is a review of scholarship that focuses on the question of social life in an online context. It covers a time period of about fifteen years, beginning in the very late 1990s and continuing to the present. I focus on this period because it represents the shift in understanding the internet as niche to internet as ordinary. It reflects the changes in demographics and purposes of online communities. Perhaps the most difficult aspect of this discussion of online communities—now spanning several decades—is to determine whether people in the 1990s are really talking about the same thing as people today. The niche-to-ordinary narrative that underscores the trajectory of this scholarship on online communities is not simply a matter of more people joining online communities. I contend that in its "becoming ordinary," what we call the internet has changed in ways that precludes us from receiving the scholarship of the 1990s uncritically, without proper cultural and historical caveats. Thus I pair the scholarship on online communities with more extensive historical and sociological work on American culture in order to situate the conversation about online communities more carefully. This is particularly relevant to the larger argument of this project (and the aims of chapter 5) concerning the American Catholic Church and its relationship to internet technology.

Bearing all of this in mind, a review of this material reveals two significant conclusions about online social interaction: (1) serious reflection on the role of the internet in social life should not make too sharp a distinction between individuals' online and offline experiences; and (2) what motivates this unhelpful distinction is an idealization of offline social life. This idealization comes in many forms, but the focus here is the particularly Catholic iteration of the local community: the Catholic neighborhood.

THE SOCIAL TIES OF ONLINE COMMUNITIES

In many ways, the scholarship from media studies about online communities confirms many of the anxieties from chapter 1. For example, in her observation of multiuser domains (MUDs) from 1999, Elizabeth Reid gives an explanation for the sometimes-vitriolic nature of computer-mediated communication (CMC). Users of MUDs are less inhibited in their arguing and verbal attacks because of a lack of negative consequences: "There seems little chance of a virtual action being met with an actual response. There is a sense that no one can be embarrassed, exposed, laughed at or hurt in their day-to-day lives."[2] Reid goes on to say, however, that this "sense" is the very same which makes true community possible in an online context. Contrary to what many of the researchers in the same volume expected, online communities regularly demonstrate the attributes of "contractibility and accountability."[3] MUDs and other online communities from the late 1990s (permanent chatrooms, listservs, etc.) relied heavily on users' willingness "to suspend the usual rules of social self-preservation, and open up to each other."[4] Indeed, the vitality of burgeoning online communities in this period was what prompted collections such as the one in which we find Reid's work. These communities relied, according to Reid, on emotional exchange. Online settings provide a set of tools whereby users are able to provide imaginatively the social context in which they interact with others. Therefore, online communities rely heavily on "the exercise of imagination," which is the collective starting point for the creation and maintenance of a viable social context.

In a sense, all social interaction relies upon an "exercise of imagination." I have things in my mind when I engage people in my everyday life; I make sense of our communication based on our shared imagination. For example, my doctor and I fall into a conversation about a particular health problem without having to establish the social context we currently inhabit. I do not have to say, "I am currently a patient, sitting in your office." Things become less intelligible to me if we do not share an imagination of the social context in which we embody. I do not, for instance, walk into a bakery and begin listing my symptoms. In these examples, the content of the conversation—the words themselves—is the key indicator of social context, but there are many others that we take for granted, such as dress, setting, and body language.[5]

The difficulty in analyzing online social contexts comes from there being significantly fewer number of indicators, including the shared physical context which imposes itself relentlessly into the social interaction. To use an example from the late 1990s, consider two chatrooms, one for single mothers of infants and the other for comic book collectors, both completely fictional. Let us imagine that these two chatrooms are hosted by the same American website, and look similar in their interfaces. They are also both English-speaking. Entering into each room, it takes a substantially longer amount of time to discern the social context. The room greets the user with English words, scrolling up the screen next to a variety of handles (screennames). One can only discern the social context of the imagined community by the words themselves, and even that may take a few lines.

Welcome to Room 546, Sociologeeist!
ASmith87: I don't know what you mean
Supermom93: they just aren't as good
ASmith87: they cost way less than usual and you're complaining?
CaliModoy: are you sure you're buying the water-resistant ones?
Supermom93: YES!!!!!!!!

This conversation could be about diapers or comic book covers. It is not the case that indicators of social context are largely absent from online contexts. It is the case, however, that there are significantly fewer indicators, and the "exercise of imagination" on which these communities are predicated is more difficult to describe in detail (for sociologists or other observers) and to enter into (for new users). When I engage the baker at the bakery, there is a very long history of economics, baking, language, etc., that we tacitly accept and acknowledge in our interaction, and that an observer could easily recognize. Were we so inclined, we could describe the various indicators of our social context to give the fullest description possible of our particular interaction. And different features of our interaction speak to these various elements: the money I use to buy my bread, the name of the bread I buy, the exchange pattern we use to complete the transaction, the physical store which smells of bread and has a case of baked goods.

For online communities, the relative lack of indicators makes discerning operative and imagined social contexts more difficult. The absence of these indicators may tempt us to determine that these communities are necessarily thin. They appear to float free of place and particularity, and we tend to attribute their more unsavory dynamics to this freedom. I would argue that online communities have a set of indicators that are more subtle and less diverse. What we cannot see immediately in the above chatroom exchange, for example, are the six years of conversations between Supermom93 and ASmith87. The three dollars I give the baker for her bread speaks to our shared imagination of the value of the American monetary system; what in the exchange of two people in a chatroom speaks to their shared social imagination?

Perhaps ASmith87 and Supermom93 are not terribly helpful examples; they've been online friends for six years. What about people who have never spoken before but engage one another directly online? The regular social engagement of strangers is one of the differences between the "ordinary" internet of today and the "niche" internet of yesterday. What can we say of the shared social imagination between less familiar users? The degree to which being social online relies upon "the exercise of imagination" can help explain the difficulty non-native users have with the internet. The internet functions as a social space (a placeless space) in which language functions analogously to all of the elements of non-virtual spaces which facilitate shared social imagination. This emphasis on language—more precisely, on text—has been cause for anxiety: critics fear that digital interaction, as mediated almost exclusively by text, is less robust than non-digital interaction. According to such critics, text also has the distinct disadvantage of being able to float free from contexts that might better situate its expression. Context—a physical location but also facial expressions, tone, inflection, volume, etc.—guards against misunderstandings and mitigates conflict. Individuals are less likely to be reduced to the words they say in non-digital contexts. Digital interaction, the critique goes, is therefore an inferior social space.

In order to evaluate online social life, we must consider at least three important sociological points. First, online communities have often included (if not assumed) offline interaction. Second, even where online communities function solely online, they are marked by a combination of "weak" and "strong" social ties, both of which are necessary for community. Third, the preference for offline communities must contend more honestly with the sociological and demographic realities of modern communities. I will discuss the first and second in some depth here, but will save the majority of the discussion of the third for the rest of the chapter, narrowing the focus to the implications for the American Catholic community.

The first point is that the social relationships maintained online are often also being maintained offline. Out of their research of online communities, Wellman and Gulia write,

> Pundits, both enthusiasts and critics of virtual community, usually speak of relationships as being solely online. Their fixation on the technology leads them to ignore the abundant accounts of community ties operating both online and offline, with the Net being just one of several ways of communicating. Despite all the talk about virtual community transcending time and space *sui generis*, much contact is between people who see each other in person and live locally.[6]

This has become even more prevalent in recent times with the proliferation of technologies that allow sustained contact online. The relationships people are sustaining online are often continuations of relationships began offline, or the relationships begun online often have offline components as well. In many cases, online interaction is not just the latest means for sustaining the relationship. Rather, it operates in a web of other kinds of communication that work together to form the infrastructure of the relationship.[7] People use social media, for all the attention given it for connecting strangers, to communicate with the people with whom they communicate and interact in other (offline) contexts.[8]

But maybe the inferiority of online community is still evident. If I sustain my relationships completely online, completely offline, or in a combination of online and offline, I might still argue that the offline communication is still superior to its online counterpart. This seems to be behind so-called technology fasts, wherein people decide to give up particular aspects of their online communication in order to focus more on the offline kind.[9] But according to Wellman and Gulia, this "treat[s] community as a zero-sum game, assuming that if people spend more time interacting online they will spend less time interacting in 'real life.'"[10] It is difficult to avoid such "zero-sum" thinking when thinking about community. This way of thinking is not exactly responsible for the persistence of the view that online social life is inferior to offline social life (admitting, for now, that they are still separable in some meaningful way). What seems more responsible is the nature of the relationships themselves.

What we are really attempting to privilege when we privilege offline social interaction is what we hope are "strong" social ties in contrast to "weak" social ties. We assume that online social ties are marked by weakness insofar as they are based on specialized interests, such as a discussion group on vegan recipes or comment thread on a particularly funny and popular video of a cat. In situations like these, people forge social ties that are "weak" because the relationship is circumscribed by specificity (soyburger sauce exchange) and/or time (Mr. Puffs the kitten goes viral for exactly 2.3 days). The internet allows us to find very specific information by finding other people producing content that is specific to whatever we want or need.[11]

According to Wellman and Gulia, however, the internet is also capable of (if not predisposed to) facilitating "strong" social ties. This is because "information is only one of many social resources that is exchanged online."[12] Other social resources include "emotional support, companionship, and advice," all of which make up "strong" social ties. One of the curious things about the internet is how people searching for specific information ("weak" ties) find each other and forge long-lasting, meaningful relationships ("strong" ties): "Even when online groups are not designed to be supportive, they tend to be. As social beings, those who use the Net seek not only information but also companionship, social support, and a sense of belonging."[13]

The conditions that allow for a move from a more informative network to a supportive community are hard to determine. It is complicated by the fact that between the specific, informative exchange and supportive, communal exchange there is another category of online social interaction, known as "generalized exchange."[14] This mechanism of generalized exchange has three elements: "(1) the obligatory transfer, (2) of inalienable objects or services, (3) between related mutually obligated transactors."[15] For our vegan recipe discussion group, generalized exchange occurs when User A answers User B's question about the use of bananas in cake recipes, with no direct benefit to User A. All of the users on the discussion group, however, understand the community as reliant on such exchanges. This common understanding facilitates later exchanges, such as when User P provides User Q with a video tutorial for her Thanksgiving Tofurkey. The mutual understanding and participation in generalized exchange can form the basis for the shared social imagination that can lead to a community of connected by "strong" ties.

Nevertheless, the internet often appears to privilege "weak" ties. Even generalized exchange can appear "weak" on the interpersonal level because it is often a singular interaction that, while contributing to the community as a whole, does little to bring individuals into meaningful contact with one another. This impression of online social interaction is not helped by recent trends of circumscribed exchanges, be they textual or visual. Currently, three of the most popular social media platforms are Twitter, Snapchat, and TikTok, all three of which mandate very specific limits on users and their exchanges. Twitter does not allow tweets (short, public, or semipublic messages) longer than 140 characters, which is no longer than about 2 short sentences.[16] Snapchat allows users to send pictures and videos (snaps) under very specific limits: videos can be no longer than ten seconds, all snaps last no longer than twenty-four hours on the platform when shared generally, and snaps sent directly between users disappear after one viewing. TikTok only allows fifteen second or one minute videos.

These circumscribed exchanges can further the impression that online social interactions express "weak" social ties. But this description can miss the many meaningful relationships and communities marked by "strong" ties that people sustain online: "We believe that critics who disparage the authenticity of such strong, online ties are being unwarrantedly snobbish in disregarding the seriousness with which Net participants take their relationships."[17] There is just no evidence that the ties of community found online are necessarily inferior to the ties of offline community in terms of their "weak" or "strong" nature. Coupled with the fact that online and offline communities have become increasingly more difficult to distinguish, the presence of both "weak" and "strong" social ties online means that critical evaluations of online communities must rely on some other premise(s).

According to Wellman and Gulia, both enthusiasts and critics of the internet are too present-minded, sometimes operating with the assumption that the nature, purposes, and requirements of human community were not questions before the phenomenon of the internet. Indeed, other technologies have been cause for raising the question of community, as well as the question of "weak" and "strong" social ties, even if framed in different terms. What discussions about the internet offer us now is a clear picture of the hopes we have for human community. Our present anxieties about technology paint us a tableau of the kinds of communities we think we prefer, but it is a picture that is not entirely grounded in reality.

Wellman and Gulia maintain that our evaluations of online community assume a "pastoralist ideal" for comparison. They write, "The standard pastoralist ideal of in-person, village-like community has depicted each community member as providing a broad range of support to all others. In this ideal situation, all can count upon all to provide companionship, emotional aid, information, services (such as child care or health care), money, or goods (be it food for the starving or a drill for the renovating)."[18] In short, when criticizing online communities, we often assume that "strong" ties more consistently mark offline communities, while "weak" ties predominate in online communities. While the distinction between "weak" and "strong" ties is helpful for understanding the variation in social communications both online and offline, perhaps it still cannot fully address the worries we have about online community. Perhaps what we are really concerned about, especially now in the "ordinary" half of the internet's story, is not about the *strength* of social ties but about whom the internet is tying together. This concern—the "who" and not just the "how"—is at the center of theologian Vincent Miller's account of media in the twenty-first century, to which we now turn.

FRAGMENTATION AND DIFFUSION

The internet lies at the intersection of several economic, political, and social currents in the stream of post-secularity. Analyzing the internet requires that one wade into the deeper cultural forces at work in the Western world since the twentieth century. Vincent Miller provides an analysis of the role of media in the contemporary "cultural ecology marked by fragmentation, polarization, and deterritorialization."[19] Miller's focus is on the effects of postsecular logics on religious traditions, particularly Christianity. In the end, he argues that the electronic media has exacerbated the heterogenization of previously integrated shared imaginations of public space. In this electronically mediated heterogeneity, fragmentation has become a matter of course and identity-making has become the goal of discourse and community. For religious traditions, this has had a deregulating effect, wherein "traditional religious authorities compete directly with new figures, popes with pundits, bishops with media personalities, theologians with bloggers."[20]

Before moving into his analysis of modern communications technology in the context of globalized post-secularity, however, Miller offers a genealogy of this "cultural ecology" by comparing our era of "electronic capitalism" to that of "print capitalism," using Benedict Anderson's *Imagined Communities*. According to Anderson, writes Miller, "nationalism emerged from the unplanned spatial transformations that print capitalism worked on the preexisting cultural foundations of clerisy and monarchy."[21] The printing press had a homogenizing effect, creating a "sense of contemporaneous time" and a "shared national memory."[22] The first is causal to the second: the medium of the newspaper (marked with a date) creates a sense of "homogenous empty time," providing the "temporal frame within which people could imagine themselves as members of a larger community comprising a vast number of members with whom they had no direct relationship."[23] The rise of nationalisms, therefore, is responsible for the creation of a "populace who imagine themselves as sharing a common heritage and destiny with the myriad others who inhabit that space, for whom they feel a 'natural' solidarity."[24] This feeling of solidarity carried a homogeneity bolstered by the imagination of shared space, of "shared political territory."[25]

The Catholic Church was forced to respond to the rise of the nation-state. It did so by means of a "mass movement."[26] This movement had various specific forms, including the rise of papal social teaching, the growth of Catholic Action, and the proliferation of "trans-local national" devotional sites (Lourdes) and practices (the rosary).[27] It also involved "constructing buildings, institutions, organizations, and formation systems necessary to counter competing ideologies and constructions of space."[28] Like the nation-states in Anderson's account, religious communities during this time are "likewise large and relatively homogeneous."[29] This allows for discourse both internal to and external to religious traditions, allowing them to bring their resources to bear on a variety of questions.

Since the 1970s, however, "technological and economic changes" have led to an "unwinding of the national scale," a trend of heterogeneity that has had and continues to have adverse effects for religious communities.[30] Like the printing press, communications technologies of the late twentieth century had a "catalyzing" effect on cultural and political imaginations.[31] The legacy of print capitalism endured well into the twentieth century, most notably in mass markets. Communications technology functions as a sort of hinge between the eras of homogeneity and heterogeneity that Miller is detailing here. Communications technologies "bore within them the seeds of the undoing of the national scale, [but] for much of the century they were nonetheless still deployed within an economy that created national-scale mass markets."[32] But communications technologies would soon be at the center of new market arrangements that encouraged the "focus on ever smaller niche markets."[33] For Miller, this focus is at the heart of the new spatial dynamics of the last four decades or so. These dynamics are marked, Miller says, by "cultural heterogenization, and a cultural geometry of disjuncture and deterritorialization."[34]

An increase in the capabilities and reach of media has led to deep fragmentation, primarily because the technology itself encourages the formation of "enclaves of like-minded."[35] Miller here refers to the example of television but the internet bears this out in even more demonstrable ways: because one is no longer limited to geographic constraints and the diversity inherent therein, one can simply find others who believe in the same conspiracy theory and spend as much time as she wishes, further concretizing the theory over vast differences. Here Miller points to the work of Van Alstyne and Brynjolfsson (1996), who provide a mathematical model for the trend of what they call "cyberbalkanization." The internet has the ability, they argue, for constructing the "global village"[36], but "it is also possible that improving communications access through emerging technology will fragment society and balkanize interactions."[37]

One of Van Alstyne and Brynjolfsson's most insightful moves is the inclusion of "bounded rationality" into their discussion of online communities. Even as distances are overcome more and more by the internet, there will always be the distance between "the computer monitor and the brain."[38] As much as we update the speed of processors, we are still limited by human processing. The reality is that while we might have access to many more people, "a citizen of cyberspace still has a finite set of 'neighbors' with whom he or she can meaningfully interact."[39] Furthermore, "these neighbors can now be chosen based on criteria other than geography."[40]

The mathematical modeling that Van Alstyne and Brynjolfsson present demonstrates that given bounded rationality, "like types have located one another and formed tightly knit communities,"[41] what Miller would call "sorting into enclaves." These communities or enclaves do not, however, typically communicate with each other as much as they utilize communication tools for intra-community communication. A lack of inter-community communication means a homogenization of isolated groups over space and time, with little need or motivation for engaging with the more diverse community of one's geographical locale. Van Alstyne and Brynjolfsson state the problem with cyberbalkanization this way:

> Individuals empowered to screen out material that does not conform to their existing preferences may form virtual cliques, insulate themselves from opposing points of view, and reinforce their biases. Internet users can seek out interactions with like-minded individuals who have similar values, and thus become less likely to trust important decisions to people whose values differ from their own. This voluntary balkanization and the loss of shared experiences and values may be harmful to the structure of democratic societies as well as decentralized organizations.[42]

The real problem with this "sorting into enclaves" is the obstacle it can present to forming social and political solidarity among a differently engaged but radically diffused[43] population. For democratic politics, the internet is a space of fragmentation that makes broad-based social action difficult and, where successful, somewhat superficial and fleeting.[44]

Miller's analysis of virtual space also includes the work of Jaron Lanier, a musician and computer scientist credited with popularizing the phrase "virtual reality." Lanier's *You Are Not a Gadget* and *Who Owns the Future?* provide critical analyses of the economic ramifications of online infrastructure. Lanier illumines the fact that the structure and norms of computer-mediated communication are not natural or inevitable, but designed by specific people for specific goals. The internet (like many technologies) is a product of military research and development. Its infrastructure, writes Lanier in *You

Are Not a Gadget, reflects its military origins, namely in what is known as "packet switching." The basic structure of the network we use every day is predicated upon a cold war desire to guard against a complete collapse of the entire system in light of a nuclear attack. The idea was that if you attack one part, it would not necessarily mean that the whole would be adversely affected. Each "packet" is a bit of information, moving toward a destination with no predetermined way of getting there: "If a particular node fails to acknowledge receipt of a packet, the node trying to pass the packet to it can try again elsewhere."[45] This gives the internet a fluidity that has given rise to a variety of biological metaphors[46] for understanding its most basic processes.

In its research and development of networks, then, the U.S. military chose packet switching as the basic process of what would become the internet. The simple but easily forgotten reality is that there is nothing inevitable about any of our technological designs; we have to recognize design and innovation as a set of historical and cultural choices. Lanier argues that this infrastructure carries libertarian ethos within the many facets of computer engineering, from hardware design to software development. Packet switching makes the internet fundamentally decentralized and delocalized, the infrastructural basis for Miller's argument about fragmentation and deterritorialization from above. Lanier's argument in *Who Owns the Future?* extrapolates on the economic ramifications of the internet's infrastructure.

Within packet switching technology, "Each node had no accountability, so nodes could accumulate in a 'friction-free' way, even though there was no such thing as a free lunch, and the friction would surely appear later on in some fashion."[47] This friction, according to Lanier, is beginning to erode the middle class. His persistent example is the rise of downloadable music, which allows certain individuals to benefit from the creative production of artists and denies artists compensation for their work. *Who Owns the Future?* is especially compelling in its economic analysis, arguing that the internet has delocalized information or data in such a way as to obscure the people who create it. Individual users are the creators of all kinds of data, from creative projects like videos and music to the more mundane data points that are created by one's web presence. According to Lanier, "Information is people in disguise, and people ought to be paid for the value they contribute that can be sent or stored on a digital network."[48]

Without this kind of compensation (which Lanier envisions in a complex system of micropayments, or "incremental wealth creation events"[49]), Lanier sees the continued erosion of the middle class. Digital configurations currently favor, Lanier argues, a "winner-take-all" distribution, wherein a few people strike it big while everyone else dreams about how to do the same. This is in contrast to a "bell curve" distribution, wherein "a bulge of average people and two tails of exceptional people, one high and one low."[50] But bell curve distributions need the help of metaphorical levees "to compensate for the madness of fluid mechanics and protect the middle class."[51] Examples include social welfare programs, unions, taxes, and other forms of economic regulation. "Levees are a rejection of unbridled algorithm," writes Lanier, "and an insertion of human will into the flow of capital."[52] Such insertion of humanity means that they are subject to the same vulnerabilities as all human enterprises. A good example is the complicated history of unions, which is marked by successes not only in justice but also in corruption.

With the erosion of these levees—an erosion that has a long history in the twentieth century[53]—Lanier understands digital configurations as the latest technology to inherit a preference for "winner-take-all" distributions: "The great oceans of capital started to form themselves into a steep, tall, winner-take-all, razor-thin tower and an emaciated long tail."[54] We are voracious in our consumption of online content, much of which used to cost real money in earlier eras. Lanier returns often to music, which provides a good example. For a small monthly fee to a streaming service, I can queue up almost any song I want to hear. The "winners" of these kinds of digital configurations are groups like programmers, companies that use data to their own commercial advantages, inventors of applications (apps), and (the much more rare) people who become famous from their YouTube videos. The successes of these people make us all dream about the fortunes possible for us as well, should we be *lucky* enough. Enough people will find my cat funny looking enough to make me rich; enough people will use the app I create for some social media reason; enough people will take notice of my blog that ad revenues will become by livable income.

Lanier's economic critique of digital infrastructure shares much with Miller's critique of the heterogenization of post-secular social life. Lanier argues that content production should be compensated even though most people never consider that they should be paid for the rather mundane things they produce online. Users never consider this because most of us just produce information about ourselves, usually in the form of communication with and to others. It does not seem like commodifiable content, even though the triumphs of "big data" show us just how much it is. In Lanier, we see an argument for the relationship between economics and social communications, two realities that globalized capitalism has long sought to make indistinguishable. The internet has expedited this process, fragmenting us further into mere consumers and diffusing whatever proclivities for solidarity by untethering us to locales.

It is this "untethering" which, somewhat ironically, cultivates the "pastoralist ideal" to which Wellman and Gulia refer in their analysis of online communities above. The pastoralist ideal is manifest in many contemporary cultural movements. One of these is the recent turn to "the local," an economic movement which privileges that which has been grown, brewed, produced, sewn, or made in one's own town or region. Frustrated by the corporations with which consumers have noticeable "weak" social ties, Americans have taken to supporting local businesses with whom it is easier to have "strong" social ties. Americans of a particular class have decided that a higher cost of goods and services is worth the possibility of "strong" economic-social ties, which are marked by a degree of transparency, kinship, community pride, and quality. Faced with market choice as the primary means of agency, Americans have thus enacted the pastoralist ideal in the turn to the local.

This "local turn" is not so much evidence against the kind of trends described by Miller and Lanier. Instead, the new focus on "the local" demonstrates precisely the globalizing effects of both technology and the market. It is simply on side of the post-secular coin, the other side of which is the proliferation of internet technology, decidedly "global" in its orientation. As we saw above, however, the social relationships that people maintain online are often extensions and reiterations of their offline (local) ones. Still, the internet allows people to transcend space and time, accessing information, people, goods, and services at any time and from almost any place. Ironically, because the turn to the local has been contemporary with the rise of e-commerce, one can quite easily tap into the economy of a place that is not local to oneself but still participates in the turn to the local. For example, I may not be able to buy a six-pack from my favorite brewery in Richmond, Virginia, at the grocery store where I live in Ohio but I can easily use the internet (through third-party sellers or other means) to purchase this "local" beer, despite its local-only distribution.

Our conversations about the local turn and the internet, together or separately, reveal the pastoralist ideal at the heart of our collective imagination of community. The pastoralist ideal is attractive to many people, including Christians. The local turn has dovetailed nicely with certain theological systems that emphasize the local church community. As a result, so much theological work being done on internet technology has tended to overemphasize the local community as the social antidote to the obvious inferiority of online community. One of the most salient points made by Wellman and Gulia, however, is that even if the pastoralist ideal ever existed (which it probably did not), "contemporary communities in the western world are quite different."[55] Research shows that the social lives of Americans (and other Westerners) are nothing like the pastoralist ideal of the "in-person, village-like community." Critics of technology might be quick to blame the internet for the discrepancy, offering images of people glued to smartphones and tablets in their homes, at restaurants and even in classrooms—virtually ignoring the "in-person" situation around them. What this critique fails to acknowledge, however, are the dramatic ways in which that situation around us has changed. Sociological studies show that our social configurations are not only changed by technology, but that the picture is much more complicated. In fact, our technological habits reflect deep changes in our social configurations.

NOTES

1. One need only remember the fiasco surrounding the healthcare.gov website following the adoption of the Affordable Care Act in 2013.
2. Elizabeth Reid, "Hierarchy and Power: Social Control in Cyberspace," in *Communities in Cyberspace*, ed. Mark A. Smith and Peter Kollock (London and New York: Routledge, 1999), 113.
3. Ibid., 114.
4. Ibid., 113.
5. The lack of nonverbal cues online is one of the biggest indicators of an incomplete or inhibited means of social communication through the medium. See the section on "presence studies" below for a brief discussion of this topic.
6. Barry Wellman and Milena Gulia, "Virtual Communities as Communities," in *Communities in Cyberspace*, ed. Mark A. Smith and Peter Kollock (London and New York: Routledge, 1999), 179.
7. Wellman and Gulia, "Virtual Communities as Communities," 170.
8. For a specific example of the online/offline relationship, see Smith et al., *Teens, Technology & Friendships*, Pew Research Forum (August 2015).
9. These have been particularly popular among Christians as a Lenten penitential practice. See Bennett, *Aquinas on the Web?* 61–66.
10. Wellman and Gulia, "Virtual Communities as Communities," 181. This is, in fact, exactly what Van Alstyne and Brynjolfsson argue: "Because time is limited, spending more time interacting with online communities necessarily means spending less time interacting with geographic communities or even family members." For a discussion of their argument, see below.
11. Again, see discussion of Alstyne and Brynjolfsson below.
12. Ibid., 172.
13. Ibid., 173.
14. Kollock, "Economies of online cooperation" quoting Ekeh (1974).
15. Ibid., 221.
16. Twitter and Tumblr make up the new medium of "microblogging," which further demonstrates the trend of circumscribed exchange I detail here.
17. Wellman and Gulia, "Virtual Communities as Communities," 181.
18. Ibid., 171.
19. Vincent Miller, "Media Constructions of the Space, the Disciplining of Religious Traditions, and the Hidden Threat of the Post-Secular," in *At the Limits of the Secular: Reflections on Faith and Public Life*, ed. William A. Barbieri, Jr. (Cambridge, UK: Eerdmans, 2011).
20. Miller, "Media Constructions," 185.

21. Ibid., 167. See Benedict Anderson, *Imagined Communities: Reflections on the Origin and Spread of Nationalism* (New York: Verso, 2006).

22. Ibid., 168. Here Miller is drawing upon the work of Elizabeth Eisenstein.

23. Ibid., 169.

24. Ibid., 170.

25. Ibid.

26. Ibid., 171. Here Miller is drawing upon the work of Charles Taylor's *A Secular Age* (Cambridge: Harvard Press, 2007).

27. Ibid., 172–173.

28. Ibid.

29. Ibid., 174.

30. Ibid.

31. Ibid.

32. Miller, "Media Constructions," 175.

33. Ibid.

34. Ibid., 176.

35. Ibid., 177.

36. See Marshall McLuhan and Bruce R. Powers, *The Global Village: Transformations in World Life and Media in the 21st Century* (New York: Oxford University Press, 1989).

37. Marshall Van Alstyne and Erik Brynjolfsson, "Electronic Communities: Global Village or Cyberbalkans?" (MIT, 1996), 3. Available online at: http://web.mit.edu/marshall/www/papers/CyberBalkans.pdf.

38. Van Alstyne and Brynjolfsson, "Electronic Communities," 4.

39. Ibid.

40. Ibid.

41. Ibid., 12.

42. Ibid., 24.

43. Miller prefers terms such as "fragmentation," "polarization," and "heterogenization." I prefer "diffusion" as the metaphor for social behaviors and organization online, and insert it into Miller's description in order to soften his critique. While I believe "diffusion" is ultimately faithful to Miller's analysis, it should be noted that this is my interpretative insertion, and that it is a substantive and not simply semantic point. I return to this point in a later section of this chapter.

44. This underlies critiques about internet "slacktivism."

45. Jaron Lanier, *You Are Not a Gadget* (New York: Vintage Books, 2010), 123.

46. "The result is that we must now measure the internet as if it were a part of nature, instead of from the inside, as if we were examining the books of a financial enterprise. We must explore it as if it were unknown territory, even though we laid it out." Lanier, *You Are Not a Gadget*, 124.

47. Jaron Lanier, *Who Owns the Future?* (New York: Simon & Schuster, 2013), 230.

48. Lanier, *Who Owns the Future?* 245.

49. Ibid., 240.

50. Ibid., 39.

51. Ibid., 43.
52. Ibid., 48.
53. Ibid., 46–52.
54. Ibid., 50.
55. Ibid.

Chapter 6

The Suburbanization of American Catholic Life

As various industries and movements capitalize on the trendy focus on local communities, sociologists continue to document the diffusion of traditional social ties in these same communities. Robert Putnam has been one of the most prominent voices in this body of work, providing compelling and extensive data on the picture of "social capital" in the United States. His most well-known work, *Bowling Alone*, provides a vast overview of the decline of traditional forms of civic participation and social engagement in American life. With coauthor David Campbell, Putnam extends *Bowling Alone*'s commentary on religious institutions into a full account of religion in American life. Both of these texts provide crucial data for understanding the current state of "community" in American culture. These texts demonstrate that the growth of online communities, with both weak and strong ties, has coincided with the decline of traditional forms of social life. Putnam's work illustrates the shifting sites of "social capital," and gestures toward a future reality wherein the local neighborhood and municipality plays a complicated and ambiguous role in the social and religious lives of its members.

"The core idea of social capital theory," writes Putnam in the early pages of *Bowling Alone*, "is that social networks have value."[1] The very concept of "social capital" is a product of the twentieth century, having been "independently invented at least six times."[2] One of the earliest definitions for social capital comes in 1916, when L. J. Hanifan writes that social capital refers to "those tangible substances [that] count for most in the daily lives of people: namely good will, fellowship, sympathy, and social intercourse among the individuals and families who make up a social unit."[3] Out of the various definitions that follow Hanifan's, Putnam surmises that social capital is essentially about both private and public goods: it is advantageous for both individuals and communities to cultivate and sustain social capital.

Among the many sites of social capital that Putnam identifies and references throughout *Bowling Alone* are political (e.g., party affiliation) and civic (publicly-oriented social activities like being a member of the National Rifle Association) activities and groups. His focus, however, is much broader than these engagements, including "the almost infinite variety of informal ties that link Americans—card parties and bowling leagues, bar cliques and ball games, picnics and parties."[4] This dense collection of social networks is what cultivates "social capital," that which Putnam demonstrates has been on a steady decline in American culture since the middle of the twentieth century.

While social capital has both benevolent and malevolent effects, Putnam is largely concerned with its "positive consequences," and the goal of the book is to present the documented erosion of these consequences. Where the sociologists of internet communities above refer to "weak" and "strong" ties, Putnam refers to "multistranded" and "singlestranded" social networks. Putnam's description here is more concrete in some ways, mostly because he has in mind communities that are geographically and physically centralized. He describes multistranded networks as "repeated" and "intensive," "like a group of steelworkers who meet for drinks every Friday night after work and see each other at mass on Sunday."[5] The singlestranded networks, he writes, tend to be "episodic" and "anonymous," "like the faintly familiar face you see several times a month in the supermarket checkout line."[6] *Bowling Alone*, as the title suggests, focuses primarily on the erosion of multistranded networks, although the trends that the data bears out applies to singlestranded networks as well. The thesis of *Bowling Alone* is as follows:

> For the first two-thirds of the twentieth century a powerful tide bore Americans into ever deeper engagement in the life of their communities, but a few decades ago—silently, without warning—that tide reversed and we were overtaken by a treacherous rip current. Without at first noticing, we have been pulled apart from one another and from our communities over the last third of the century.

At this point, it may appear as if Putnam's work can be easily used to refute whatever argument is advanced here regarding the relative value of online (nontraditional) communities. It is, indeed, possible to read and utilize Putnam's invaluable work this way. What I am attempting to demonstrate here, however, is that the trend of erosion with regard to social capital that Putnam so clearly demonstrates has a reciprocal relationship with the technological advances made in the same historical period. Technological habits and developments that extend the social networks of individuals beyond the spaces Putnam studies are both *responsible for* and a *possible answer to* the trend that Putnam details in *Bowling Alone*. These habits, however, are also symptomatic of important social and economic changes in the same period Putnam analyzes.

Let us give due time to the "responsible for" aspect of the above thesis. Putnam devotes an entire chapter to "Technology and Mass Media," wherein he notes the relationship between readers of print news and those who are civically engaged. Consumers of TV news are less engaged than their print-reading counterparts, but "news watchers are nevertheless more civic than most other Americans."[7] But news-watching only makes up a fraction of the time the subjects in Putnam's studies spent with their televisions. Entertainment makes up a far bigger segment of television-watching. Putnam cites the exponential growth of television-watching after 1950, and argues that "the single most important consequence of the television revolution has been to bring us home."[8] This is material to his larger argument about waning civic engagement primarily because television-watching has replaced many of the leisure activities that brought people together in the kinds of civic activities Putnam has in mind: bowling leagues, lodges, clubs, etc. He writes that the increase in television-watching has meant a decrease in "virtually every form of civic participation and social involvement."[9]

So the rise of the family television has drawn people into their homes, in relative isolation, and away from the social activities of our predecessors. But Putnam acknowledges the very important fact that "correlation is not causation,"[10] and that there is a way to read the relationship between television and social disengagement differently: "People who are social isolates to begin with gravitate toward the tube as the line of leisurely least resistance."[11] He goes on to provide substantial data against this reading, specifically from a study in Canada that compared communities with various means of access to television. Ultimately, Putnam remains convinced that "dependence on televised entertainment" has been a major factor in the civic and social disengagement that is the subject of *Bowling Alone*.

Putnam's analysis of television is relevant for considering the internet for at least two reasons. First, it demonstrates the effects that technology can have on social behavior in concrete ways. But more importantly, his work represents the sociological data that gets deployed against the internet, without much justification for the direct transfer from television. In an earlier chapter, in fact, Putnam avoids this temptation by commenting on the internet and its future in a measured, albeit insufficient, way. Putnam argues that there are three counter trends to the phenomenon he is describing, and that the internet is "by all odds the most important."[12]

In the end, Putnam's account of the internet is relatively optimistic. This is due in large part to his optimism about the recovery of social capital more generally. He writes that the internet is capable—primarily because of computer-mediated communication—of being a positive answer to the problem of social disengagement: "I conclude that the Internet [sic] will not automatically offset the decline in more conventional forms of social capital, but that it has that potential. In fact, it is hard to imagine solving our contemporary civic dilemmas without computer-mediated communication."[13] His conclusion here is owing in large part to his use of Wellman and Gulia (discussed in chapter 5), whose sociological data demonstrate the communal benefits and complexity of computer-mediated communication. Putnam also helpfully situates his discussion of the internet within the context of the history of the telephone, comparing the conjecture surrounding the telephone's effect on social life to contemporary discussions about the possibilities and problems of the internet. He writes that "the astounding series of poor predictions about the social consequences of the telephone is a deeply cautionary tale."[14] When telephone usage increased, many assumed that it would function in isolating ways, decreasing the amount of non-telephonic ("face-to-face") social interaction. Instead, the telephone had mostly the effect of "reinforcing, not transforming or replacing, existing personal networks."[15] So too might be the case for computer-mediated communication, says Putnam.

In Putnam's narrative, the relationship between technology and social capital is largely one of cause and effect: television drew people into their homes and away from civic activities, and the internet has the potential to do more of the same. Putnam does state, however, that "the Internet will not *automatically* offset the decline in more conventional forms of social capital, but that it has that potential."[16]

But the cultural phenomenon of something like television is never so squarely at home in the "cause" position of the cause-effect relationship here. Putnam's work is detailed and comprehensive enough to bear this out but he does not attend well enough here in his analysis of television on the ways in which our technological habits—beginning with radio and television and continuing through the social media which dominates contemporary life—can also be seen as *symptomatic* of broader cultural changes. To be more specific, important *spatial* reconfigurations preceded and motivated our technological habits regarding mass media, and these spatial realities continue to influence the attraction to social media. Lizabeth Cohen's *A Consumer's Republic* provides a narrative picture of the relevant spatial reconfigurations, and does so in a manner that allows us to attend more closely to the economic aspects of both mass and social media.

The driving thesis of Cohen's work is that mass consumption functioned as the primary way in which American culture reidentified itself after World War II. Consumerism became linked to good citizenship, and spending money became the primary activity of the "good" American in the postwar years. One of the clearest sites for mass consumption, according to Cohen, is the explosive expansion of the American suburb, which she refers to as the "landscape of mass consumption."[17] According to Cohen, "Between 1947 and 1953 the suburban population increased by 43 percent."[18] Even more telling, however, is the relationship of the suburban neighborhood to the city neighborhood. She writes, "Over the course of the 1950s, in the twenty largest metropolitan areas, cities would grow only by .1 percent, their suburbs by an explosive 45 percent."[19] Such massive growth in the suburbs had several enabling factors, all of which imply spatial changes that are relevant to the social lives of Americans since 1945.

Cohen's narrative notes that the move to the suburbs has some historical precedents, namely "Victorian streetcar and garden suburbs and the bungalow building of the 1920s."[20] Unlike these early suburban trends, however, the building of the postwar American suburb had the advantage of "mass auto ownership and federally funded highways."[21] The rise in car ownership during this time meant a kind of physical mobility that allowed people to live relatively near but not in the cities of their parents and grandparents. Cohen uses the suburbs of New York and New Jersey as an illustrative example, writing that

> increasingly, people from long-established, often highly industrialized, and, by the end of the war, congested and deteriorating urban centers . . . left homes near jobs, relatives, and long-established ethnic and religious communities to move to newly built houses further out . . . much the way Americans of an earlier era had left farms and small towns for beckoning cities.[22]

This exodus from cities by the American middle and upper class reconfigured the social lives of many Americans. It reoriented their lives in important and impactful ways. One of these reorientations is, as Putnam notes, toward the screen. The television, purchased under the new code of the being a good American via consumption, becomes the primary site not only for entertainment but also for marketing.[23] This is the era of market segmentation,[24] and the explosion of advertising that targeted particular demographics through print and television.

The suburbanization of American life is a particularly important moment in Catholic history in the United States. The exodus from urban Catholic neighborhoods to the suburbs set a precedent of mobility and marked a new milestone in cultural assimilation for Catholics of European origin in the United States. This laid the groundwork for the experience of so many descendants of European Catholic immigrants, whose only experience of the tightly knit and closely located parish community is that which is found in family photo albums and oral histories. For many American Catholics of a certain age, walking to Mass on Sunday is a quaint vestige of the era of the Catholic neighborhood. Owing in no small part to the voluntarism and consumerism of American religious life, one's parish is probably much more determined by one's preferences (for the pastor, for the music, or even for the cry-rooms) than by geography. The drive to and from Mass has become as natural and essential as finding a pew.

Pew Research data shows that Americans are pretty evenly distributed through different kinds of landscapes: 20 percent live in rural areas, 22 percent live in large cities, 21 percent live in suburbs near a large city, and 37 percent live in a "small city or town."[25] What are we to make of Cohen's historical narrative in light of these numbers? The spatial reconfiguration—from urban to suburban—of the mid-twentieth century is but one part of a much larger cultural dynamic that Cohen attempts to capture with the category of the "Consumer's Republic." What she really wants to convey is the matrix of cultural, economic, racial, and political currents that give rise to so many aspects of American life in the late twentieth and early twenty-first centuries. I want to suggest that although Americans live in a variety of places, many if not most Americans have been thoroughly "suburbanized."

To be "suburbanized" is to accept as normal a spatial and social reality that fundamentally lacks a localized center, be it economic, cultural, or religious. One can come at this in a variety of ways, and a popular way of thinking about the phenomenon I am describing here has been through discussions of globalization. A globalized economy promises the availability of goods largely irrespective of geographic location. To use Lanier's image regarding packet switching, globalization promises "frictionless" economic access. Thus we see the overlapping logic of our economic and technological lives, both predicated on the idea that access is to be unmitigated by geographical limitations.

The suburbanization of the spaces themselves is quite easy to see: American suburbs hundreds of miles apart have startling similarities, and even towns and cities begin to look, sound, smell, and taste the same. This homogenization of spaces deemphasizes the importance of the local, often into obsolescence. In concrete terms, the economic factors at play have meant the demise of smaller businesses that simply cannot compete with the lower prices of national and multinational corporations. Despite where we live, Americans are a suburban people, unconstrained by geography, and, for the most part, living without a center. Both Miller and Lanier understand media and technology within the context of globalization, and rightly so. What I do not think they attend to fully, however, is the mid-century ethos that Cohen describes, and the way in which the "Consumer's Republic" gives rise to and exacerbates the technological advances that continue to suburbanize our living spaces and spatial imaginations.

Miller uses several concepts in his work to describe the relationship between economics and media today: "fragmentation," "deterritorialization," "heterogenization." Van Alstyne and Brynjolfsson prefer "balkanization" and offer compelling evidence for the homogeneity of online communities. The situation in which we are now living, it seems, is radically heterogeneous and individualistic, and to the extent we form them at all, we form communities that are homogeneous and we do so over sometimes vast distances. I want to add "diffusion" to this growing list of descriptors, primarily as a way of combining the insights of both Putnam and Cohen and incorporating them into the more specified conversation about technology. Owing in large part to the cultural values embodied by the Consumer's Republic of postwar America, we have experienced a suburbanization of our imaginations that has resulted in a *diffusion* of social capital (a la Putnam). Social ties are not "weak" where they once were "strong" (to use Wellman and Gulia's terms). Instead, all ties are diffuse, in that they are no longer situated within localized, centralized institutions, be they religious or otherwise. If postwar Americans enthusiastically embraced the new spatial reality of the diffuse suburb, we have inherited this diffusion and reflect it in our social, economic, and religious lives.

This more general notion of "suburbanization," therefore, can help us understand the particular situation of American Catholics. Again, despite the fact that Catholics live in all kinds of places, I would argue that the dominant experience of American Catholics is actually "Suburban Catholicism." Parish communities often no longer represent the social and cultural center of American Catholic life, any more than they represent the geographic center.[26] Even parishes whose physical structures are still firmly in the middle of old neighborhoods no longer boast the thick communal life of earlier (pre-Consumer's Republic) eras. This diffusion of American social life is important for understanding the experience of American Catholics today, especially young Catholics, who are disaffiliating from the church in greater numbers than ever before.

According to sociologist Patricia Wittberg, current data from the General Social Survey demonstrate that young Catholics (Gen X and Millennial generations) are far less religious than their predecessors. Thanks to immigration from Latin America, the Catholic population in the United States has remained stable, despite what can only be described as a mass exodus by non-Hispanic Catholics. For Wittberg, the most disturbing aspect of this trend is the fact that "Millennial women are slightly more likely than Catholic men their age to say that they never attend Mass," making them the first generation of American Catholic women for whom this is the case.[27] Wittberg finds this demographically disturbing for the American church because she knows what other sociologists of religion know: women keep people (i.e., families) in religious communities.

There are, of course, too many factors at play to responsibly speculate the reasons for decline in religiosity among Catholics.[28] Some of them are obvious: general decline in religiosity on a national scale; the rise of the "nones," a category which denotes a lack of religious affiliation but may also include less traditional forms of religion, like loosely organized Christian communities; the perception that conservative politics and religion are inextricably linked, effectively making issues like gay marriage and climate change function like ultimatums in the minds of young people. Some people may even want to blame technology for a decline in religiosity among young people, citing it as either a symptom of their self-absorption and apathy or its efficient cause.[29]

Millennials are the generation for whom the Catholic neighborhood is encountered almost exclusively through the nostalgia of families and parish halls. But the relationship of Millennials[30] to the suburbs is complicated. According to the Pew Research Center, young people are more likely to be urbanites than older people:

> Urban populations skew much younger than those of other types of communities. One-third of urban residents are between 18 and 29 years of age, compared with two in 10 or fewer in each of the other types of communities. More than four in 10 large city residents are "Generation Y" (ages 18–34) [also known as "Millennials"], which is significantly higher than the proportion of young adults living in other types of communities.[31]

While this kind of data supports the perception that Millennials are a hypermobile generation with strong urban preferences, other data complicates this image. A Wells Fargo[32] marketing report from April 2015 details the living preferences of Millennials with great precision, arguing that they are moving less and less, and still prefer the suburbs to urban living. The persistence of the "urban-loving Millennial" image might be due in some part to Millennials themselves, who retain a kind of ambivalence toward the suburbs. *The New York Times* article "Creating Hipsturbia" provides an illuminating look into the trend of urbanizing suburban spaces.[33] Even when they stay in or move to the suburbs, Williams writes, Millennials are urbanizing them, bringing yoga studios, farm-to-table restaurants and boutiques usually found in urban spaces to suburban ones. This helps "to ward off the nagging sense that a move to the suburbs is tantamount to becoming like one's parents."

What I think Cohen's narrative provides us in this context is a way of thinking about the spatial and economic realities of American Catholics as important aspects in the experience of young people grappling with the church. One must consider the obstacles to the communal ideal inherent to suburban American Catholicism. Furthermore, the technologies that dominate the lives of many young Americans (even across racial and class differences) are not only causes or effects of the decline in social capital detailed by Putnam. They are also symptomatic of the spatial reconfigurations that prize decentralization. We should not be surprised, therefore, that young people understand the ways in which internet and digital technologies overcome great distances as not only good and useful but as almost entirely unproblematic. This is the ethos of suburban America, the great inheritance of Cohen's Consumer's Republic. This is also the experience of many American Catholics, whose church communities are held together not by neighborhood, nationality of origin, or social activities outside of Mass but by any number of diffuse and maybe even unrelated reasons: love for pastor; proximity to favorite brunch place; the choices of the music director; or convenient Mass times.

THE CHURCH, PRESENTLY

I first want to explain the relationship between technology and the American church more explicitly. This is the sociological reality of the modern church that makes media studies essential for the church's vitality. Secondly, I want to introduce the somewhat startling notion that our current technological situation can actually help illumine some of the tradition's most basic truths, namely the mediating presence of the church and its Eucharistic center. This is the focus of the next chapter, but it requires an introduction here in order to demonstrate its relationship to the scholarship reviewed in this chapter and the sociological situation of the American church in particular.

The review of Putnam and Cohen above gestured at the relationship between technology, economics, and space. In particular, Cohen's narrative shows us the suburbanization of American life, a spatial reconfiguration that both resulted from and perpetuated the consumerist ethos of the postwar era. What is particularly helpful about this narrative from a Catholic perspective is that it disrupts the Catholic version of the "pastoralist ideal": the Catholic neighborhood.[34]

The assimilated Catholic experience of many white American Catholics today sits uncomfortably in the identity politics of the twenty-first century. In response, some Catholic theologians have been attracted to (mostly Protestant) theologies and ecclesiologies[35] that argue for an intense focus on the local community, and this sometimes turns into a nostalgia for the thick communal ties of the ethnic Catholic neighborhood.[36] This nostalgia is easy to understand, given the experience of American Catholics today. Catholicism is no longer the glue that holds one's social life together as it would have been for Catholics in the 1930s, for example. This social "glue" had many instantiations, including lay sodalities, baseball leagues, church basement bars, and bowling teams. In fact, so much of what Putnam discusses in *Bowling Alone* can be mapped onto the Catholic neighborhood. One's daily activities were related to the parish that it functioned as a social center for the neighborhood, binding the spatial reality of one's living space to the communal reality of one's social activities to the theological reality of one's worship. All of this can appear to younger,[37] suburbanized Catholics as a kind of gold age of

American Catholicism, where a seamless integration of one's social and religious life that built and sustained an unassailable identity.

Just as the "local turn" demonstrates our desire for local community in the face of our globalized reality, this coincidental "local turn" in theology shows us what we want and expect from the community of the church. What I hope to have demonstrated here is that sustained reflection on our technological lives should not simply dismiss the global nature of online communication as necessarily inferior to the local community we find in our churches. To do so is to miss the fact that (1) online communication often complements offline communication; (2) online communication can sustain real relationships, even in and perhaps because of their of transcendence local communities; and (3) our preference for offline communication over online communication often relies on a pastoralist ideal that has probably never been realized and certainly is not the case in most places in the twenty-first century. For Catholics, asking questions about online communities does not simply reify parish communities; it can bring to light all of the ways in which we actually fail to live up to the ideals we have in mind for Christ's church.

To use a more general example of the relationship between our expectations for community and their effect on our evaluation of virtual space, let us briefly return to Van Alstyne and Brynjolfsson. Within their compelling mathematical analysis of online communities, they include an irksome sentence that betrays the assumption of so much work done on online communication: "Because time is limited, spending more time interacting with online communities necessarily means spending less time interacting with geographic communities or even family members."[38] This statement seems rational enough: time *is* limited, after all. Time is like a pie chart, with pieces being occupied by one thing or the other. One cannot simply create more time. Therefore, whatever time a person spends communicating online necessarily cuts into the other pieces of the pie, including the piece representing communicating offline. What this line of thinking fails to account for, however, is the degree to which it relies on the "pastoralist ideal."

When we go to critique online communities, we often cannot help but conjure the best possible image of our offline communities. Van Alstyne and Brynjolfsson, therefore, are analyzing online communities against the best possible version of offline communities they can imagine. But part of the prevailing discourse about the internet—one that is present even in Van Alstyne and Brynjolfsson's same article—is that the internet provides greater access to and for a greater number of people than earlier means of communication. This means that there is not a one-for-one relationship between interlocutors in different media. From a Catholic perspective, this tendency must make us aware of the ways in which we may be misrepresenting (or misremembering, from a historical perspective) our faith communities. In fact, what may be interesting to theologians and ministers about internet technology may be the very question of community, and how the questions we ask about online communities actually press us into hard questions about our faith communities.

Drawing from the work of researchers like Wellman and Gulia, Catholics can analyze contemporary parishes and dioceses with the categories of "weak" and "strong" social ties. My contention is that we imagine religious communities to be held together by "strong" social ties, which is not only socially untenable but also wildly untrue. We have to come to terms with the fact that communities of all kinds are a mix of weak and strong social ties, and that dismissing online communities as "weak" does not necessarily mean that our offline worshipping communities are "strong."

Subjecting our faith communities to Wellman and Gulia's categories can account for some of its sociological facets, but it cannot fully account for these communities theologically. I believe sociological analyses remain valuable for locating the church in its cultural and historical context. The distinction between weak ties and strong ties, however, does not do enough to explain the complexity of relationships within religious communities generally and the Catholic Church particularly. There exists a burgeoning conversation around the idea of "presence" that moves beyond the idea of weak and strong ties, and opens new opportunities for theology to engage with multiple disciplines in a common quest for seeking the truth about human community.

Researchers of online social behavior have been developing a subfield dedicated to the concept of "presence," a category that is broad enough to capture the complexity of online experience and with enough philosophical implication to reach beyond sociological categories. The idea of "presence" appeals to a variety of disciplines, including psychology, philosophy, and the arts. There is an incredible opportunity here for theology to join the conversation about "presence," especially given the tradition of mediation described in the preceding chapter.

So what exactly do these scholars mean by "presence"? Most of them use "social presence" and "presence" interchangeably, demonstrating that they are almost exclusively concerned with the degree to which users *feel* present to or with *other users*. Early research in presence studies relied on media richness theory, the notion that social presence is determined by the relationship between the medium itself and its ability to execute the task at hand (e.g., communication). According to media richness theory, social presence is defined as "the extent to which a medium is perceived as warm, sociable, personal, or intimate when used to communicate with someone else."[39] The distinguishing feature of media richness theory is that researchers and analysts pay close attention to the medium itself. Other scholars, particularly Biocca et al., rely on a more complex theory of social presence, which they argue is composed of three dimensions: (1) copresence (mutual awareness);

(2) psychological factors (like empathy); and (3) behavioral interaction, such as mutual assistance.[40] The research undertaken within this theoretical framework tends to require more attention toward individual users, making the research more labor intensive and logistically complicated.[41]

One of the foundational texts for presence studies is from Lombard and Ditton, who provide a helpful overview of the emerging definitions of "presence" in studies of mediation. What these many definitions share, they argue, is the simple idea that presence is "the perceptual illusion of nonmediation."[42] The emergence of this subfield has added more psychological and conceptual perspectives to the studies of online social behavior. It also invites—by virtue of its interest in more abstract concepts like "perception," "illusion," and "nonmediation"—the interest of scholars of fields like philosophy, religious studies, and theology. The very category of "presence" is a provocative invitation into the conversation on mediation, as the metaphysical connotations and implications of such an idea is simply too tempting to ignore.

From a Catholic theological perspective, the idea of "presence" is especially suggestive, given the role of "presence" in the sacramental life of the church. Chapter 3 has already argued for a hermeneutic of virtuality for interpreting the broader sacramental imagination of the church. The field of media studies allows us to understand both the historical and eternal realities of the church in new and theologically rich ways. For now, suffice it to say that the questions of online communities and Christian communities seem to have the same concern at their center: to what extent are individuals truly present to one another in meaningful and socially productive ways? For the Catholic Church, this presence is always understood in the theological matrix of the church and its sacraments.

NOTES

1. Robert Putnam, *Bowling Alone* (New York: Simon and Schuster, 2000), 19.
2. Putnam, *Bowling Alone*.
3. Quoted in Ibid., 19.
4. Ibid., 27. I like to think of these as the referents of what one commonly finds at thrift stores: old bowling league shirts with names like "Jim" on the patch, T-shirts from picnics and family reunions, glassware that reads things like "Sons of Herman—Akron, Ohio."
5. Ibid., 22.
6. Ibid.
7. Ibid., 220.
8. Ibid., 223.
9. Ibid., 228.
10. Ibid., 235

11. Ibid.
12. Ibid., 166.
13. Ibid., 180.
14. Ibid., 166.
15. Ibid., 168.
16. Ibid., 180.
17. Lizabeth Cohen, *A Consumer's Republic: The Politics of Mass Consumption in Postwar America* (New York: Vintage Books, 2003), 6.
18. Cohen, *A Consumer's Republic*, 195.
19. Ibid.
20. Ibid., 196.
21. Ibid.
22. Ibid., 197.
23. Cohen notes that during the building of the "landscape of mass consumption," marketing becomes intertwined with social science and psychology, resulting in targeted advertising campaigns that no long imagines mass markets but highly segmented groups of people or even specific individuals (chapter 7).
24. Wendell Smith proposes "an alternative to mass marketing that made his article in the *Journal of Marketing* a landmark: market segmentation." Smith proposed market segmentation in 1956, and by 1970, it "had become the indisputable rule." See Cohen, *A Consumer's Republic*, 295–296.
25. Carolyn Miller et al., "How People Get Local News and Information in Different Communities," Pew Research Center, Pew Internet and American Life Project, Project for Excellence in Journalism, Knight Foundation (September 26, 2012), 6.
26. See Philip Gleason, *Keeping the Faith: American Catholicism Past and Present* (South Bend: University of Notre Dame Press, 1987), 29.
27. Patricia Wittberg, "A Lost Generation?" *America*, February 20, 2012. See also Wittberg, *Building Strong Church Communities: A Sociological Overview* (New York: Paulist Press, 2013).
28. For an overview of the many theories for these trends among Catholics, see Robert Booth Fowler, "The Roman Catholic Church in 'Protestant' America Today," *The Forum* 11, no. 4 (2014): 721–742.
29. One is inundated with articles, op-eds, and blog posts about the technology-obsessed Millennials and their political and religious apathy, entitlement, and self-absorption, although this narrative is beginning to change. Even where it is complicated, however, the narrative for Millennials often includes statements like the following: "For a generation digitally wired from childhood, and reared on apocalyptic videos and computer-generated movie epics, not to mention the exploits of hackers, these events showed the real world to be as tightly networked, and for that reason as easily disrupted as the virtual one, even as the grown-ups in charge, the guardians of order, seemed overwhelmed and overmatched, always a step behind. It is no surprise, as Pew reported, that the millennial generation is skeptical of institutions—political and religious—and prefers to improvise solutions to the challenges of the moment. It is one thing to own a smartphone, as so many of us do. It is quite another to have mastered its uses at age 10." Sam Tanenhaus, "Generation Nice," *New York Times*, August 15, 2014.

30. Born between 1985 and 1995, although some will put the generation as early as 1977.

31. Miller et al., "How People Get Local News and Information in Different Communities," 7.

32. Because they are now the largest generation of Americans, all kinds of companies are paying attention to the preferences of Millennials.

33. Alex Williams, "Creating Hipsturbia," *The New York Times*, February 15, 2013.

34. It may be more helpful to use the word "ghetto" here to describe the neighborhood I have in mind. I am attempting to be sensitive to all of the racial and economic connotations of this word, by using the word "neighborhood." While "ghetto" is a better descriptor for the isolated nature of these neighborhoods, as well as their relationship to the rest of American culture, I think that "neighborhood" remains an appropriate word, given the historical and sociological argument I am advancing here. It's quite obvious that the Catholic ghetto no longer exists, but neither does the Catholic neighborhood, even in a less isolated and segregated way.

35. I have in mind here theological trends that would best be called "post-liberal." However, one can see this nostalgia quite clearly in the work of a scholar like Jay Dolan, whose *American Catholic Experience* points to these neighborhoods as bastions of lay agency. Theologians of different ages and ideological temperaments, therefore, have found the neighborhood of the prewar era to be an interesting site for reflection on their own hopes and desires for Catholic communities.

36. This has also dovetailed nicely with the "local turn" mentioned above.

37. Really, "younger" here means any Catholics who grew up after the dissolution of the Catholic neighborhood of the prewar era, and not just "Millennials."

38. Van Alstyne and Brynjolfsson, "Electronic Communities," 5.

39. Anne Sivunen and Emma Nordback, "Social Presence as a Multi-Dimensional Group Construct in 3D Virtual Environments," *Journal of Computer-Mediated Communication* 20 (2015): 20.

40. F. Biocca, C. Harms, and J. K. Burgoon, "Toward a More Robust Theory and Measure of Social Presence: Review and Suggested Criteria," *Presence: Teleoperators & Virutal Environments* 12, no. 5 (2003): 456–480.

41. See Sivunen and Nordback, "Social Presence as a Multi-Dimensional Group Construct in 3D Virtual Environments," 19–36.

42. Matthew Lombard and Theresa Ditton, "At the Heart of It All: The Concept of Presence," *Journal of Computer-Mediated Communication* 3, no. 7 (September 1997).

Chapter 7

The Standards of Communion

This chapter focuses on the second doctrinal locus often employed in theological accounts of technology: the church. I have attempted to demonstrate that the sacramental imagination of the Catholic Church reflects a virtual logic. This chapter draws together both the sacramental and social dimensions of the church by means of the Eucharistic assembly. It focuses the argument of the virtual logic found in the sacramentality of the church on the very particular sacramental practice of the Eucharist. Discussion of the Eucharist demands a discussion of the church's self-understanding, especially in light of the centrality of communion ecclesiology following the Second Vatican Council.

The first section focuses on the work of Henri de Lubac. In de Lubac, we find great optimism for the social aspect of the church. His ecclesial optimism comes to the fore especially in his discussion of his view of history and his view of the sacraments. I will discuss the role of history and the sacraments in de Lubac's work in order to demonstrate his optimism. Because of this optimism, de Lubac's system is susceptible to readings that reify the local community. De Lubac's argument about the social nature of the church and its sacraments reflects an implied confidence in ancillary social spaces that are eroding or altogether absent from the American church at present.

The second section focuses on the work of sacramental theologian Louis-Marie Chauvet. In Chauvet, we find a theological account of mediation that is the foundation for the sacramental life of the church. Given this account of mediation, Chauvet's theological system provides a framework for understanding the internet. It focuses on the productive dynamic between presence and absence, a dynamic I argue is the defining feature of the "virtual." Furthermore, Chauvet's discussion of symbolic exchange provides a set of theological criteria by which we can evaluate the possibilities for communion, both within the church and extra-ecclesial social spaces such as the internet.

Understood in the context of its capacity to transform what it means to be social, the internet represents a cultural phenomenon greatly in need of theological critique. Using the two theological frameworks of Henri de Lubac and Louis-Marie Chauvet, this chapter argues that the internet is related analogically to the virtual logic of the church's mediating apparatuses, especially the Eucharist and the sacramental system of which it is the center. This sharing in virtual logic has important sociological and theological implications for the church. Theologies of the internet can provide means by which to critique the challenges facing the church, such as suburbanization of the American church described above. In de Lubac and Chauvet, we can determine the importance of ancillary spaces for symbolic exchange crucial to the social life of the church.

THE ECCLESIAL OPTIMISM OF HENRI DE LUBAC

Henri de Lubac spent much of his theological career on the question of the natural/supernatural distinction in the Scholastic tradition. He critiqued the notion of "pure nature," which he understood to assume a dualistic understanding of the cosmos. This dualism was unacceptable for de Lubac, who "saw it as downgrading the faith and as contributing to the secularism of the day."[1] In 1946, he published *Surnaturel*, his treatise against the idea of "pure nature."

De Lubac came to the discussion of the natural/supernatural, however, only after he had written about the church and its sacramental life. These earlier writings were motivated by de Lubac's concern about the effects of modern individualism on the church, a corrosive trend that he saw as symptomatic of and exacerbated by the idea of "pure nature." This argument was at odds with those in de Lubac's time who attempted to blame the church for being an obstacle to the secular social unity they sought. According to Raymond Moloney, SJ, "What particularly galled [de Lubac] was that this individualism was sometimes laid at the door of Christianity by those who were anxious to promote a greater social awareness in contemporary society."[2] In response, de Lubac argued for the essentially social nature of the church.

De Lubac's thesis that the church has an "eminently social character" has implications for the church's self-understanding (ecclesiology) as well as its worship and ritual (sacramental theology).[3] By using the adverb "eminently" (and elsewhere "essentially"), de Lubac means to present the church not just as a good or strong form of sociality but as the *truest* form of sociality. The church is thus connected to other social realities insofar as those realities reflect the social longings of the human person that only the church can satisfy. He describes secular efforts for unity as "the subject of some of the deepest yearnings of our age."[4] De Lubac was here responding to the apparent unity wrought by the early days of nationalism, what he terms the "age of Europe's expansion"[5] and what Charles Taylor calls "the age of mobilization."[6] The church "lays no claim to cultural imperialism" and other forms of violence that have characterized economic and political expansion. The church's mission, however, is "to purify and give fresh life to each of the [varieties of spiritual experience]."[7]

In his discussion about the age of mobilization, we see in de Lubac a great optimism about both the efforts for unity outside of the church and the church's ability to subsume these forms of unity into the true unity of the church. "Nothing authentically human, whatever its origin," writes de Lubac, "can be alien to [the church]."[8] Furthermore, it is in the church that humanity finds not only its true unity but its true self: "Catholicism is religion itself. It is the form that humanity must put on in order to finally be itself."[9] De Lubac's response to the secular effort toward the unity of the human race, therefore, is to see in it the longing for social unity that only the church can truly and fully deliver.

While a Catholic cannot just baptize these efforts and accept them as they are, s/he can use them to "lead men of good will to the threshold of Catholicism, which *alone can effect this unity in its highest sense.*"[10] This is an incredibly optimistic view of the church that relies upon very particular assumptions about history and the sacraments, specifically the Eucharist. In both cases, we will see how de Lubac's work can serve as a guide for engaging questions of culture, including the issue of the internet.

De Lubac's view of history pervades his work. He draws on sources from many different centuries, mining the tradition for its timeless richness without reifying any particular epoch of the church. This is an important distinction between de Lubac and his Scholastic interlocutors, whom he critiqued for proposing views of nature and grace that were uninterested in the historical particularities of the church in time: "For him the issue is not about what our destiny has to be in virtue of our finite nature as such, or what it might be in another world order, but about what is actually is in the only world order known to us, which is also the one revealed to us in the sources of the faith."[11] De Lubac refuses to forgo sources from the past while simultaneously refusing to cast them as belonging to a more privileged age than ours.[12]

More than his commitment to *ressourcement*, however, de Lubac's view of history is theological and eschatological. This is particularly evident in his reflections on the social nature of the church found in *Catholicism* from 1938. History is theological because "God acts in history and reveals himself through history. Or rather, God inserts himself in history and so bestows on it a 'religious consecration' which compels us to treat it with due respect."[13] The eschatological framework of *Catholicism* is evidenced by its subtitle: *Christ and the Common Destiny of Man*. De Lubac understands history within this framework, writing that all of history is a "preparation for this destiny," meaning the coming of God into the world through Christ.[14] "The world," he writes, "has a purpose and consequently a meaning, that is to say, both direction and significance."[15] Following the fathers, de Lubac describes the Bible as a history of the world, revealing that direction and significance, namely the collective salvation of humankind.

De Lubac's view of history is helpful for a theology of the internet insofar as it reminds us that it is only in history that salvation is found. The timeless truths of the traditions, therefore, are subject to the inflections and interpretations of the age in which they find their concrete expression. If we assume with de Lubac that the Catholic and the salvation we find in her is essentially social, we are bound to pursue the truths of what it means to be "social" in our particular time and culture.[16] As the world opened for de Lubac within the conflicts and progress of the twentieth century, his theology bears the accent of his milieu. Or, as de Lubac would put it,

> [A]lthough the church rests on eternal foundations, it is in a continual state of rebuilding, and since the Fathers' time it has undergone many changes in style; and without in any way considering ourselves better than our Fathers, what we in turn have to build for our own use must be built in our own style, that is, one that is adapted to our own needs and problems.[17]

The transformation of social life we now witness in the church in the United States because of the internet represents both a need and a problem for theology. Our theological "style" regarding the eternal foundations of the church must reflect our media ecology, which shapes so much of our society. As I argued in chapter 3, this means understanding the sacramental life of the church as virtual. Here, I argue that we can understand the ecclesiology of the church as virtual as well, given the relationship between the sacraments and the church proposed by de Lubac.[18]

To say that the church is social is not a matter of mere sociology for de Lubac but it is a matter of salvation.[19] The church represents the fact that "God did not desire to save mankind as a wreck is salvaged," but instead ordained human participation as a requisite aspect of the sacramental economy.[20] He continues, "The law of redemption is here a reproduction of the law of creation: man's cooperation was always necessary if his exalted destiny was to be reached, and his cooperation is necessary now for his redemption."[21] This cooperation includes human activity broadly, but finds its highest purpose in the sacramental life of the church.

The sacraments join us not only to Christ but also to each other. De Lubac writes that the sacraments "make real" the union with Christ and with the community. But the latter is not necessarily inferior to the former: "It is through union with the community that the Christian is united to Christ."[22] As David Grummett explains, "There is, de Lubac repeatedly insists, no private Christianity."[23] De Lubac explains the social nature of baptism and reconciliation before turning to the *sacramentum sacramentorum*, the Eucharist. The Eucharist establishes "real unity," in the words of John Damascene. In fact, says de Lubac, thinkers in the Middle Ages all agreed that "the result of the sacrament is unity."[24] De Lubac notes that the sense of this true unity, effected by the Eucharist, was forgotten in the Middle Ages, "like the slow atrophy of an unused sense."[25] This slow atrophy would be the subject of *Corpus Mysticum*, de Lubac's developed historical treatment of the Eucharist.

Following the controversy over the Eucharist of which Berengar of Tours was the central figure, there was untethering of the church from the Eucharist that persisted in de Lubac's time (and ours). The effect of this untethering which is an over-emphasis on the Body of Christ on the altar and an obfuscation of the reality of Body of Christ in the assembly. The sacramental Body and Body "born of Mary" are deemed *real* and *proper* while the communal Body of Christ is *mystical*.[26] "From the moment when it became the *mystical body*," writes de Lubac, "the ecclesial body was already detaching itself from the Eucharist."[27]

In *Catholicism*, de Lubac reminds us that before the twelfth century, theologians and others did not make this distinction between the sacramental/real and the communal/mystical: "They unhesitatingly understood that by their reception of the Eucharist they would be incorporated the more into the church. They could see a profound identity between the mysteries of the 'real presence' and of the 'mystical body.'"[28] The consequence of recovering this "profound identity," whether or not de Lubac could anticipate it or not, was a renewed interest in the site of encounter with the Eucharistic assembly, the local church community. It is precisely on the notion of the "assembly once constituted" that de Lubac's work can speak to the idea of the social. De Lubac insists that the church is "the sacrament of Christ, as Christ himself, in his humanity, is for us the sacrament of God."[29] The church is the "tabernacle of his presence," the keeper of the light without which we remain in the darkness.[30] As the mediation of Christ, it is only in the church that we find complete unity, though we attempt it elsewhere.[31] The mission of the church is to present Christ to the world, and it is in this making-present that the church is the sacrament of Christ.

The place of materiality in the sacramental economy imbues all materiality with a potentially sacramental character. Analogously, if the church, essentially social, is the sacrament of Christ, this imbues the rest of social life with a potentially sacramental character. De Lubac is fond of the image of "living stones" for the church, which allows him to emphasize the social character of the church without neglecting individual spirituality. These living stones are fully alive on earth when gathered as the Eucharistic assembly. But what of these stones when they are not? By saying that the church and its sacraments are essentially social, de Lubac wants to critique purely sociological accounts of the church.[32] In so doing, however, he manages to direct us back toward sociological questions by giving us the Eucharistic standard by which to judge social life. That Eucharistic standard consists, for de Lubac, in what Moloney calls "spiritual interdependence."[33] De Lubac provides a notion of the church as a "level of spiritual belonging and mutual responsibility," "the level on which we are all members of one another and mediators to one another of the life of God shared with us."[34]

It should come as no surprise that the Eucharistic assembly in its local form has become the benchmark by which Catholic theologians evaluate social realities.[35] The optimism of the Second Vatican Council ecclesiology, drawing heavily on de Lubac's work, has resulted in a hope about the Eucharistic assembly with regard to the social lives of its members. Given the theology of the Eucharist within the church, this seems right and true. Gathered around the table to consume the Body of Christ, we become, through grace, consumed by the Eucharist and transformed into the Body of Christ in the world.[36] To the extent that the church has adopted de Lubac's work on the Body of Christ, there has been a retrieval of the relationship between the Eucharistic table and the Eucharistic assembly. This seems clear from the work of the council, especially in *Lumen Gentium* and the communion ecclesiology that has emerged from it. It has meant a renewed emphasis on the Body of Christ in the church.

De Lubac is sensitive to the dynamic between the local and universal church, but the emphasis on determining a stronger relationship between the sacramental Body and the ecclesial Body has resulted in an over-emphasis on the local community. The editors of the English translation of *Corpus Mysticum*, Laurence Paul Hemming and Susan Frank Parsons, state this new problem well in their preface. There has been, following de Lubac's work, "a correctional shift away from the appearance of the 'objectified' host to a concentration on the worshipping community."[37] Hemming and Parsons go on to say that the effect of this correctional shift "has been the fetishisation, not of the Sacred Species, the host, but of the community itself, the one that has assembled for the Eucharist."[38] Somewhat tragically, then, the individualistic piety surrounding the sacramental Body that provided, in at least some degree, the impetus for de Lubac's return to the sources has resulted in a different form of individualism, "a turning-in on our selves," making the assembly the subject and the Eucharist merely the object.[39]

This, of course, runs counter to de Lubac's entire project in *Corpus Mysticum*, as well as the sacramental theology he puts forth elsewhere. In *The Splendor of the church,* he draws on Yves Congar to address this issue. Some in the church, "'anxious to turn to full account' her 'visible organism' and 'whatever in her is an institution or means of grace', end up (for example) by making the sacramental cultus 'a sort of end in itself.'"[40] This cannot be so for de Lubac, given that the present sacramental economy is a matter of the temporal order, not the eternal.[41]

Again, Hemming brings de Lubac into the modern ecclesial context with his commentary on *Corpus Mysticum*. He helpfully places de Lubac's work on the sacraments in the context of pluralism:

> The difficulty is that the community that has assembled (as we now understand it, especially in an age when to be regularly at Mass is to make a choice for something and often against what everyone else is doing on a Sunday morning) is a community that often understand itself to have chosen to be there, not the community—the body proper—that we must assume has been chosen and assembled by God.[42]

While Hemming is right to characterize the contemporary ecclesial moment in this way, de Lubac himself nuances the assembly a bit more in *The Splendor of the church*. He says that the church is indeed "the divine calling-together," giving God the subjectivity in the way that Hemming wants to emphasize. However, de Lubac writes that the church is also the "community of the called-together." He goes on to say that "the active sense is primary, but the passive is no less necessary and no less important."[43] De Lubac makes this distinction clearer, saying that the Greek εκκλησια has a dual Latin translation of *convocatio* and *congregatio*. The duality that de Lubac means to press upon here is that when we consider the assembly of the church, we must consider both the assembly called together and the "assembly once constituted."[44] To minimize or exclude either aspect would be to succumb to an ecclesial Monophysitism, as we noted earlier.

Hemming's focus on voluntaristic religious affiliation is well founded, but it is only part of the cultural story. De Lubac's insistence on the church as social highlights issues beyond the problem of voluntarism, challenging us to discern the degree to which the church functions, in its cultural and historical particularity, as the Body of "spiritual belonging and mutual responsibility." De Lubac's vision of the relationship between the sacraments and the church, and their eminently social nature, reflects an incarnational ecclesiology that holds the eternal and temporal in creative tension. In so doing, however, it compels the church into the messiness of the cultures in which it finds itself, unable to untether its universal truths from its particular mediations, just as

"Christ existing before all things cannot be separated from Christ born of the woman, who died and rose again."[45]

Hemming represents one possible trajectory of the optimism in de Lubac's work. In his insistence that the church is the form of sociality which no other human enterprise can deliver, de Lubac lays a foundation for an ecclesial triumphalism that actually runs counter to his own sensitivities to the historical particularity of the church. What becomes evident in this trajectory is the degree to which de Lubac assumed dense social structures within which the church presents itself as the social form par excellence. In his discussion of the church's relationship to temporal "societies" of which the members are a part, de Lubac grants that such societies have autonomy insofar as it is not the mission of the church to "take the place of statesmen and formulate 'programs.'"[46] It is also not the case that members of the Body will be authorities on or reformers of social matters. On this point, however, de Lubac shows the very implication about the church's relationship to social life that I have been attempting to demonstrate here. He writes, "But even on the plane of earthly societies the church contributes, in fact, much more than a program, and her authentic children contribute to the best of programs much more than an outward agreement or a mere technical competency."[47] De Lubac envisions that the church—specifically in its Eucharistic practice—animates the lives of its members in such a way so as to provide a "preparation for social tasks."[48] De Lubac thus proposes a theological relationship between the church and the social spaces of its members that betrays a particular vision of social life in which individuals assume a connection between their social and ecclesial lives.

Even in his own fractured context, de Lubac could present his optimistic ecclesial vision precisely because of the social structures that are inferior to the "eminently social" church. As de Lubac observes the social spaces surrounding the church—especially those evolving as a result of the age of mobilization—he is filled with great optimism in the church's ability to relate to these spaces in positive ways. As peoples and traditions increasingly come into contact with one another, there remains a temptation within the church to simply reject "false religions" and to "change and refashion everything, put everything down and build afresh."[49] De Lubac rejects this position because he understands the church's mission as transformative, not destructive in its relationship to forms of social life that appear antithetical to the church. De Lubac's understanding of the mission of the church allows him to see these movements toward secular unity with great optimism: "How marvelous it is to see the 'elements of the world' slowly forming, growing to maturity, evolving—no man knowing—to provide a body for the Christianity of the future!"[50] For de Lubac, although secular forms of sociality are always inferior to the sociality of the church, they are thus not competitive with but contributive to eschatological communion. He is confident that the church exists in a complex network of human sociality whereby the church provides the highest version of that sociality. In terms of ancillary spaces, he assumes a connection between the ordinary social spaces inhabited by the members of the Body and the visible structures of the church, including the liturgy. In fact de Lubac is so sure of this connection that he understands it eschatologically: all of the social spaces surrounding and supporting the social life of the church are contributing to "the Christianity of the future."

As infectious as de Lubac's optimism can be on this point, he gives little indication of the precise means by which the church effects social unity in the here and now. He is, of course, very clear that the Eucharist makes the church and is therefore the center of the social unity of the church. One wonders, however, about the content and practice of this unity outside of the Eucharistic assembly. This is essentially the question of how the Body of Christ in the assembly relates to the Body of Christ on the altar. De Lubac devotes *Corpus Mysticum* to precisely this question, and yet the mechanics of the relationship remain rather obscure. This is particularly evident when one considers forms of being social outside of the Eucharistic assembly. More to the point, it is unclear how de Lubac's confidence in Eucharistic unity can account for the fractured relationship between the majority of one's social life and the sacramental life of the church in the suburbanized experience of contemporary American Catholicism.

We can continue to say with de Lubac that the church and sacraments are social, but the ramifications of this in the larger sense of what it means to be social here and now remain to be seen. As much as de Lubac fights against a purely sociological understanding of the church, his work is confronted by sociological realities that put new pressures on the social dimensions of the church. When the church is gathered around the Eucharistic table, the assembly is surely the sign (sacrament) of the Body of Christ. But what of the Body, made of "living stones," outside of this liturgical moment? For the American Catholic Church, these "living stones" exist within the age of suburbanization discussed in chapter 4. In de Lubac, there is an implied confidence in social spaces that are ancillary but related to the Eucharistic assembly. These ancillary spaces stretch out from the church in concentric circles, made of the same "living stones," which are, again, most fully alive at the Eucharistic table. These ancillary spaces constitute the broader social nature of the church without being the cause of it. It is difficult to imagine what the church can be without social spaces that allow for the practice and cultivation of that which is learned in the liturgy. Thus while the Eucharist will always be the climax of the church's encounter with grace, this grace flows from this center into secondary, supportive, non-liturgical spaces to vivify the social reality that we call the church.

These spaces, however, are more than *supportive* of the Eucharistic assembly. They also often function as liminal spaces that, as per the Latin root *limen*, function as thresholds or doorways. These spaces are liminal insofar as they facilitate and encourage movement of individual Catholics: individuals have spaces that are Eucharistically referential in which to enact ecclesial unity, and these spaces create a dense, extra-ecclesial social context for liturgical participation. Therefore, these spaces can be conduits for the church's engagement with the world, as well as conduits for the community's engagements with the liturgical life of the church.

De Lubac is not detailed on the content of these spaces but he nonetheless expresses great confidence in the church's ability to transform the social lives of the members of the Body of Christ, social enterprises that he understands eschatologically, as we saw above. Redemption, says de Lubac, restores not only the unity between humanity and God "but equally of the unity of men among themselves."[51] He goes on to quote St. Maximus, who uses the image of "friendship" to describe the relationship between the members of the Body. Maximus says that in the church "no one is in the slightest degree separated from the community, all are fused together, so to speak, one in another, by the mere and undivided strength of faith."[52] De Lubac recapitulates Maximus' vision by saying that the "mystic reality" of the church has a "visible result of fraternal charity, a radiant novelty in the midst of a world grown old in its divisions."[53]

For de Lubac (and his sources) there is great confidence in the close relationship between the unity of the church and the social lives of its members. It is unclear that this closeness can be assumed in the age of suburbanized Catholicism. Be it aspirational or nostalgic, de Lubac's optimism for the unifying effects of the Eucharist outside the assembly itself makes his work somewhat foreign to the modern American reader. Given the age of fracture in which many American Catholics understand their social identity vis-à-vis the church, de Lubac's work cannot speak fully to a reality wherein what they do on Sunday morning has little relationship to the rest of their social lives outside of individual morality and spirituality.

In chapter 6, the primary ancillary space at issue was the parish neighborhood. There are many more of these spaces, however, and they change with place and time. In addition to the formal spaces of the church such as schools and hospitals, there are other spaces that enjoy (or have enjoyed) an informal yet referential relationship to the church's liturgical life. Such spaces may be formal in their own right, such as labor unions full of Catholic members who interpret their place in terms of the church's social teaching. They can also be informal, loosely structured associations that foster social relationships that incarnate the unity effected by the Eucharist in the liturgy. These are not precisely apostolic structures but they are spaces in which members of the Body of Christ are apostolic.

The story of pluralism and its concomitant voluntarism, therefore, is incomplete without an accounting of the erosion or absence of ancillary social spaces that form a dense network in which members of the Body understand themselves and their faith. Moreover, even where these spaces still exist, they have lost their liminality: these spaces no longer function as thresholds by which individuals and communities find passage from the church to the world or from the world to the church. These spaces are not equivalent to the sacramental economy, but they are sacramental insofar as they facilitate the unity of the church in the world. They provide the "where" of the enactment of unity that is effected in the liturgical life of the church. This unity precedes the making-present of Christ in the world that de Lubac says is the "unique mission" of the church.[54]

Admitting the absence of spaces that are ancillary but related to the Eucharistic assembly, and the disappearance of their liminality, is a crucial step in reading the cultural moment in which the American church finds itself. Members of the Body live within a media ecology that is a cause of and response to shifts in social space. The internet continues to provide spaces for social life that no longer exist and in some cases, never existed. Internet culture highlights the absences in traditional spaces of social life such as religious communities. While these absences do not affect the doctrinal truth of the sacraments, they do bear strongly on the religious lives of the members of the Body and the degree to which they may understand the truly social nature of the church.

The internet does more than simply reflect the absence of traditional social spaces; it also provides contexts for new versions of them, sometimes good and sometimes bad in their novelty. The church needs ancillary social spaces for its flourishing. These are the spaces for "spiritual belonging and mutual responsibility." These are the spaces for a Christian life based on charity, a life marked by the sacraments insofar as it reflects what sacramental theologian Louis-Marie Chauvet calls "symbolic exchange."

PRESENCE AND ABSENCE IN THE EUCHARISTIC ASSEMBLY

Henri de Lubac's insistence on the sociality of the church is an optimistic ecclesial vision that assumes a theological reading of history and an ecclesiology centered on the unifying efficacy of the Eucharist. He argues that the logic of the church is at odds with the pervasive individualism he observed in the culture around him. Individualism continues to prove a cultural force that has real and damaging effects on the church. Bishops and theologians have attended to this concern, although many have enhanced the theological discussion of individualism by contextualizing it in consumer culture.[55] In the critique of consumerism, the liturgy provides a concrete moment wherein theologians can contrast the logic of the church with the logic of the market.[56] I will follow these scholars by delving deeper into the sacramental life of the church as a means by which to further explore its social nature. Although his work is predominantly about the assembly gathered for the Eucharist, de Lubac's view of the church carries an implicit confidence in what I term "ancillary social spaces" that do not affect sacramental efficacy but do impact the church in its broader social nature.

I want to press upon the relationship between the Eucharistic assembly and these ancillary social spaces. I assert with de Lubac that the church is essentially social, I understand this to extend beyond the confines of the liturgical assembly. Grummett notes that "De Lubac's ecclesiology is fundamentally motivated by his desire to make the Christian faith available in all its richness and power both within the church and beyond the visible boundaries of the church."[57] I would argue the same on this point, given de Lubac's optimism for the church as the truest form of human sociality. However, I submit that within de Lubac's ecclesial optimism there is a sociological assumption in extra-liturgical Catholic social spaces that existed in de Lubac's context that may not exist in ours. He assumes the presence of viable spaces for the instantiation of Catholic unity, the relative absence and erosion of which presents challenges unique to the twenty-first century American church.

De Lubac argued for the social nature of the church in a theological mode so as to subvert purely sociological descriptions of the church. But the church must always contend with the realities of the time and place in which it exists, a point with which de Lubac himself agrees: "My love is for the Holy City, not only as it is ideally, but also as it appears in history, and particularly as it appears to us at present."[58] In the spirit of de Lubac's work, I will demonstrate the *theological* relationship between the Eucharist and ancillary Catholic social spaces. I argue that these spaces support the liturgical life of the church insofar as they allow for the exercise and application of the sacramental logic of symbolic exchange performed in and learned through the Eucharist.

This section employs the work of sacramental theologian Louis-Marie Chauvet, a French thinker whose negotiations with postmodern and linguistic philosophy prove very helpful for understanding mediation in a theological mode. First, I will give a brief account of Chauvet's sacramental system, drawing primarily on the 1995 English translation of *Symbol and Sacrament*. I will focus on Chauvet's use of the category of *symbol* and its importance for the sacramental life of the church. Second, I will describe Chauvet's idea of "symbolic exchange" as the logic of the Eucharist. Third, I will argue that Chauvet understands symbolic exchange as the logic of the church beyond the Eucharistic assembly. This will provide the basis for the final section of this chapter, wherein I employ the idea of "symbolic exchange" to develop a standard for evaluating the viability of ancillary social spaces in the church.

Symbol and the Sacraments

As his title suggests, *symbol* is the central category of Chauvet's sacramental theology. He offers the sacraments as *symbols* as a corrective paradigm to the sacraments as *instruments*.[59] Chauvet provides a critique of the metaphysical system that is the foundation for the long tradition of sacramental instrumentalism, a tradition that has dominated because of Scholastic sacramental theology. Chauvet takes issue with a system for understanding the sacraments that Thomas Aquinas adopts from Augustine, namely that a sacrament is "the sign of a sacred thing."[60] In his attempt to explain how sacraments effect what they signify, Thomas says that they have "*the virtue of producing* [causative] *grace*."[61] Therefore, writes Chauvet, "The whole question is conceived according to the model of an '*instrument*,'" despite Thomas' attempt to escape efficient causality.[62]

Thomists will insist that this schema of instrumental causality is merely an analogy. To this Chauvet replies: "Even when purified by the reminder that it is only an analogy, these terms all serve to build up an ever-present *scheme* of representation that we call *technical* or *productionist*."[63] But Chauvet argues that Aquinas merely inherits this productionist mode of thinking about the relationship of subjects to God from Western metaphysics. He argues, quite boldly, "Western thought is unable to represent to itself the relations between subjects or of subjects with God in any way other than one according to a technical mode of cause and effect."[64] The problem with this representation is that it can obscure the graciousness and gratuitousness of grace.

On this point, commentator Glenn Ambrose clarifies, "The real problem for Chauvet lies in the metaphor of production that still overshadows his later understanding of grace."[65] The metaphor of production makes the sacraments susceptible to idolatry, not only of the sacrament itself but also of those who administer it.[66] Describing the stakes of this discussion, Ambrose explains Chauvet's ultimate purpose here: "The sacraments are understood to be instrumental means by which we conveniently come into God's favor and presence and not a possible site for a frequently disruptive encounter with God's presence and absence understood from the perspective of symbolic exchange."[67] Returning to the sacraments as symbol, therefore, can rescue the sacraments from the metaphor of production.

Although Aquinas is the real foil for Chauvet's sacramental theology in later chapters, Chauvet is, in effect and practice, taking on the philosophical tradition upon which most of (Western) Christian thought is based.[68] One of the major culprits in Chauvet's eyes is Plato. Chauvet uses Plato to

136   *Chapter 7*

demonstrate what he calls the "*metaphysical bent* of Western philosophy."[69] What Chauvet finds in Plato and in the philosophical tradition of which he is a primary benefactor is a fundamental aversion to impermanence: "*Any thought which would not come to rest in a final term*, a final significance, a recognizable and ultimate truth, such a thought, in [Plato's] eyes, is *unthinkable*."[70] It is incompleteness and interminability that are illogical for Plato and the Platonic tradition, and it is just these that Chauvet understands as the heart of the relationship between God and the human being. In a word, that relationship is *symbolic* for Chauvet.

Chauvet understands a symbol as the act of "making-present," which he assumes to be central to the human experience. If we focus only on the act of "making-present," however, we miss the fact that within the very act of making (or attempting to make) present is the acknowledgment of absence. Admittedly, underlying symbols of all kinds, including the symbols that make up virtual space, there is an impetus to deny absence and, indeed, embark upon the hubristic endeavor to overcome it altogether. At every turn, however, the symbolic will always bear witness to absence: "The symbol cannot carry out this task except in its role as witness to the founding faith of humanity: the law of distance, of lack, of otherness, of the 'vacant place' where the real belongs to an order different from the immediate data or the available value."[71] To assent to mediation is to relinquish control, "a true mourning for this desire to be all-powerful."[72] In short, to assent to mediation is to accept one's place as a creature and not creator.

At this point, Chauvet must discuss our most basic of symbolic systems: language. Here he engages German philosopher Martin Heidegger, who characterizes the dualistic influence of Western philosophy on our conception of language thusly: "It is no longer the very place where the world happens; it is the world's reflection. Or rather, the things of this world are now no more than the shadows cast by the 'ideal' realities represented by thought and objectified by language."[73] We tend to understand language as an instrument of the real, thereby standing as a perpetual reminder of our *distance* from the real. But for Chauvet, this misunderstands language because it gives the impression that "humans have language, instead of being originally possessed and constituted by it."[74] It gives the illusion that human beings can somehow be outside of language and "use" it. Rather, both Chauvet and Heidegger argue that we are always-already in a system of language by which our subjectivity is constituted. As Glenn Ambrose explains, "As a carrier of a world, language in its signifying dimension brings to our attention a world outside our skin. . . . Language is a body in which subjects produce and receive themselves."[75]

The consequences of the perception of language with which Chauvet takes issue are far-reaching. To understand language as the thing that stands in our way of the real is to come to resent and to suspect language. What's more, "we discern a further suspicion of the very *corporality* and *historicity* of humankind: such is the unconscious paradigm that seems to control the metaphysical way of thinking."[76] Chauvet is after a "positive evaluation" of language and the body, an evaluation he deems "impossible" under these philosophical conditions.

Chauvet argues that *symbol* provides a way out of the "resentment of the necessity of a mediation" produced by Platonic dualism.[77] This resentment—a catch-all for the inheritance of Western metaphysics—will always stand in the way of a sacramental theology other than instrumental causality. One cannot resent mediation if one is to understand the sacramental economy entrusted to the church for the salvation of the world. Chauvet makes this point clear in the smaller edition of his sacramental theology: "In order to accede to the faith, the two disciples of Emmaus have had to overturn their own Jewish convictions and accept something monstrous for any good Jew, a Messiah who would have to go through death. You too must convert your desire for immediacy and *assent to the mediation of the church*."[78]

"To assent to mediation" means overcoming a fear of incompleteness and interminability. In truth, it means overcoming a fear of absence. Absence is distressing. We are compelled by a desire for the real, and it will always be tempting to shirk mediation (as if it were possible) to be in its presence. "But thinking on the question of God comes alive," Chauvet writes as he echoes Heidegger, "only insofar as it consents to the 'distress' of this absence."[79] As creatures longing for a reunion with our Creator, we bear the mark of insisting on a presence that actually speaks to absence. According to Chauvet, the acceptance of absence is necessary for understanding grace. It requires an appreciation for and a welcoming of absence, of emptiness, of the many ways we can describe our fundamental distance from God. "Emptiness," explains Chauvet, "is not nothing; the absence is precisely the place from which humans can come to their truth by overcoming all the barriers of objectifying and calculating reason."[80] By coming to terms with absence, a person comes to terms with her own finitude. This coming to terms with absence is more process than a one-time affair, as we will always be tempted to control, dominate, and objectify.[81]

If we assume with Chauvet that we harbor such nostalgia for immediacy with God, self, and others, this will affect our approach to more than just the sacraments. To the extent that the sacramental economy constitutes the economy of salvation, they have a privileged place in our understanding of mediation. However, Chauvet's assertions are *anthropological* because they posit mediation as the fundamental task of the human being. But we must be clear: saying mediation is fundamental does not mean to say that all mediation is ordered to the good.

The nostalgia for immediacy—one that is essentially illusory—drives a desire toward our own selfish ends as much if not more than it drives a desire for communion with God and each other. Chauvet accounts for this in his distinction between symbol and Jacques Lacan's imaginary. He writes, "The *imaginary* is the psychic agency that tends to deny the lack, to erase the difference, to fill up the distance separating humans from the real."[82] In short, the desire for the imaginary is a desire for immediacy that refuses to admit the necessity of mediation, thereby refusing the symbolic order. As Ambrose explains, "Living in the imaginary order can only be accomplished by means of an act of denial which attempts to repress the tie to every other, whether that other is objects outside our skin, one's body, or other people."[83] Such attempts at repression within the temptation toward imaginary leads Chauvet to caution that "left to itself, the imaginary is deadly."[84] It is antithetical to the sacramental imagination—it can undermine the entire enterprise of the church, which demands ties precisely to "objects outside our skin, one's body, [and] other people."

Inasmuch as the sacraments are meant to bring us into the presence of God, they are also meant to remind us of God's absence. To deny the distance between ourselves and God—the source of the real—is a basic definition for sin. We followed (and follow) our own selfish desires for as immediate an experience of the real as we could conjure: not just knowing God but being gods ourselves. In tragic irony, we fell into a state of perpetual mediation and remediation; we no longer enjoy the immediate (unmediated) communion with both God and each other. But mediation is not just a mark of our distance; it is also the means by which God draws us back to him and to each other. Mediation is the means of our salvation.

The salient point from Chauvet's reflections on absence up to this point is that, to the degree that symbols are mediations of presence that speak also to absence, symbol-making is *the* human task.[85] Always taking language as the fundamental system of symbols, Chauvet writes, "The communication of grace is to be understood, not according to the 'metaphysical' scheme of cause and effect, but according to the symbolic scheme of communication through language."[86] Calling to mind his earlier assertion that humans do not have language so much as they are had by language—they are constructed as subjects by it—Chauvet draws an analogy between the mediation of language and the sacraments: "To speak theologically of the sacraments not as instruments but as mediations, that is to say, as expressive media in which the identification and thus the coming-to-be of subjects as believers take place."[87] For Chauvet, the church is a "socio-linguistic matrix" within which members know themselves and know each other. This matrix is a complex system of symbols in which believers express and understand their identity, relative to themselves and to each other.

The sacraments are a symbolic system of actions, words, and objects that embody both presence and absence. Their corporality bespeaks the grace of God in Christ, who takes flesh to redeem us. And their corporality bespeaks God's absence from us by pointing us back to the mediation that marks our humanity and our distance from God this side of the eschaton. It is precisely here that the sacraments reveal themselves as virtual: they are suspended in the productive and uncomfortable space between presence and absence. To emphasize presence over absence is to covet a closure of the distance between creature and Creator; to emphasize absence over presence is to doubt the apostolic witness of that God dwelt among us in a real way.

Symbolic Exchange

Chauvet critiques the productionist mode of sacramental theology because one need not look far to find it entrenched in the church. It is the prevailing means by which we understand and explain the sacraments in catechetical situations of all kinds, exacerbated by modes of thought formed by and sustaining a culture of market exchange. These two tidal waves—Western metaphysics and capitalist economics—dominate the sea of sacramental theology in which all Catholics swim.

Chauvet wants to assert the gratuitousness of grace and rescue it from the instrumental causality that has dominated sacramental theology. He does so by means of a contrast between two logics: "that of the marketplace and value, based on objects in themselves, and that of symbolic exchange, before or beyond the realm of worth and based on the relations between subjects as such."[88] That is, he wants to distinguish between exchanges that emphasize the object being exchanged and exchanges that emphasize the subjects doing the exchanging, with the object as a symbol of that exchange. He differentiates sign and symbol, using Edmond Ortigues to describe a symbol as that which "introduces us into a realm to which itself belongs."[89] The symbol also "brings with itself the entire socio-cultural system to which it belongs."[90]

Symbols are fundamentally about the relationship between subjects for Chauvet, for they are meant to "join the persons who produce or receive it with their cultural world (social, religious, economic . . .) and so to identify them as subjects in their relations with other subjects."[91] Symbols are not mere representations of another reality; they are a "function of summons or challenge, of coming-to-presence . . . of communication between subjects."[92] Contrasted with the logic of market exchange, then, "the symbol is by its nature outside *the realm of value*. What is important is not the utility of the object, but the exchange that it permits between the subjects."[93] In symbolic exchange, the "true objective of these trades was the establishment of a subject's identity and place in society."[94] They were beyond value as objects and functioned instead as an exchange that constructed the identities of those in the exchange and their places in the community.

Symbolic exchange is not just about the circumscribed sacramental ritual or the unity that both he and de Lubac insist that it effects. The logic of symbolic exchange has an "immediate *ethical* implication."[95] Furthermore, this ethical implication is not simply a by-product of the sacramental activity of the church.[96] Rather, "to become historically and eschatologically the body of him whom they are offering sacramentally, the members of the assembly are committed to live out their own oblation of themselves in self-giving to others as Christ did, a self-giving called *agape between brothers and sisters*."[97] He explains more clearly the relationship of the liturgy to the ethical lives of the members of the Body, saying, "The liturgy is *the powerful pedagogy where we learn to consent to the presence of the absence of God, who obliges us to give him a body in the world*, thereby giving the sacraments their plenitude in 'the liturgy of the neighbor' and giving the ritual memory of Jesus Christ its plenitude in our existential memory."[98] The Eucharist is a "powerful pedagogy" and the lesson it teaches is the logic of symbolic exchange wherein those gathered around the table learn to exchange not objects but their very selves. But in what context do the members practice the *agapic* love that they learn in the Eucharistic liturgy? This implies extra-liturgical ecclesial contexts for the practice of symbolic exchange. Of course the ethical life extends to the whole of one's life. As a community committed to self-giving, however, there must be extra-liturgical spaces that are ancillary to the Eucharist but constitutive of its "intrinsic" ethical dimension. These are the spaces implied in de Lubac's ecclesial optimism, and that link Chauvet's sacramental and moral theology. These are the ancillary social spaces whose erosion threatens the viability of the American Catholic Church and whose twentieth-century forms must evolve into new spaces for the practice of symbolic exchange in the twenty-first century.

Criteria of Symbolic Exchange and Communion

Chauvet insists that we understand the Eucharist as a "powerful pedagogy" wherein we are formed in the logic of symbolic exchange. Therefore, symbolic exchange provides criteria by which we can evaluate potential sites for communion, both within and outside the church. Symbolic exchange gives us at least three criteria for such evaluation: (1) mediating structures that reflect the desire for the immediate and the inevitability of mediation; (2) the productive tension between presence and absence that I call *virtual*; and (3) the possibility for exchange that follows the logic of the gift economy with regard to subjectivity.

Let us first apply these criteria to the church in search of potential communion. (1) Both the church itself and the sacramental economy that it preserves throughout history speak to the centrality of mediation to the human experience. Mediation is an anthropological and theological reality for the church, particularly because of the experience of God incarnate in Jesus Christ. The Incarnation forms the basis for more than just an assent to mediation within Catholicism; indeed, an incarnational imagination seeks and desires mediation. While the specific modalities of this desire may be particular to Christianity, the centrality of mediation has its roots in the Jewish experience of God in history and revealed scripture.

(2) The sacramental economy and the local church that preserves it and is animated by it rely on a virtual logic that requires a giving-in to absence. Truly, it requires consent to living in the distressing space between presence and absence. This expands the definition of the virtual beyond the context of the digital network while retaining the ability to understand the internet in these terms. Thus understood, the virtual moves away from its somewhat benign definition to a hermeneutic for the church as well as the internet. We must determine the degree to which our communities remain suspended in the dynamism of presence and absence, a suspension that requires constant self-reflection and persistent humility. In short, to what extent is the community, ecclesial or otherwise, truly *virtual*?

In addition to drawing members of the Body of Christ together by means of the Eucharistic table, this community cannot be separated from its eschatological context as it concerns the *who* of the assembly. The community is virtual insofar as the Eucharist is celebrated not only with and for those present in the building of its ritual but in unity with and for two other communities as well: all members of the Body of Christ throughout the earth, and the Communion of Saints. The first acknowledges absence as the church extends over space. The second acknowledges absence as the church extends throughout time. Both rely on a virtual logic insofar as they make present the Body of Christ in the sacrament while simultaneously giving consent to the absence of that Body. This is what de Lubac means when he calls the church "virtual" himself: "Though only one cell of the whole body is actually present, the whole body is there virtually. The church is in many places, yet there are not several churches."[99]

It is thus within ritual itself that members of the Body of Christ experience the instantiation and pedagogical space of symbolic exchange. These rituals, says Chauvet, are meant to "function symbolically." By "functioning symbolically" he means operating on the level of symbolic exchange, which requires an assent to the "presence of absence." We must accept incompleteness and imperfection. It is only in submitting to absence that we can understand symbols, which bring into present that which cannot be immediate. Ritual is pedagogical insofar as it teaches us how to encounter the Other without succumbing to the temptation of believing that the Other is immediately knowable. Theologically, the ritual transforms and trains our vision to preserve God's absence while drawing us into his presence. Furthermore, it teaches us a discourse whereby we aim to exchange our very selves in kenotic love of the other.

(3) The third and final criterion of the possibility for symbolic exchange is the criterion for which thinkers like de Lubac have great hope and the criterion in which we find the greatest challenges. As the fullest form of what it means to be social, the church has great potential for the exercise of the exchange of subjects that operates on the level of the gift economy. It is within the Eucharist that we learn what it means to give freely and completely of oneself to the other, and it is this self-giving that is the way of the God to whom we are joined in the sacrifice of Christ on the Cross and altar.

Communion is the social effect of symbolic exchange lived in community. Symbolic exchange is learned in the ritual-pedagogical space of the Eucharist. The community needs extra-liturgical spaces in which to practice and live out symbolic exchange. Chauvet's discussion of ethics as an integral aspect of the sacramental economy demonstrates the sacramental nature of all of human life, insofar as the sacraments function as the means by which we learn the obligatory gratuitousness that we take into the rest of our lives. I want to reflect, however, on liminal spaces between non-liturgical spaces like work, school, friendships, etc., and the circumscribed liturgical space of the Eucharistic assembly. It is precisely in these ancillary Catholic spaces where the ecclesial unity that de Lubac envisions comes to fruition. These spaces are at the very center of the sociological picture presented in chapter 4. We live, regardless of literal location, in a suburbanized economic culture, wherein twentieth-century forms of social life have become simply one aspect among many from which to choose, if chosen at all. This means that religion, too, is suburbanized, insofar as religious communities no longer function as the center of neighborhoods, cities, and towns, and therefore no longer function as the center of one's social life.

Given these sociological challenges, understanding the virtual as a theological category can open creative ways to reengage the social life. I propose that we diagnose our current social moment in the church by means of the following analogical question: what is the *theological* relationship between the altar or sanctuary and the vestibule or fellowship hall? The latter are liminal ecclesial spaces that can function as strong symbols of the church/world relationship. Religious traditions have at certain points in their history enjoyed a great variety of these spaces, with the liminality extending beyond the vestibule or hall and into neighborhoods, cities, and even the nation-state. The importance of recognizing the suburbanized experience of American churchgoers lies precisely in the erosion or weakening in these liminal spaces. To the degree that American religious communities are suburbanized, one cannot rely on the traditional ancillary social spaces which are the literal neighborhoods and cities, but are also a complex network of associations and activities that reinforced the church as the center of one's life. Rendered a choice among many in the logic of market exchange, the church is thrust now into a system whose logic is alien to its own. The church needs ancillary social spaces to thrive, and it can no longer count on previous sites for these spaces.

I proceed with these final comments about local communities with full acknowledgment that there are people both as volunteers and employees who spend most of their waking hours working on this very aspect of the church. I intend in no way to denigrate or belittle their efforts to bring people together in moments of communion. My suspicion, however, is that we are susceptible to idealizing our local churches in such a way as to obfuscate the ways in which it lacks the robust community envisioned by someone like de Lubac. What it would require is a multitude of sites for symbolic exchange that would provide the formation for communion. I fear that Catholics in the contemporary American church find themselves desirous of these sites—as might be evidenced by their rapid adoption of technology which purports to provide it—and often find the church wanting.

To close, I want to provide the very beginning of a way forward on this point. Each local parish will have to answer the question of symbolic exchange for itself. The first step, then, would be to pose the question itself: Where are our sites for symbolic exchange and what are they? The idea is that as communities, we need to be honest about the relationships we find (or do not find) in the Eucharistic assembly. To be sure, these relationships in no way impact the reality of the sacrament. They do, however, affect the viability of the church in history, and the spiritual lives of those for whom the church is the sacrament of Christ.

We need spaces in which to practice what the Eucharist teaches us as members of the Body. With the erosion or absence of extra-ecclesial spaces wherein we might practice what we learn, the symbolic exchange par excellence in which we participate in the Eucharist is short-circuited. The Eucharist has become a precious, exceptional moment of social unity in an otherwise divided social existence. That unity, however, often has no content outside of the ritual itself, and thus while the sacramental efficacy may be preserved, the stakes are high with regard to the viability of the church. Chauvet demonstrates these high stakes when he writes, "Stuck in the rubrical orbit of the unchangeable, isolated from the cultural values that nourish the modern ethos breathed in by everyone, willy-nilly, along with the air of the time, these liturgical rites, excessively foreign to the surrounding world, could only become meaningless."[100]

This is not meant to imply that the church does not still maintain many sites for symbolic exchange. What we have to be honest about, however, is the apparent fact that many people who were baptized in the church are finding their community (and communion) elsewhere. This, of course, is always the case as the church does not exist in a cultural vacuum but within contexts that are always making demands on members of the Body of Christ. For the church in the United States at this moment, however, the exodus and absence of these members has become a particularly acute ecclesial wound. To ignore this wound and soothe ourselves with the assurances of orthodoxy is inadequate and theologically irresponsible. What Chauvet provides on this point is the simple but convicting reminder that the church is not free from the values of cultural particularities. At present, the various phenomena of internet culture penetrate, threaten, embolden, and affect the church in too many ways to count. If our theology is not isolated from this cultural matrix, then the values of this cultural matrix are open to theological description and critique.

The dense networks of social communication that sustained a robust liminal space symbolized by the vestibule or hall have become weak, nonexistent, or replaced by new means of connection in this technological paradigm. But we cannot simply name this a crisis and double down on doctrine. What is before us is a moment of great opportunity, wherein the church pays careful attention to the ancillary social spaces being created and maintained by and among the members of the Body through technology.

Let us then apply the criteria of symbolic exchange to the various forms of online social life. (1) Chauvet argues that assenting to mediation means we must *"let go of the desire to see-touch-find."*[101] On the one hand, the migration of so much of our lives to virtual space represents a desire in precisely the opposite direction that Chauvet highlights here. On the other hand, this same migration, in both its involuntary and voluntary forms, highlights the inevitability and importance of mediation. In pursuing social lives online, users assent to mediation insofar as they assent to a mediated experience of the other, despite the driving desire for an immediate experience. By giving the original matrix of symbolic exchange, language, a highly visible nature, the internet places mediation itself into sharp relief. We have on display within internet culture the most fundamental human task of mediation.

(2) This assent to mediation requires that we give in to absence. We have long been quick to indict technological culture, driven by market logic, for its presentist aspirations. We point to all sorts of virtual artifacts as further evidence of the very nostalgia Chauvet says has run amok. When we can just google everything, we might say, we have no awareness of limitations. When we can leave our opinions, unfounded and ill-informed, wherever we please online, we have no humility or charity. When we trade stories, images, and videos of exploited people in too many contexts to count, we have no understanding of the dignity of human beings. In all of these instances, our pursuit of presence—of immediacy—is reinforced and even rewarded.

What this narrative alone fails to consider, however, are the various ways in which the internet is a pedagogy of absence. Is it at all possible, for example, that the limitations imposed by the virtual spaces in which we now spend so much time can bring us back into an awareness of the necessity of absence? The dialectic between immediacy and hypermediacy, between presence and absence, is not frictionless. We feel it acutely in moments of miscommunication, dropped connections, and imperfect mediations. This friction highlights absence and acknowledging absence is the grounds for communion through the logic of symbolic exchange.

(3) In chapter 4, the work of sociologists and psychologists demonstrated that there are features to online community that do not neatly fit our expectations. We find people doing things for each other with no observable benefit by the standards of market exchange. Perhaps even more than when much of the work above was completed, we now witness a robust internet culture that is predicated largely on the creative (if often misguided or frivolous) energy of individual users who understand their social lives relative to the internet in ways that are more complicated than market exchange.

In Chauvet's sacramental theology, grace operates on the logic of symbolic exchange because it is always gratuitous. One operates within the logic of symbolic exchange when one consents to the obligatory gratuitousness that comes with the receipt of a gift. Gifts are valuable as objects. Instead, the gift is characterized "by the relationship of alliance, friendship, affection, recognition, gratitude it creates or recreates between the partners."[102] This is the only way to understand the relationship between God and humans because this relationship is within the order of love. Love cannot be understood within the realm of value; love is only intelligible in the realm of the gift economy. Where there is obligatory gratuitousness, there is the possibility for communion.

Is it possible to find moments of communion within the casual, day-to-day exchange of online communities? To answer this, we must talk about online communities in a more specific way. The rise of social media allows us to look carefully at the particular ways in which people exchange information online. It also reminds us that it might be possible that information is not the primary "thing" that they are exchanging; it might be possible that they are actually exchanging themselves. This has both positive and negative connotations, as the overwhelming amount of discussion about pornography can attest. But one should not emphasize the negative over the positive. We might pay attention here to what people think they are doing online, but this has been a particularly difficult set of data to capture. Sociologists and psychologists have long tried to determine the self-reflection of online behavior, with any number of obstacles in their quest. What appears to be the case is that there are moments of online transaction (such that it is) which follow the logic not primarily of the market but of something like symbolic exchange, whether or not users are conscious of it.

We should assert, once again, that the symbolic exchange of the sacramental tradition of the Catholic Church has a theological and anthropological priority to other forms and sites of symbolic exchange. The sacraments are symbolic exchange par excellence. But we may find within our own imperfect human culture—its artifacts, systems, discourses—analogies of symbolic exchange. If we can find moments of symbolic exchange within online discourse, we might then be able to suggest some degree, however small, of communion.

Let us take for a preliminary example the culture and practices of Wikipedia. With its persistent reminders for donation, Wikipedia reminds us constantly that it is not outside the logic of the market. But Wikipedia shows us that individual users online form themselves into communities that are committed to truth, however contested. Wikipedia is a self-correcting community, not unlike some of the oldest online communities and the new platforms modeled upon them. The ethos of a community like Wikipedia prizes truth. Critics will be quick to remind us that Wikipedia operates with a predominantly Enlightenment mentality with regard to truth, which is duly noted. However, as the sociological work in chapter 5 can attest, the "value" for an individual user who contributes to Wikipedia seems to be outside the logic of strictly market exchange. In fact, it seems closer to what Chauvet describes as symbolic exchange in traditional societies. This may be shocking, given that we may assume there is nothing further from a traditional society than the technocratic society of the internet. Our assumptions need not obscure the complexity of online communities unless we insist on retaining them despite the reality before us.

What users "get" from something like Wikipedia is beyond market value, and it may even be beyond the value of identity-construction given its anonymity.[103] Contributing to a community like Wikipedia (and any number of wiki sites like it), a user offers the "gift" of edits as a means of contributing oneself to a community. This community is more than just an aggregate of self-interested users; it carries a definite set of expectations, carefully circumscribed by a tradition of exchanges by the individuals themselves. This is the self-correcting and self-policing nature of online communities that gives them form and shape in addition to their algorithmic confines. One might even say that the Wikipedia contributor community has rites and rituals. For Chauvet, ritual programming is pre-reflective. It is on the level of action, not discourse. Although online exchanges are always somewhat beholden to discourse, given their largely textual nature, is it possible that they function closer to ritual than we have thus far been willing to admit? If so, this may be one possible explanation for the elusiveness of user self-reflection.

What would it mean for us to say that digital life has its own rites and rituals, supported by actions, gestures and narratives to construct a community and individual identity vis-à-vis that community? This is not to imply that such communities replace the church but that they function analogously to the church's sacramental life in terms of symbolic exchange. Online communities move toward communion, glimpsing it even if never fully attaining it.

But Wikipedia represents a rather passive form of online community. What if one were to apply the metric of symbolic exchange to the more common platforms for online community, social media networking sites? By 2015, a full 90 percent of American adults aged eighteen to twenty-nine used social media sites. The most popular of these sites are Facebook and Twitter. I maintain that it is possible to understand the communities initiated and sustained by Facebook and Twitter as capable and demonstrative of communion.

Facebook remains more popular than Twitter in the United States, with 71 percent of American adult internet users on Facebook.[104] Of that population, 70 percent report using the site "daily."[105] This makes Facebook a significant factor in the social lives of Americans. I want to consider two aspects of the Facebook community: relationship-building and political/ideological identity. In both cases, the challenges of the social media context are obvious, while the moments for communion are fleeting. The aim is not to baptize Facebook or to operate with the assumption that it is a tool to be used for good or bad. Rather, the aim is to highlight aspects of Facebook culture that demonstrate a capacity for symbolic exchange.

Facebook functions for many internet users as a key means for maintaining family relationships and friendships over space and time. Only 39 percent of Facebook users report being Facebook friends with people whom they have never met in person.[106] This means that a majority of Facebook users have offline experiences of their online relationships. As important as Facebook has become for the social lives of Americans, its drawbacks are obvious and numerous. Facebook is known for facilitating the inane, the frustrating, and the vile. The distance one finds from real social consequences is often enough to embolden the worst kinds of exchanges between individuals and among communities. Facebook is also a very particular interface with regulations that have been known to favor privileged populations over marginal ones.[107]

So to what degree might the relationship-sustaining aspect of Facebook reflect the communion we seek? We must first admit that Facebook is changing what it means to be social. Friendships and families are changing because the mediation of their relationships is taking new forms. And we cannot underestimate the power of the network on our social lives. In 2014, a controversial study tested the viability of "emotional contagion" on Facebook. The study was based on the idea that "emotional states can be transferred to other via emotional contagion, leading people to experience the same emotions without their awareness."[108] The researchers found that the appearance of positive posts on one's Facebook News Feed (a main page of posts from one's friends) resulted in more positive posting on the part of the user, and more negative posts in the News Feed resulted in more negative posts.

Facebook is more than a repository for emotions. Facebook has become an essential mediator—and in some cases, the primary mediator—for the connective tissue of family and friendly relationships for millions of people. It has become the family photo album, the coffee shop, the salon, and the classroom. Wherever there are moments of kindness, motivated by a genuine desire for the good of another, there is the chance for communion. These moments are banal and largely unnoticed, because that's what communion requires. The kind of communion gifted to the church, after all, is the theological treasure of *agapic* love that makes itself known in exchanges that take place between subjects as subjects. What people find on Facebook is a means by which they can share themselves. They are searching for what Chauvet would call a "coming-to-presence" of themselves to others and others to themselves. This coming-to-presence is fraught with difficulty and temptation for self-aggrandizement but the desire for it reflects our desire for the immediacy we lost in the Garden. By acting on our desires for unmediated presence, we consent to absence. Our striving for immediacy with each other means mediation, and we consent to mediation because we know we have no other choice. To be human is to be mediated, and we follow these desires to the places—digital and otherwise—where presence and absence meet in order to glimpse the communion we've lost.

If we understand digital content as symbols, an online community like Facebook can indeed reflect the symbolic exchange of a gift economy. The symbols of Facebook are text comments, pictures, videos, and shared links (usually to more text). Chauvet maintains that language is the most basic form of symbolic exchange. It is possible to understand these various digital artifacts as the vocabulary of internet language. When another user (Facebook friend) shares a photo with me, she does so outside the realm of value. I receive the photo under the obligation for a return gift. What is of value here, however, is not the photo itself, but the degree to which we have engaged in an exchange that constitutes us as subjects to each other and within the larger community.

Being a member of the Facebook community, I am not free to refuse gifts (digital artifacts) or to refuse gifting, lest I place myself outside of that community. Refusals amount to what Chauvet calls "short-circuiting" the economy of gift upon which the community relies. To be "on Facebook" really is to consent to a gift economy whereby I am obligated to return gift within the community upon receipt of gift. These gifts take many different forms, including ones that are ideologically motivated.

Facebook has become a forum for political and ideological activity. Political activity takes several forms on Facebook. The simplest is probably posting comments on others' posts, including personal statements, articles, pictures, or videos. Another would be posting content itself, especially politically charged content that will generate discussion.[109] A third means of political Facebook activity involves changing one's profile picture for a particular cause, issue, or idea. Some researchers have posited that Facebook provides fertile ground for political expression because online social interaction creates a "major reservoir of civic energy."[110] But others have argued that Facebook activism only serves the purposes of identity-making and reputation-building, with little observable effect on issues themselves.[111] In its more popular and less scholarly form, this argument often calls Facebook political activity "slacktivism," which gestures toward the low cost of political activity online relative to its social benefits. Among these social benefits are appearing compassionate or well informed, as well as initiating or strengthening relationships based on common ideology. Incidentally, this is the case for offline activism as well.

One of the most well-known of these Facebook political activities is changing one's profile picture. Each Facebook user has his or her own page with two photos at the top: a profile picture in a small square and a "cover photo" that is large and takes up the entire top part of the screen. For now, the cover photo has not become a common site for political activity. But the profile picture has. One such example is the Red Equal Sign Profile Picture (RESPP) campaign from 2013. In March of that year, the US Supreme Court heard arguments regarding the Defense of Marriage Act and California's Proposition 8. Both pieces of legislation dealt with the legalization of gay marriage. The Human Rights Campaign asked "its supporters to show their support for marriage equality during the hearings by changing their profile pictures to a simple image of an equal sign on a red background symbolizing love (a variation of the group's standard blue-and-yellow logo)."[112] Penney's research on this particular campaign gives us insight into the motivations and culture of online activism.

The traditional interpretive paradigm for activism is based on efficacy, meaning that a campaign like RESPP would be evaluated for its ability to affect the Supreme Court's decisions. However, this qualitative study demonstrates that, at least where participant motivations are concerned, this paradigm is inadequate. Instead, online gestures that are politically or ideologically motivated fall more neatly into a "cultural theory of change,"[113] whereby one's gesture is meant to incrementally contribute to a change in cultural values by reaching multiple publics through one's social media presence. Furthermore, as one's Facebook network is by and large made up of individuals with whom one shares (to varying degree) knowledge and trust, the opportunity for influencing the values and opinions of one's network is greater than it might be in more traditional but more impersonal settings. For example, a stranger knocking on my door to sign a petition may be less mediated than my Facebook friends engaging in something like the RESPP but it is not necessarily more personal.

The emergence of online activism, however small, within the cultural theory of change is an important development for those interested in solidarity. What is of particular note is its relationship to the more traditional "legislative theory of change," which understands political action on the basis of something like legislative efficacy. The legislative theory of change continues to dominate our discourse about political activity online. However, this interpretive paradigm misses not only participant self-understanding but the complexities of political action in social networks, both online and offline.

Facebook has begun to change what it means to have friends, to be in touch with family, and to present oneself in public or semi-public ways. One of the most intriguing aspects of this new social space has been the impulse to *do* politics, owing in no small part to the relative ease with which it now means to do something political. We should not be content to measure political activity by the static metrics of what it demands of us and what it produces. It is entirely possible that the new paradigm of Facebook activism may present a legitimate challenge to these productionist understandings of what it means to involve oneself in politics. Often, solidarity does not "look" effective. It looks weak and ineffective to the capitalist cultural values in which it often operates. But solidarity focuses less on measurable outcomes than on fostering relationships between human beings grounded in compassion, empathy, and respect for the dignity of all people. What this implies, therefore, is that online "slacktivism" may actually be a move in the direction of solidarity.[114]

Symbolic exchange is thus the standard for solidarity online. To the extent that one engages with mediating structures as a means by which to exchange oneself—that is, to seek communion with another. One contributes to the political discourse of an online community under the realm of the symbol: what one is contributing is not a particular object but one's subjectivity as a member of that community. This need not be the case for every politically motivated Facebook action for it to be true at least in possibility. The contribution of a symbol is an attempt at the coming-to-presence of the subject; a user changes her profile picture as an act of subjectivity because she is contributing herself to the community as witness to a particular value.[115]

Facebook facilitates many things in digital space, including the building and maintenance of relationships and political activity. To the extent that they follow the circuit of a gift economy, both of these transactional spaces are capable of operating on the order of symbolic exchange and cultivating communion. But Facebook is not alone in this capacity.

Facebook continues to hold the honor of first place among social media platforms, with Twitter hot on its heels. But for all their competitive energy, Facebook and Twitter operate with different logics with regard to the social networks they mean to construct. In general, Facebook tends to be social networking for the familiar, whereas Twitter opens users to larger, less familiar networks. Burgess makes note of this when discussing the evolution of social media: "Tellingly, once logged in [to Twitter] the user is invited to answer the question 'What's happening?', rather than 'What are you doing?', indicating a preference for the less personal or self-absorbed, but also less immediate and intimate, and more externally focused and informational uses of the platform."[116] This is not to say that Facebook is not used for broader networking or that close friends do not use Twitter to communicate. However, it must be noted that Twitter is not just Facebook operated by a different company. It is precisely in their differences where we might find traces of communion sustained by symbolic exchange.

Twitter tends to be a network of more loosely connected users, many of whom have probably not met one another.[117] Twitter differs from Facebook in many ways, the most obvious of which is the size and nature of the public that one engages. Let me begin with the admission that Twitter is an even scarier place than Facebook. At least the nasty comment threads on Facebook have the guise of social repercussions, given the offline ties between so many of its users. Twitter allows for more contact with more kinds of users than Facebook. The social group that one enters when tweeting is much more vast. This vastness is both its attractiveness and its repulsiveness. Unless one sets the privacy settings extremely high, social exchange on Twitter is not determined by the formal invitation and acceptance of something like a Facebook friend request. This means that one can be engaged by or engage with a stranger—someone one has never spoken to online or offline—at almost any time.

These interactions can be positive or negative, and they are notorious for tending toward the latter. While the vitriolic nature of Twitter has become something of a commonly held joke, I do not want to downplay its severity. There are plenty of instances on Twitter that are violent and hateful, and law enforcement is trying hard to keep up with this new and interesting way we have found to hurt other people.[118] But our inability to handle the stranger well should come as no surprise, especially to the theologically minded. Is the contentious Twitter exchange not the newest iteration of our sinful response to strangers throughout human history? I offer this context for digital sinfulness not to dismiss it but to engage it more fully and more honestly. We are woefully inadequate as creatures at engaging the stranger, but we have our moments. We have moments of charity and humility, even online. We have moments where we defend the innocent and speak truth to power. What Twitter has provided is a new means by which to encounter the stranger. We should not be surprised that we usually fail at communion. But we should also not be surprised to find genuine moments of symbolic exchange, wherein subjects share their very selves to the degree they can with those they encounter.

One of the biggest hurdles that online spaces like Twitter have for facilitating symbolic exchange is the fact that their underlying logics are still driven by market exchange. Individual dignity and worth on Twitter (and Facebook, for that matter) is often measured in followers, retweets, favorites, and mentions. Twitter is the space of marketing oneself and being marketed to. It is difficult, although not impossible, to escape market logic when the platform is predicated upon it.

Twitter's capacity for stranger-engaging highlights an important aspect of Chauvet's discussion of symbol. He writes that all language is "caught between sign and symbol."[119] He means that any discourse can function either as a symbol, which provides "foundation of the identity of the group and individuals, and an agent of cohesion between subjects within their cultural world," or as a sign, which is only about the exchange of information and judgments. Even the most banal conversation has a purpose in symbolic exchange insofar as it is about establishing a relationship between subjects. In the case of social media, that relationship is often contentious and not exactly what a theological critique would understand as grounded in Christian charity. What can Chauvet's comments here about symbol and language help us understand about Twitter and virtual communion?

For the more vitriolic moments of online discourse, language edges closer to symbol, and therefore closer to symbolic exchange, because it functions as the mediation of subjectivity, not just information.[120] In its brighter moments, a tweet (a short comment published to all of one's followers) and the response tweets (the line of conversation that follows from an original comment) can demonstrate a relationship of positive cohesion such as friendship, collegial respect, or common interests. In its darker moments, tweets and response tweets demonstrate relationships of hate, domination, and abuse. Surely this is not ground for communion. However, I think we can indeed understand this discourse, even in its most vile form, as exhibiting the potential as site for communion.

The circuit of symbolic exchange helps us understand the exchange of subjects themselves, not objects such as words or pictures. By recognizing discourse as symbolic exchange, we can recognize the building of relationships, both positive and negative. When an exchange moves in the direction of the obligatory gratuitousness that imitates the love of God, it then moves in the direction of communion. Without the visibility made possible by the mediation of symbols, the process of communion cannot begin.

I want to provide two small examples of the potential for communion for the church itself within virtual space. I do not consider these moments of communion within virtual space to be new or unique but as the modern instantiation of the historically virtual nature of the Catholic imagination. In both of the following cases, online space became the site of symbolic exchange insofar as the symbols (primarily words but also pictures) became secondary to the exchange of the subjects themselves. This kind of exchange expresses a Eucharistic logic, the practice of which requires liminal spaces for the manifestation of Christian unity outside of the liturgical rite.

James Martin is a Jesuit priest, the editor of *America* media, and one of the internet's favorite American Catholics. He maintains active Facebook, Twitter, and Instagram accounts, through which he offers news, insights, spiritual guidance, and prophetic witness to the demands of justice. Fr. Martin is generally unafraid to post or share provocative church-related news that garners attention from Catholics who are very willing to share their opinion in the comments. Most of Fr. Martin's posts include the following: "NB: Two post limit. No ad hominem. Keep on topic."[121] Fr. Martin's recurring *nota bene* is an acknowledgment of the debates that can ensue in the comments, and an effort to allow for them without allowing the vitriol that characterizes comment debates online.

Some of Fr. Martin's most popular posts deal with the issue of homosexuality and the church. After the largest mass shooting in the United States at an Orlando LGBT night club, Fr. Martin posted a video on Facebook wherein he says, "For too long, Catholics have treated the LGBT community as 'other.' For the Christian, there is no 'other.' There is no 'them.' There is only 'us.' . . . Those who are invisible to the community are seen by Jesus. . . . Catholics have a responsibility, I feel, to make everyone feel visible and valuable."[122] The comment thread following this video had many of the typical debates among Catholics regarding homosexuality. At several points, however, the comments reflected a different tone. In addition to many openly gay Catholics thanking Fr. Martin for his message, a few commenters talked about their own estrangement from the church. Commenter Brent Whitestone writes, "If I knew Catholics like you when I was growing up I would have never left the Catholic church."[123] His comment is followed by 163 replies, one of which is Fr. Martin: "Brent Whitestone: Come home. You're welcome. Find a welcoming parish and be welcomed back, as Christ desires."[124] Virtual space has thus allowed for a moment so desperately needed in the church: Catholics (including clergy) speaking to one another in open and honest ways, and in a way that exhibits the love of Christ. The words on this one comment thread are symbols to be exchanged, but what is truly exchanged here (be it ever so briefly) is the subjectivities of the members of the Body of Christ. I understand the exchange of subjectivity to occur in this context when one person offers the gift of themselves by means of a word given in honesty and in earnest desire to be received by the other. This need not be through deep conversations about the interior of one's heart. Indeed, we know that friendship is built on banal but true moments of exchange. What is central is the coming-to-presence of subjectivity, an offering however small of who one is to another.

These might have been the conversations in the liminal social spaces of the neighborhood bar, bowling league, or union hall of some other time. Communities need such spaces for practicing exchange, learning what builds friendship in charity (symbolic exchange) and what only leaves us disconnected and even at odds with each other. In a word, communities need spaces to practice communion. In the absence of these spaces and in the absence of their liminality with the church, the baptized are in need of sites for symbolic exchange, many of which can now only be found online.

The second example of symbolic exchange online regards a personal exchange I had on Twitter. Pope Francis recently implied that, because couples lack full awareness of that to which they are agreeing, many modern sacramental marriages are probably null.[125] I became involved in a discussion of marriage preparation in the church with a few lay people and a priest on Twitter. We shared stories of our own marriage preparation experiences, most of which were at best insufficient and at worst inappropriate. After sharing my story and divulging that my husband had been raised Jewish, a young woman responded to me that she was engaged to a non-Christian. I responded by saying that she was welcome to private message ("PM") me if she wanted to talk about the process. She did message me and we talked online for about twenty minutes about the process and marriage itself. In this moment, she and I were able to engage in symbolic exchange with another member of the Body of Christ in virtual space. She and I did so with full awareness that we would never meet, nor did our ability to engage in symbolic exchange require that we meet in person. I was able to have the exchange that parish halls and neighborhoods so rarely now accommodate: open and honest conversations of shared experiences, fears, and hopes about one's place in the church and its sacramental life. It is this type of exchange upon which communities are built and sustained. It is this kind of exchange that is taught in the liturgy, and needs spaces in which to flourish outside of it.

In both Fr. Martin's comment thread and my personal exchange on Twitter, I witnessed the possibilities of symbolic exchange within virtual space. These spaces are not always liminal to the church but they often can be. For both clergy and lay people, the internet provides the spaces—and sometimes the *only* spaces—for the practice of symbolic exchange. It provides extra-ecclesial spaces that, regardless of geographic location and often asynchronously, are the spaces for living the unity effected by the Eucharist. Virtual space has thus become the space for the potential of communion.

By acknowledging the centrality of mediation within Catholicism we begin to see points of convergence between our ecclesial and technological lives.

In addition, contemporary social communications technology points once again to the perpetual longing for community. Henri de Lubac provides an optimistic view of the church, the only social reality in which this longing can be fully sated. Such optimism, however, is susceptible to an idealization of the local community that fails to acknowledge real sociological challenges facing the extra-liturgical life of the church—challenges that now frame so much of the American Catholic ecclesial experience.

With his emphasis on the integral relationship between sacrament and ethics, Louis-Marie Chauvet's sacramental theology offers a way forward in our understanding of the sacramental and social life of the church. By arguing for symbolic exchange as the central logic of the sacraments, Chauvet opens new possibilities for understanding other sites of communion by the standard of symbolic exchange. Chauvet's insistence on the place of absence cautions all theology, especially that which offers a critique of technology, against presentist modes of thinking. Modern social media such as Facebook and Twitter show us clearly that our desires for immediacy remain, and many times we follow these desires to violent and otherwise disastrous ends. These media also cultivate spaces, however, for engaging with one another symbolically and highlighting the reality of absence.

In the absence of twentieth-century versions of liminal spaces whereby members of the Body of Christ engage in symbolic exchange, the internet has become a potential site for communion. While not ignoring the overwhelmingly vitriolic, divisive, and even violent nature of online social communication, it is possible to see moments of symbolic exchange that reflect the gratuitous love of God we learn in the Eucharist. By acknowledging this potential, we allow for the cultivation of liminality within such spaces, constructing new thresholds whereby the church engages the world and the world meets the church.

NOTES

1. Raymond Moloney, SJ, "De Lubac and Lonergan on the Supernatural," *Theological* Studies 69 (2008): 511.
2. Raymond Moloney, SJ, "Henri de Lubac on church and Eucharist," *Irish Theological Quarterly* 70, no. 4 (December 2005): 334.
3. Henri de Lubac, *Catholicism: Christ and the Common Destiny of Man*, trans. Lancelot C. Sheppard and Sr. Elizabeth Englund, OCD (San Francisco: Ignatius Press, 1988), 18.
4. de Lubac, *Catholicism*, 353.
5. Ibid., 293.
6. See Taylor, *A Secular Age*. See especially Chapter 12.
7. De Lubac, *Catholicism*, 294.

8. Ibid., 297.

9. Ibid., 298.

10. Ibid. Italics mine.

11. Moloney, "De Lubac and Lonergan," 512.

12. De Lubac disliked the term "*nouvelle theologie*" precisely on this point, "because it contradicted the very impetus of the movement which was to renew theology by a return to its biblical and patristic sources." Susan K. Wood, *Spiritual Exegesis and the Church in the Theology of Henri de Lubac* (Grand Rapids, MI: Eerdmans, 1998), 6. See de Lubac, *Catholicism*, 323: "So too shall we reject the notion that the modern age has experienced outside the church only error and decadence. That is an illusion, a temptation to which we have yielded only too often."

13. De Lubac, *Catholicism*, 165. De Lubac understood a lack of respect for history to be both the consequence and a cause of the idea of "pure nature" that he critiques elsewhere: "The last word in Christian progress and the entry into adulthood would then appear to consist in a total secularization which would expel God not merely from the life of society, but from culture and even from personal relationships." *The Mystery of the Supernatural*, trans. Rosemary Sheed (New York: Herder & Herder, 2012), xxxv. The French original is *Le mystere du surnaturel* (Paris: F. Aubier, 1965).

14. De Lubac, *Catholicism*, 141.

15. Ibid., 142.

16. See de Lubac, *Splendor*, 46: "The mystery of the church is all Mystery in miniature; it is our own mystery par excellence. It lays hold on the whole of us. It surrounds us on all sides, for it is in his church that God looks upon us and loves us, in her that he desires us and we encounter him, and in her that we cleave to him and are made blessed by him."

17. De Lubac, *Catholicism*, 321–322.

18. De Lubac quotes Pseudo-Haymo in *Catholicism*: "Sacramenta faciunt ecclesiam," ("Sacraments make the church"), 87.

19. On this point, see Moloney, "Henri de Lubac on church and Eucharist," 334: "Apostolically he wished to provide various Catholic social movements of the day with a theology of the corporate which would ground their activities in the sources of the faith. Doctrinally he wished not only to open up Christians to their social responsibilities but also to the basis of those responsibilities in the spiritual interdependence which binds the members of Christ's body into one. Grace is not just individual and invisible; it is concrete and communal, as we see in the actual church and the actual Eucharist. Our Christian destiny is not just to save the individual soul but to do so by entering more fully into our role within the body of Christ. Christ loves us, he tells us, individually but not separately."

20. De Lubac, *Catholicism*, 226.

21. Ibid.

22. Ibid., 82.

23. David Grummett, *De Lubac: A Guide for the Perplexed* (New York: T & T Clark, 2007), 73.

24. De Lubac, *Catholicism*, 93.

25. Ibid., 99.

26. See de Lubac, *Corpus Mysticum*, 103: "It would be noted that sacramental and mystical, which until recently had still been considered synonymous, and are basically the same word, were now separated and placed in opposition to one another."

27. De Lubac, *Corpus Mysticum*, 246.

28. Ibid., 101.

29. De Lubac, *Splendor*, 202.

30. Ibid., 209–210.

31. De Lubac, *Catholicism*, 225: "Outside Christianity, again, humanity tries to collect its members together into unity. Throughout the centuries a powerful instinct compels it through an apparent chaos of dispersal and conflict, collisions and strivings, social integration and disintegration, toward a 'common life', an outward expression of that unity which is obscurely felt within."

32. See *Catholicism*, 15: "We are accused of being individualists even in spite of ourselves, by the logic of our faith, whereas in reality Catholicism is essentially social. It is social in the deepest sense of the word: *not merely in its applications in the field of natural institutions* but first and foremost in itself, in the heart of its mystery, in the essence of its dogma. It is social in a sense which should have made the expression 'social Catholicism' pleonastic." Italics mine.

33. Moloney, "Henri de Lubac on Church and Eucharist," 334.

34. Ibid., 342.

35. In addition to the various ecclesiological trajectories subsequent to the council, I have in mind here the trajectory of Catholic theology that is heavily influenced by postliberal theology. For example, the Catholic students of Stanley Hauerwas, such as William Cavanaugh, adapt the predominantly Protestant focus on the local community to the local particularity of the Catholic sacramental assembly: If the Eucharist is the site of effected unity, it makes sense to make the local community qua Eucharistic assembly the standard of community and communion by which we critique the rest of social life.

36. See Grummett, *De Lubac*, 57, who quotes *The Splendor of the Church*, 130.

37. Hemming and Parsons, Editors' Preface, *Corpus Mysticum*, xiii.

38. Ibid., xiii–xiv.

39. Ibid., xiv.

40. De Lubac, *Splendor*, 73.

41. See de Lubac, *Splendor*, 73: "Human mediation, now indispensable and of primary importance, will have no *raison d'être* in the Heavenly Jerusalem; there, everyone will hear God's voice directly and everyone will respond to it spontaneously, just as everyone will see God face to face."

42. Laurence Paul Hemming, "Henri de Lubac: Reading *Corpus Mysticum*," *New Blackfriars* (2009): 528.

43. De Lubac, *Splendor*, 104.

44. Ibid., 103.

45. De Lubac, *Catholicism*, 174.

46. Ibid., 304. One should not assume that de Lubac means "statesmen" here as an indication that these societies are merely nation-states or political configurations.

47. *Catholicism*, 364.
48. Ibid.
49. *Catholicism*, 283.
50. Ibid., 285.
51. *Catholicism*, 35.
52. *Mystagogia*, c. 1 (PG 91, 665–668), qtd. in *Catholicism*, 54.
53. *Catholicism*, 54.
54. De Lubac, *Splendor*, 219.
55. "The 1975 General Instruction of the Roman Missal explicitly warns against the 'appearance of individualism' at Mass; this warning is repeated in the 2002 Instruction." Timothy Brunk, "Consumer Culture and the Body: Chauvet's Perspective," *Worship* 82, no. 4 (July 2008): 297. From the 1975 Instruction that Brunk references: "They therefore are to shun any appearance of individualism or division, keeping before their mind that they have the one Father in heaven and therefore are all brothers and sisters to each other."
56. See Brunk, "Consumer Culture and the Body," 298: "In a culture wherein people are trained to view life in terms of *my* needs and wanted (urged on by a cycle of production and consumption that is only too happy to point out new needs and wants), in a culture that mass-produces 'devices' that challenge what it means to be 'together,' doing the *public* work of liturgy (work that is not itself part of the cycle of production and consumption) . . . how does one persevere and promote the understanding of Christian worship and Christian existence as in essence communal?" See also Vincent J. Miller, "The Liturgy and Popular Culture," *Liturgical Ministry* (Summer 2006): 161–170.
57. Grummett, *De Lubac*, 54.
58. Henri de Lubac, *The Splendor of the Church*, trans. Michael Mason (San Francisco: Ignatius, 1986), 9.
59. See Megan L. Willis, "Language as the Sanctuary of Being: A Theological Exploration with Louis-Marie Chauvet," *The Heythrop Journal* LI (2001): 872: "Louis-Marie Chauvet's postmodern theology suggests a paradigm shift from the conception of Divine Presence established by ancient Western notions of being which laid the foundation for the church's causal sacramentology."
60. Louis-Marie Chauvet, *Symbol and Sacrament: A Sacramental Reinterpretation of Christian Existence*, trans. Patrick Madigan, S.J. and Madeleine Beaumont (Collegeville, MN: Liturgical Press, 1995), 13.
61. Thomas qtd. in Chauvet . . . ST III, q. 62., a. 3
62. See Chauvet's discussion of Hugh of Saint-Victor, 11.
63. Ibid., 22. Italics in text.
64. Ibid., 22.
65. Glenn Ambrose, *The Theology of Louis-Marie Chauvet: Overcoming Ontotheology with the Sacramental Tradition* (Burlington, VT: Ashgate, 2012), 48.
66. Ambrose, *The Theology of Louis-Marie Chauvet*. Both minister and the church itself.
67. Ibid.

68. Some take issue, unsurprisingly, with Chauvet's characterization of Aquinas. See Joseph Mudd, *Eucharist as Meaning: Critical Metaphysics and Contemporary Sacramental Theology* (Collegeville, MN: Liturgical Press, 2014).

69. Chauvet, *Sacrament and Symbol*, 24. Italics in text.

70. Ibid., 24. Italics in text.

71. Ibid., 117. The phrase "founding faith of humanity" is provocative. Following this line of thinking, it would be possible to understand all of human efforts to grab and hold "the real" and further witness of its absence. This is especially interesting as a way to read the Enlightenment and the intellectual heritage it bequeaths to the West. These deeper anthropological statements provide a fuller description of the phenomenon of remediation provided by Bolter and Grusin, who appear at once too historical and not historical enough in their account.

72. Ibid., 88.

73. Ibid., 29.

74. Ibid., 33.

75. Ambrose, *The Theology of Louis-Marie Chauvet*, 93.

76. Ibid., 34.

77. Ibid.

78. Louis-Marie Chauvet, *The Sacraments: The Word of God at the Mercy of the Body*, trans. Madeleine Beaumont (Collegeville, MN: Liturgical Press, 2001), 28. Italics in text. Later, Chauvet writes that "the assembly, which is his present body of humanity, is the *active sacramental mediation of his action*" (33). Italics mine.

79. Chauvet, *Symbol and Sacrament*, 62.

80. Ibid., 63.

81. Chauvet notes that this is truly what is meant by the "theological act," which is not so much about knowledge but about witness. He writes, "This amounts to slow work of apprenticeship in the art of 'un-mastery,' a permanent work of *mourning* where, *free of resentment*, a 'serene' consent to the '*presence of the absence*,' takes place within us little by little." *Sacrament and Symbol*, 74. Italics in text.

82. Chauvet, *Symbol and Sacrament*, 96.

83. Ambrose, *The Theology of Louis-Marie Chauvet*, 62.

84. Chauvet, *Sacraments*, 15.

85. "The consent to mediation . . . is the fundamental human task." Ibid., 145.

86. Chauvet, *Symbol and Sacrament*, 139.

87. Ibid., 110.

88. Ibid., 111.

89. Ibid., 112.

90. Ibid., 115.

91. Ibid., 121.

92. Ibid.

93. Ibid., 129.

94. Ambrose, *The Theology of Louis-Marie Chauvet*, 89.

95. Chauvet, *Symbol and Sacrament*, 277. Italics in text.

96. "This ethical dimension is not simply an extrinsic consequence of the Eucharistic process; it belongs to it as an *intrinsic* element . . . it is precisely ethics that must become authentically 'Eucharistic.'" Ibid. Italics in text.

97. Ibid. Italics in text.

98. Ibid., 265. Italics in text.

99. De Lubac, *The Splendor of the Church*, 149.

100. Chauvet, *Symbol and Sacrament*, 335.

101. Ibid., 162. Italics in text.

102. Chauvet, *Symbol and Sacrament*, 107.

103. Note here how the anonymous feature of online discourse actually allows for an exchange online that moves toward the good.

104. M. Duggan, N. B. Ellison, C. Lampe, A. Lenhart, and M. Madden, "Social Media Update 2014," Pew Research Center (January 2015), 4–5. http://www.pewinternet.org/2015/01/09/social-media-update-2014/.

105. Duggan et al., "Social Media Update 2014."

106. Ibid., 5.

107. See Lingel and Golub, "In Face on Facebook: Brooklyn's Drag Community and Sociotechnical Practices of Online Communication," *Journal of Computer-Mediated Communication* 20 (2015).

108. Kramer, Guillory, and Hancock, "Experimental Evidence of Massive-Scale Emotional Contagion through Social Networks," *Proceedings of the National Academy of Sciences* 111, no. 24 (June 17, 2014): 8788.

109. Under this category I would also place the curious case of the internet meme, which can be political or ideological but is often not. See Segev et al., "Families and Networks of Internet Memes: The Relationship Between Cohesiveness, Uniqueness, and Quiddity Concreteness," *Journal of Computer-Mediated Communication* 20 (2015).

110. See Maria Bakardijeva, "Subactivism: Lifeworld and Politics in the Age of the Internet," *Information Society* (March 5, 2009): 91–104.

111. See Erik Bucy and Kimberly Gregson, "Media Participation: A Legitimizing Mechanism of Mass Democracy," *New Media & Society* 3 (September 2001): 357–380.

112. Joel Penney, "Social Media and Symbolic Action: Exploring Participation in the Facebook Red Equal Sign Profile Picture Campaign," *Journal of Computer-Mediated Communication* 20 (2015): 56.

113. See Ethan Zuckerman, "Understanding Digital Civics," *My Heart's in Accra*, August 30, 2012.

114. According to Pope John Paul II in *Sollucitudo Rei Socialis* (1987), solidarity "is not a feeling of vague compassion or shallow distress at the misfortunes of so many people, both near and far. On the contrary, it is a firm and persevering determination to commit oneself to the common good; that is to say to the good of all and of each individual, because we are all really responsible for all." §38 We can use his distinction here to distinguish between "slacktivism" and true expressions of solidarity, although these are as difficult to ascertain as personal intentions.

115. In Pope John Paul II's terms, the person is changing her picture in order to express her commitment to the common good.

116. Jean Burgess, "From 'Broadcast Yourself' to 'Follow Your Interests': Making Over Social Media," *International Journal of Cultural Studies* 18, no. 3 (2015): 283.

117. On a related note, Pew Research reports that Twitter users frequent the site less than they frequent Facebook, with 36 percent of Twitter users visiting daily compared to 70 percent of Facebook users who visit daily (Duggan).

118. Take the case of Anita Sarkeesian, popular feminist blogger who incurs daily death and rape threats from mostly male gamers who do not appreciate her critiques of video games. Sarkeesian has been on the forefront of a growing movement to get Twitter to take more responsibility for hate speech on its platform. She has also been part of an effort to educate law enforcement on social media in order to begin prosecuting her attackers and others like them. See Charlotte Alter, "Anita Sarkeesian: Don't Give Twitter 'a Cookie' For Their New Harassment Policy," *Time.com*, April 24, 2015.

119. Chauvet, *Sacrament and Symbol*, 126.

120. It is possible sometimes to see the very moment in an online conversation when the discourse moves from the assumption of the sign (conveying information) to symbol (the coming-to-presence of subjectivity). It is a turning point in tone, vocabulary, and other means of expression including pictures, internet references or jokes, and community-specific artifacts such as hashtags.

121. Facebook page, Public Figure, "Fr. James Martin, SJ."

122. Fr. James Martin, SJ., "Standing in Solidarity with Our LGBT Brothers and Sisters," June 13, 2016.

123. June 13, 2016. 1:57 p.m.

124. June 13, 2016. 2:58 p.m.

125. A revised text tries to clarify his statement by changing "the great majority of our sacramental marriages are null," to "a portion of our sacramental marriages are null." "Updated: Most marriages today are invalid, Pope Francis suggests," *Catholic News Agency*, June 16, 2016.

Conclusion

The dissolution of anything resembling an American Catholic subculture—and many other subcultures, for that matter—has left the church in a precarious situation. For all of the reasons in the rise of the Nones (the religiously unaffiliated), I would argue that a lack of a dense social network into which the church and its liturgical particularities can fit has at least some role to play. We find ourselves grasping, often awkwardly, at what will remake the church into a "relevant" entity, trying to fit the life of the church back into the rest of life. What we fail to see, however, are the ways in which it is a simple lack of connection, not relevance, that lead many young people away from the church. In many cases, their response is not a defined "No," but a shrug, if a response at all.

I have attempted to argue here that despite the challenges posed by digital technology, there is much to be hopeful for from a Catholic perspective. First and foremost, the preference for images over text in online culture could mean a renewal of the sacramental sense that so many have argued was lost in the modern period. I have attempted to demonstrate the congruity here by re-capitulating the church's sacramentality within the category of virtuality. By doing so, I hope to demonstrate moments of hope for the church. Additionally, I have proposed that the church lacks ancillary spaces for the living out of Eucharistic principles. In short, people need to see and live in communities that have meaningful connections to their ecclesial life. Without these communities, the church appears superfluous, if not overly burdensome, to the modern mind.

Economic realities have made the construction and maintenance of such ancillary spaces difficult if not impossible. The suburbanization of American Catholicism, in particular, has meant a decentering of social life that structures it around little else than consumer choice. In the absence of this center, we witness a desperate need and desire for community. I have argued elsewhere that this is presenting itself in surprising but familiar ways, most of which do not disrupt or challenge the market ideology that has driven the dissolution of nonmarket-based community in the first place. My suggestion is that digital spaces can and are providing the new means for living out lives framed by the Eucharist. Indeed, the symbolic exchange exemplified by the Eucharistic assembly is the standard to which God calls us to commune with one another. It is a standard that has always been difficult, but whose difficulty is not foreign to the narrow gate of Jesus. It is the standard for offline and online relationships, and while many want to argue that it is only possible in the former, I have attempted to insist that this need not be the case. In fact, the way in which digital topography collapses space and time has deep resonance with the church's own understanding of the Communion of Saints and the *ekklesia*. That is, we as Christians have always been called to engage with our brothers and sisters across aisles, across borders, and even beyond the grave.

This project has been an attempt to provide a systematic theological account of the internet in a way that responds to and is faithful to these dynamics long within the tradition. I determined that two doctrinal loci dominate the theological landscape on these matters: the Incarnation and the church. The doctrine of the Incarnation centers much of the discussion on questions of embodiment and materiality. The doctrine of the church as the mediator of God's grace through the sacramental economy locates the discussion of the internet within the context of the local church community, or parish. This is due not only to the doctrine itself but to trends in theology following the Second Vatican Council, which has favored a Eucharistic ecclesiology centered on the local assembly.

In light of these loci, I have attempted to provide an account of Catholic sacramentality within the category of the virtual. I provided a theological account of mediation by drawing on the work of computer scientists and media scholars who have noted the dialectic of immediacy and hypermediacy within the media ecology of Western culture. We can understand this dialectic in terms of the desire for presence and the requisite absence of that which is mediated as a response to that desire. It is precisely within this relationship between presence and absence, especially in its necessary tension, that the mediation of Catholic sacramentality finds its genesis.

At the heart of so much theological reflection about the internet is its ability to promote or inhibit true (variously conceived) community. Using the descriptors of sociological accounts of digital community, online community does in fact offer the possibility of "strong" social ties. Such social ties must be considered in light of a further historical and sociological description of American life. The cultural and economic dynamism of suburbanization has had profound effects on the sociological realities facing the American Catholic Church. It is precisely within the context of the suburbanization of the American Catholic Church that I have undertaken this theology of the internet as a Catholic theologian.

In order to consider the social realities of the particularly American church, I suggest that we return to the nexus of ecclesiology and sacramental theology. Henri de Lubac's Eucharistic-centered ecclesiology has had substantial influence at the Second Vatican Council and beyond, and his ability to bring the theological and social together provide a rich source for our conversation, despite the age of his work. Although profound and theologically rich, de Lubac's vision for the church assumes the presence and flourishing of social structures that support the properly liturgical life of the church.

In the end, I suggest that the work of Louis-Marie Chauvet is helpful for understanding the sacramental life of the church, as well as its social implications, on a continuum of mediation that can accommodate new, digital forms. Chauvet's work place the church's sacramental life in a broader context of symbol and mediation. From Chauvet, three criteria emerge by which we might measure communion, whether found in the church or in the ancillary social structures that it needs to thrive, including the internet. These three criteria were (1) an acceptance of mediation; (2) the productive tension between presence and absence; and (3) the possibility for symbolic exchange. These criteria offer a framework for understanding the social dynamics of life online.

Of all of the theological concerns mentioned in chapter 1, one remains particularly difficult for any discussion of contemporary digital life. The vitriolic tendencies of life online have always had detrimental effects on human lives. Considering the positive potential of online life has only become more challenging in recent years, as racism and sexism have reached new heights in these contexts, encouraging more outward expression and making more and more forays into mainstream culture. We have no choice, however, but to engage vitriolic elements in the very same spaces. This requires careful attention to the relationship between digital spaces—what I have termed "ancillary spaces"—and institutions that exist around them.

The question of "ancillary spaces" is the heart of the argument set forth above. Americans face a crisis of social spaces, both within the church and outside of it. The fluidity and accessibility of digital spaces give them great potential for supporting, encouraging, and facilitating the meaningful critique of institutions like democratic processes, higher education, and religious communities. They also present a challenge to these same institutions for the way in which they offer a means by which groups of individuals can create alternative communities to such institutions. It is not just the church that must consider the myriad ways in which individuals encounter one another and the spaces in which they do so on a daily, hourly, or moment-to-moment basis.

I set out in this project to bring the logics of the culture in which we live into dialogue with the ancient logics of the Catholic Church. While I am deeply sympathetic to the many worries and concerns that the internet brings into our lives, I hope to have offered here a theological treatment of the internet that does not reduce this complex social phenomenon to its worst elements. I propose that there is much to explore theologically within technological and internet culture. This culture shows us many things about our desires, fears, shortcomings, and capabilities. The church thrives when it can speak to these complex social realities, and while the sociological picture of the Catholic Church in the United States reflects many challenges ahead, the burgeoning spaces for encountering one another might also fill us with hope for communion.

Bibliography

Ambrose, Glenn P. "Eucharist as a Means for 'Overcoming' Onto-Theology? The Sacramental Theology of Louis-Marie Chauvet." PhD diss., Graduate Theological Union, 2001.

———. "Psychoanalysis, Social Psychology, and the Sacramental Theology of Louis-Marie Chauvet." Paper presented at the annual meeting of the College Theology Society, Portland, Oregon, 3–6 June 2010.

———. *The Theology of Louis-Marie Chauvet: Overcoming Onto-Theology with the Sacramental Tradition.* Burlington, VT: Ashgate, 2012.

Aquinas, Thomas. *Summa Theologiae.* http://www.corpusthomisticum.org/sth0000.html.

Bailey, Kenneth. *Paul Through Mediterranean Eyes: Cultural Studies in 1 Corinthians.* Downers Grove, IL: InterVarsity Press, 2011.

Bakardijeva, Maria. "Subactivism: Lifeworld and Politics in the Age of the Internet." *Information Society* (March 5, 2009): 91–104.

Benedict XVI. "Message for the 46th World Day of Communications: Silence and Word: Path of Evangelization." January 24, 2012.

Bennett, Jana Marguerite. *Aquinas on the Web? Doing Theology in an Internet Age.* New York: T & T Clark, 2012.

Brunk, Timothy. "Consumer Culture and the Body: Chauvet's Perspective." *Worship* 82, no. 4 (July 2008): 290–310.

———. *Liturgy and Life: The Unity of Sacraments and Ethics in the Theology of Louis-Marie Chauvet.* American University Studies, VII: Theology and Religion. New York: Peter Lang, 2007.

Bucy, Erik and Kimberly Gregson. "Media Participation: A Legitimizing Mechanism of Mass Democracy." *New Media & Society* 3 (September 2001): 357–380.

Burgess, Jean. "From 'Broadcast Yourself' to 'Follow Your Interests': Making Over Social Media." *International Journal of Cultural Studies* 18, no. 3 (2015): 281–285.

Cavanaugh, William T. *Torture and Eucharist: Theology, Politics, and the Body of Christ.* Malden, MA: Blackwell Publishing, 1998.

Chauvet, Louis-Marie. *The Sacraments: The Word of God at the Mercy of the Body*. Translated by Madeleine Beaumont. Collegeville, MN: Liturgical Press, 2001.

———. *Symbol and Sacrament: A Sacramental Reinterpretation of Christian Existence*. Translated by Patrick Madigan, S.J. and Madeleine Beaumont. Collegeville, MN: Liturgical Press, 1995.

Cicero. *Rhetorica ad Herennium*. Book III. Loeb Classical Library. Cambridge: Harvard University Press, 1954.

Clement XIII. *Christianae Republicae: On the Dangers of Anti-Christian Writings*. November 25, 1766.

Cohen, Lizabeth. *A Consumer's Republic: The Politics of Mass Consumption in Postwar America*. New York: Random House, 2003.

Copeland, Adam. "The Ten Commandments 2.0." *Word & World* 32, no. 3 (Summer 2012): 217–226.

de Certeau, Michel. *The Mystic Fable: The Sixteenth and Seventeenth Centuries*. Chicago: University of Chicago Press, 1992. French original, 1982.

de Lubac, Henri. *Catholicism: Christ and the Common Destiny of Man*. Translated by Elizabeth Englund. San Francisco: Ignatius Press, 1988.

———. *Church: Paradox and Mystery*. Translated by James R. Dunne. New York: Ecclesia Press, 1969. French original, 1967.

———. *Corpus Mysticum: The Eucharist and the Church in the Middle Ages*. Translated by Gemma Simmonds with Richard Price and Christopher Stephens. Notre Dame: University of Notre Dame Press, 2006.

———. *The Splendor of the Church*. Translated by Michael Mason. San Francisco: Ignatius Press, 1986.

Detweiler, Craig. *iGods: How Technology Shapes Our Spiritual and Social Lives*. Grand Rapids, MI: Brazos Press, 2013.

Dodge, Martin and Rob Kitchin. *Mapping Cyberspace*. London: Routledge, 2001.

Doyle, Dennis M. *The Church Emerging from Vatican II: A Popular Approach to Contemporary Catholicism*. Mystic, CT: Twenty-Third Publications, 1992.

———. *Communion Ecclesiology: Vision and Versions*. Maryknoll, NY: Orbis, 2000.

———. "Henri de Lubac and the Roots of Communion Ecclesiology." *Theological Studies* 60, no. 2 (1999): 209–227.

Duggan, M., N. B. Ellison, C. Lampe, A. Lenhart, and M. Madden. "Social Media Update 2014." Pew Research Center (January 2015), 4–5. http://www.pewinternet.org/2015/01/09/social-media-update-2014/.

Ebel, Eva. "The Life of Paul." In *Paul: Life, Setting, Work, Letters*, edited by Oda Wischmeyer, translated by Helen S. Heron, 97–110. New York: Continuum, 2012a.

———. "Paul's Missionary Activity." In *Paul: Life, Setting, Work, Letters*, edited by Oda Wischmeyer, translated by Helen S. Heron, 111–120. New York: Continuum, 2012b.

Eilers, Franz-Josef, SVD, ed. *Church and Social Communication: Basic Documents*. Second Edition. Manila: Logos (Divine Word) Publications, Inc., 1997.

Eisenstein, Elizabeth. *The Printing Revolution in Early Modern Europe*. New York: Cambridge, 1983.

Fowler, Robert Booth. "The Roman Catholic Church in 'Protestant' America Today." *The Forum* 11, no. 4 (2014): 721–742.

Francis. *Evangelii Gaudium* (Apostolic Exhortation). November 24, 2013.

———. *Laudato Si* (Encyclical Letter on Care for Our Common Home). May 24, 2015.

———. "Message for the 48th World Day of Communications: Communication at the Service of an Authentic Culture of Encounter." June 1, 2014.

Gaillardetz, Richard R. "The New E-Magisterium." *America* 182, no. 16 (May 6, 2000): 7–9.

Gamble, Harry. *Books and Readers in the Early Church*. New Haven: Yale, 1995.

Gleason, Philip. *Keeping the Faith: American Catholicism Past and Present*. South Bend: University of Notre Dame Press, 1987.

Godzieba, Anthony. "Quaestio Disputata: The Magisterium in an Age of Digital Reproduction." In *When the Magisterium Intervenes: The Magisterium and Theologians in Today's Church*, edited by Richard R. Gaillardetz, 140–153. Collegeville, MN: Liturgical Press, 2012.

Grummett, David. *De Lubac: A Guide for the Perplexed*. New York: T & T Clark, 2007.

Haskell, Rob. "eVangelism: The Gospel and the World of the Internet." *Evangelical Review of Theology* 34, no. 3 (2010): 279–285.

Heil, Paul. *The Letters of Paul as Rituals of Worship*. Eugene, OR: Cascade Books, 2011.

Hollenbaugh, Erin E. and Marcia K. Everett. "The Effects of Anonymity on Self-Disclosure in Blogs: An Application of the Online Disinhibition Effect." *Journal of Computer Mediated-Communication* 18, no. 3 (April 2013): 283–302.

John Paul II. "Message for the 36th World Day of Communications: Internet: A New Forum for Proclaiming the Gospel." May 12, 2002.

———. "Message for the 24th World Day of Communications: The Christian Message in a Computer Culture." May 27, 1990.

Kappeler, Warren A. *Communications Habits for the Pilgrim Church*. New York: Peter Lang Publishing, 2009.

Karaflogka, Anastasia. *E-Religion: A Critical Appraisal of Religious Discourse on the World Wide Web*. London: Equinox, 2006.

Kollock, Peter and Marc Smith. *Communities in Cyberspace*. New York: Routledge, 1999.

Konijn, Elly A., et al. *Mediated Interpersonal Communication*. New York: Routledge, 2008.

Lanier, Jaron. "Jaron's World: Virtual Horizon." *Discover*, May 11, 2007.

———. *Who Owns the Future?* New York: Simon & Schuster, 2013.

———. *You Are Not a Gadget: A Manifesto*. New York: Vintage Books, 2010.

Lombard, Matthew and Theresa Ditton. "At the Heart of It All: The Concept of Presence." *Journal of Computer-Mediated Communication* 3, no. 2 (September 1997): n.p.

Lubac, Henri de. *Catholicism: Christ and the Common Destiny of Man*. Translated by Lancelot G. Sheppard and Sister Elizabeth Englund, OCD. San Francisco: Ignatius, 1988.

———. *Corpus Mysticum: The Eucharist and the Church in the Middle Ages*. Translated by Gemma Simmonds, C.J. South Bend, IN: University of Notre Dame Press, 2007.

———. *The Splendor of the Church*. Translated by Michael Mason. New York: Sheed and Ward, 1956.
Marquis, Timothy Luckritz. *Transient Apostle: Paul, Travel, and the Rhetoric of Empire*. New Haven: Yale University Press, 2013.
Mayer, Paul A. *Computer Media and Communication: A Reader*. Oxford: Oxford University Press, 2000.
McDannell, Colleen. *Material Christianity: Religion and Popular Culture in America*. New Haven, CT: Yale University Press, 1998.
McLuhan, Marshall and Bruce R. Powers. *The Global Village: Transformations in World Life and Media in the 21st Century*. New York: Oxford University Press, 1989.
Miller, Carolyn, et al. "How People Get Local News and Information in Different Communities." Pew Research Center, Pew Internet and American Life Project, Project for Excellence in Journalism, Knight Foundation (September 26, 2012).
Miller, Vincent J. "Media Constructions of Space, the Disciplining of Religious Traditions, and the Hidden Threat of the Post-Secular." In *At the Limits of the Secular: Reflections on Faith and Public Life*, edited by William A. Barbieri, Jr., 162–198. Grand Rapids, MI: Eerdmans, 2014.
———. "When Mediating Structure Change: Transformations of Magisterial Authority in Digital Culture." In *When the Magisterium Intervenes: The Magisterium and Theologians in Today's Church*, edited by Richard R. Gaillardetz, 154–174. Collegeville, MN: Liturgical Press, 2012.
Moloney, Raymond S. J. "De Lubac and Lonergan on the Supernatural." *Theological Studies* 69 (2008): 509–527.
———. "Henri de Lubac on Church and Eucharist." *Irish Theological Quarterly* 70, no. 4 (December 2005): 331–342.
Montgomery, Scott. "Beyond Comments: Finding Better Ways To Connect With You." NPR.org. August 17, 2016.
Moore, Brenna. "How to Awaken the Dead: Michel de Certeau, Henri de Lubac, and the Instabilities between the Past and the Present." *Spiritus* 12 (Fall 2012): 172–179.
Norris, Pippa. *Digital Divide? Civic Engagement, Information Poverty and the Internet in the Democratic Societies*. New York, NY: Cambridge University Press, 2001.
Ong, Walter J. *Orality and Literacy: The Technologizing of the Word*. 30th Anniversary Edition. New York: Routledge, 1982; 2012.
"Our Digital Future." Editorial. *America*, February 17, 2014.
Penney, Joel. "Social Media and Symbolic Action: Exploring Participation in the Facebook Red Equal Sign Profile Picture Campaign." *Journal of Computer-Mediated Communication* 20 (2015): 52–66.
Pinckaers, Servais. *The Sources of Christian Ethics*. Translated by Sr. Mary Thomas Noble, O.P. Washington, DC: The Catholic University of America Press, 1995.
Pius XI. *Divini illius Magistri* (On Christian Education). December 31, 1929.
Putnam, Robert. *Bowling Alone: The Collapse and Revival of American Community*. New York: Simon & Schuster, 2000.

Qian, Hua and Craig R. Scott. "Anonymity and Self-Disclosure on Weblogs." *Journal of Computer Mediated-Communication* 12, no. 4 (July 2007): 1428–1451.

Radio Vaticana. "Pope Francis: His First Words." Accessed June 24, 2015. http://en.radiovaticana.va/storico/2013/03/13/pope_francis_his_first_words_/en1-673112.

Randels, George. "Cyberspace and Christian Ethics: The Virtuous and/in/of the Virtual." *Annual of the Society of Christian Ethics* 20 (2008): 165–179.

Root, Andrew. "A Screen-Based World: Finding the Real in the Hyper-Real." *Word & World* 32, no. 3 (Summer 2012): 237–244.

Rudy, Kathryn M. *Virtual Pilgrimages in the Convent: Imagining Jerusalem in the Late Middle Ages*. Turnhout, Belgium: Brepols, 2011.

Scully, J. Eileen. "The Theology of the Mystical Body of Christ in French Language Theology 1930–1950: A Review and Assessment." *Irish Theological Quarterly* 58, no. 1 (March 1992): 58–74.

Sivunen, Anna and Emma Nordback. "Social Presence as a Multi-Dimensional Group Construct in 3D Virtual Environments." *Journal of Computer-Mediated Communication* 20 (2015): 19–36.

Smith, Anthony Burke. *The Look of Catholics: Portrayals in Popular Culture from the Great Depression to the Cold War*. Lawrence, KA: University Press of Kansas, 2010.

Soukup, Paul, ed. *Media, Culture and Catholicism*. Kansas City, MO: Sheed and Ward, 1997.

Spring, Michael B. "Informating with Virtual Reality." In *Virtual Reality: Theory, Practice, and Promise*, edited by Helsel and Roth, 5–13. London: Meckler, 1991.

Tanenhaus, Sam. "Generation Nice." *New York Times*, August 15, 2014.

Tanner, Norman. *The Councils of the Church: A Short History*. New York: The Crossroad Publishing Company, 2001.

Taylor, Charles. *A Secular Age*. Cambridge: Harvard University Press, 2007.

Thompson, Phillip M. *Returning to Reality: Thomas Merton's Wisdom for a Technological World*. Eugene, OR: Cascade Books, 2012.

Van Alstyne, Marshall and Erik Brynjolfsson. "Electronic Communities: Global Village or Cyberbalkans?" MIT, 1996. http://web.mit.edu/marshall/www/papers/CyberBalkans.pdf.

Ward, Graham. "Between Virtue and Virtuality." *Theology Today* 59, no. 1 (2002): 55–70.

Williams, Alex. "Creating Hipsturbia." *The New York Times*, February 15, 2013.

Wittberg, Patricia. *Building Strong Church Communities: A Sociological Overview*. New York: Paulist Press, 2013.

———. "A Lost Generation?" *America*, February 20, 2012.

Wood, Susan K. *Spiritual Exegesis and the Church in the Theology of Henri de Lubac*. Grand Rapids, MI: Eerdmans, 1998.

Woolley, Benjamin. *Virtual Worlds: A Journey in Hope and Hyperreality*. Cambridge: Blackwell, 1992.

Wright, N. T. *Paul in Fresh Perspective*. Minneapolis: Fortress Press, 2005.

Index

absence, xiii, 19, 60, 62, 64–68, 71–76, 87, 141, 145, 155; and Paul's letters, 77–84; and the sacraments, 135–39
access: internet, 3, 12–15, 59, 91, 100, 101, 104; mass media, 33–34, 111, 114, 118, 165; printed books, 28
anonymity, 3–6, 19–20, 40; and pseudonymity, 3, 5
authority, 8–12; and church documents, 9, 43

Benedict XVI, Pope, 26–27, 41, 46–48
Bennett, Jana, 4–7; on digital divide, 12; on Powers and Principalities, 11, 13, 18
Body of Christ: ecclesial, 4, 50, 129–33, 140, 144, 154; historical, 67–68, 127; sacramental, 127–28, 131, 141. *See also* communion

Christological councils, 66
Clement XIII, Pope, 25–26
Cohen, Lisabeth, 112–17
communion: and desire for immediacy, 62, 65, 81, 87, 138; ecclesial documents and, 26, 28–29, 37, 48, 53; online, 124, 150, 152–57, 166; and symbolic exchange, 140, 142–48, 165

cyberbalkanization, 100–101, 114

de Certeau, Michel, 67–68
de Lubac, Henri, 67, 165; ecclesiology of, 123–34, 142; Eucharistic theology of, 127–29
digital divide, 12
disembodiment, 5, 15–18, 47; and embodiment, 48, 65, 67, 164

Eucharist, 52–53, 66–67, 82, 117, 123, 127–35, 140–43

Facebook, 147–51, 153
Francis, Pope, xi, 48–52; and encounter, 42, 45, 48, 51–53; *Laudato Si*, 49

globalization, 10, 48, 52, 114
Godzieba, Anthony, 9–11, 43

Incarnation, xiii, 1–7, 11, 18, 19, 26–27, 31, 37–39, 65–67, 75–77, 129, 141, 164

John Paul II, Pope Saint, 9, 26, 41, 43–46

labor unions, 103, 132

language, 17, 77, 82–83, 95, 136–38, 144, 148, 152
Lanier, Jaron, 60, 101–4, 114
Legion of Decency, 25–26
Leo XIII, Pope, 29
liturgy, 8, 80, 131–34, 140, 154
Lourdes, 60, 84–87, 100

Martin, James, 153–54
mediation, xii–xiii, 17, 19, 60, 136–41, 144, 147–48, 152, 164–65
Miller, Vincent, 9–11, 13, 43; on heterogenization, 10, 99–100, 103, 114
Mount St. Mary's, 85–86

Paul, Saint, 66, 76–84; letters, 79, 81, 82, 83; life, travel, 78
Paul VI, Pope, 42–43
pilgrimage: Lourdes and replicas, 86; the pilgrim church, 42, 68; virtual, 71–76, 83–85
Pius XI, Pope: *Divini illius Magistri*, 28–29; *Vigilanti Cura*, 27–28
Pius XII, Pope: *Miranda Prorsus*, 29–32
Pontifical Council (Commission) for Social Communications, 26; *Aetatis Novae*, 38–40; *The Church and Internet*, 39–40; *Communio et Progessio*, 36–38, 42–44, 48; establishment of, 32; *Ethics in Internet*, 39–40
presence, 19, 60, 62, 71, 73, 77, 117, 119–20, 127, 133, 164–65; and absence, xiii, 19–20, 61, 64–68, 76, 87, 123, 139–41; studies, 119. *See also* virtual
printing press, 8, 79, 99–100

Putnam, Robert, 109–12, 115, 117

relics, 72, 75, 85; metric, 71–73
remediation, 61–68, 138
Rudy, Kathyrn, 71–76, 78, 85

sacrament: sacramental economy, xiv, 11, 15, 18–19, 26–31, 124, 126, 135, 141–42, 155, 164; sacramentality, 60, 62, 63, 66, 75, 77, 84, 86–87, 163, 165
Second Vatican Council, 25–26, 37, 45, 123, 128, 165; *Gaudium et Spes*, 1–2, 25, 35–36, 39, 46, 48; *Inter Mirifica*, 32–36, 40, 43; *Lumen Gentium*, 128
suburbanization, 113–17, 124, 131, 163
symbolic exchange, 123–24, 139–44; and the internet, 144–53, 164–65; and sacraments, 139–40

Taylor, Charles, 125
Twitter, 52, 98, 147, 151–52, 154

virtual: and Catholicism, 19–20, 60, 63–64, 66, 76, 86–87, 123–24, 136, 139–45, 163–64; and Paul, 79–84; reality, 18, 59–60. *See also* absence; presence
vitriol, 6–7; and social media, 59, 93, 151–53, 155

Wellman and Gulia, 96–98; pastoralist ideal, 98, 103–4; weak ties and strong ties, 97, 112, 115, 119
World Communications Day, 40–51; establishment of, 28, 37; topics, 41

About the Author

Katherine G. Schmidt is assistant professor of theology and religious studies at Molloy College (New York). Her work focuses on the relationship between Catholicism and digital culture. She teaches courses in both ethics and religion at Molloy College and lives in Queens, New York.

Made in United States
North Haven, CT
14 June 2022